Praise for
SNAKE DRIVER!

"A balanced, forthright and readable account of some of the most dedicated soldiers that have ever worn the uniform of this great nation ... This book captures the spirit and soul of the men who love the challenge of flying."
— Lt. General Calvin A. H. Waller (Ret.)
Deputy Commander, Desert Storm

"Army aviation came of age in Vietnam. Bob Rosenburgh has added an important chapter in the history of those heroic aviators who answered many an infantryman's call for help. The *whop-whop-whop* of approaching choppers was always a welcome sound, but the shout 'The snakes are coming' was special—and very reassuring."
— Lt. General William H. Harrison (Ret.)

D1019646

SNAKE DRIVER!

Cobras in Vietnam

Bob Rosenburgh

IVY BOOKS • NEW YORK

Ivy Books
Published by Ballantine Books
Copyright © 1993 by Robert Rosenburgh

Library of Congress Catalog Card Number: 93-91591

ISBN 0-8041-0538-3

Manufactured in the United States of America

First Edition: November 1993

Dedication

This book is dedicated to my father, Durwood E. Rosenburgh. He was a man of courage and kindness, wisdom and wit. Those who knew Rosey treasure his memory, and my life's great fortune was to be his son.

Table of Contents

Acknowledgments..ix

Introduction..1

1. Door Gunner (Jerry Ballantyne)........................7
2. Huey Gunship (Jim Kreutz) 25
3. Birth of the Snake...41
4. A Deadly New Toy (Tom Meeks).....................55
5. Vung Tau Transition (Chuck Nole) 64
6. Air Cavalry Squadron (Tom Wie) 73
7. Aerial Rocket Artillery (Rex Swartz).............90
8. Cobra Company Commander (Lou Bouault)...........113
9. ARA Commander (Jake Benjamin) 143
10. The Pink Panthers (John Cole)........................160
11. Task Force Garry Owen (Roger Fox).......................181

Glossary 203

Bibliography..207

Acknowledgments

I found that a nonfiction like this can be as much work researching as it is writing. The task was eased by those people and organizations who graciously responded to my requests for information and pictures. I spent many hours at the excellent Grandstaff Library on Fort Lewis, digging for details, which, I hope, are factually incorporated into the text. Many thanks to Library Director Pattie Lauterbach. My thanks to my wife, Elvia, for patience and assistance, helping make a space in my day for writing, and for encouragement when I faltered. She conceived the original idea and convinced me I could write *Snake Driver*.

At Ivy Books, Owen Lock presented me with the opportunity, and Steve Sterns and Ellen Key Harris kept my contract ball rolling and focused. Fred Martin of the *U.S. Army Aviation Digest* staff sent me some of the best historical material on Cobras I have. Bob Leder, of Bell Helicopter, Textron, sent me the greatest total volume of photos, books, brochures and fact sheets, making my research easier and more thorough. At the Patton Museum of Fort Knox, Kentucky, Dave Holt and John Purdy provided excellent photos of the Cobra prototype. Lt. Col. F. C. Peck of the USMC Media Branch at the Pentagon was particularly generous in his assistance, too.

The hardest part, though, were the interviews. Twelve men, some strangers and others longtime friends, invited me into their homes and relived their worst nightmares for my little tape recorder. Some were comfortable with the past and had little difficulty relating the old battles. Others buried their demons and never looked back. To exhume the old memories now, especially in the entirety I asked for, was often an emotional ordeal. As a Vietnam veteran myself, I found we carry scars that aren't visible, but deep nonetheless. Two of the pilots are not featured in *Snake Driver*, Ed Rickabaugh and Mark Hanson. Ed was a great help to me, providing a wealth of information that went into other chapters, and Mark is slated for my next book, *Loach*. I thank each of them for their candor and hope the nation has learned gratitude for their courage and service.

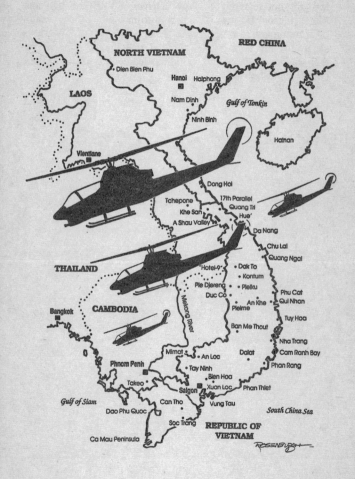

Introduction

The saga of the Cobra helicopter began with the genesis of the U.S. Army's airmobile divisions, from the early 1950s into the midsixties. This radically new type of fighting force laid the ground work that developed into a need for the Cobra. The AH-1 Cobra was a new class of weapons system, the attack helicopter, built to fill a critical gap in the revolutionary concept of the airmobile infantry divisions being battle tested in Vietnam.

The concept started not as a singular blueprint drawn from a brilliant flash of inspiration but rather from a series of reports, projects, and military boards. And, despite continuing resistance from a deeply entrenched bureaucracy, it was the foresight and perseverance of a few visionary officers that ensured the eventual fielding of the new forces.

Following World War II and the Korean War, there were clear signs indicating significant potential for expanding the role of helicopters in modern warfare.

The French used helicopters in the Indochina war until their tragic defeat at Dien Bien Phu, then later in Algeria. The United States had tested the use of weapons in some helicopters in Korea, but it was the French that first put this new idea to regular field use in actual combat.

By then the stage was set for planners at the Pentagon to develop a new kind of army unit, based on helicopters, for all the battlefield utilities of supply, maneuver, and attack.

In June 1956, Brig. Gen. Carl I. Hutton, commandant of the aviation school at Fort Rucker, Alabama, formed a studies group under the stewardship of Col. Jay D. Vanderpool, chief of the aviation school combat development office. This group, which was soon to be known as "Vanderpool's Fools," was expected to create a kind of "Sky Cav" and accelerate the speed at which traditional cavalry missions could be accomplished on the modern battlefield.

General Hutton began the studies-group project on the premise that helicopters could provide excellent mobility for the infantry and fire support to boot, so he pressed on with his plan.

Colonel Vanderpool's team developed and built a wide variety of nonstandard weapons systems for their aircraft.

It was an anything-goes atmosphere that produced some decidedly curious contraptions along the way to more successful applications. As the weapons were designed, so, too, were tactics for their successful employment in combat.

By March 1958, the Sky Cav had become an official army unit. General Hutton's dream had become a reality, at least as a prototype unit.

Over time, the unit would be redesignated several times: as the 8305th Aerial Combat Reconnaissance Company; Troop D (Air), 17th Cavalry; Troop D, 3d Squadron, 17th Cavalry; and finally as the famous 1st Squadron, 9th Cavalry of the 1st Cavalry Division (Airmobile) when it was sent to Vietnam in 1965.

By 1960, other organizations within the army, taking the lead from Colonel Vanderpool and General Hutton, were trying out their own ideas for arming helicopters.

This lack of structure made it difficult to pursue the airmobile concept, tactics, doctrine, and organization until those issues were resolved. And, it would be a formidable task to convince the U.S. Congress to fund any program that wasn't clearly spelled out.

To put their aviation house in order, the army initiated the aircraft development plan to provide specific guidance for research and development through the next decade. The plan included three broad areas of development objectives known as Army Study Requirements. They forecasted a need for a light observation helicopter, manned surveillance, and tactical transport. Notably absent was mention of the need for an attack helicopter, since the addition of armaments to the other types was considered adequate to convert them for the task.

The army had grown from just over seven hundred aircraft in the early 1950s to more than five thousand aircraft of fifteen different types by 1960. Watching the army acquire an evermore sophisticated fleet of rotary-wing and fixed-wing aircraft, air force officers became nervous that they could eventually be relegated to merely maintaining the nuclear deterrent. In a congressional committee hearing, they were even referred to at one time as "the silent silo-sitters of the seventies." Their concerns ultimately resulted in disarming all army fixed-wing aircraft and the transfer to the air force of the C-7 Caribou in 1967.

The army formed a formal board, chaired by Lt. Gen. Gordon B. Rogers, on January 15, 1960 to examine the army aircraft development plan. This group was critical in the early development of the airmobile division and, although it was called the army aircraft requirements review board, it is generally referred to as the Rogers Board. In February 1960, forty-five manufacturers submitted 116 different designs developed according to Army Study Requirements.

After completing technical and operational evaluations of the many entries, the board met from February 29 to March 6 at Fort Monroe, Virginia, before making their recommendations. The first was to begin an immediate design competition for a light observation helicopter to replace the L-19 Bird Dog fixed-wing aircraft and the OH-13 and OH-23 helicopters.

Second, the Rogers Board recommended that more research be conducted on sensory and surveillance systems before specifications could be made for a penetration surveillance aircraft.

Finally, a replacement was recommended for the CH-47 Chinook helicopter and the C-7 Caribou transport aircraft.

The Rogers Board made two additional recommendations; one of which had far-reaching consequences. One suggestion was that each type of aircraft should be considered for replacement every ten years, based on technology advances and proven performance, or lack of it.

The other recommendation was to determine whether the concept of airmobile fighting units was even practical! That dovetailed nicely with General Hutton's aerial combat reconnaissance company, since the board also provided for a test unit to evaluate the concept and its feasibility.

The real value of the Rogers Board was to start the official United States Army bureaucracy on the path to formally creating what would become the airmobile division, providing the needed guidance on planning for aviation development, procurement, and manning.

Another renaissance had begun in 1959 and was coming to fruition at about the same time. Bell Helicopter, under contract from the army to produce a new helicopter ambulance, had developed a single-engine utility helicopter called the XH-40. The resulting aircraft was redesignated as the HU-1 Iroquois when deliveries first began in June 1959. Nicknamed "Heuy," it was later redesignated UH-1A, but the moniker stuck. The new helicopter was powered by a turbine engine.

Instead of the elaborate contraptions with piston engines that previous helicopters were, this one was fairly sleek, reliable, needed less maintenance, performed markedly better, and carried more troops and cargo.

Development of the UH-1 was a turning point in military history. Like the famous battleship *Dreadnought* that altered forever the design of the world's navies, the Huey demonstrated that turbine engines were the only choice for military helicopters.

The airmobile concept might have taken many more years to develop had it not been for the escalation of the war in Vietnam in the early sixties.

It was on December 11, 1961, that the 57th Transportation Company (Light Helicopter) from Fort Lewis, Washington, and the 8th Transportation Company (Light Helicopter) from Fort Bragg, North Carolina, arrived at a dock in Saigon on the aircraft carrier USNS *Card*.

Through the rest of 1961 and into 1962, American aviation units continued to trickle into South Vietnam to support the Army of the Republic of Vietnam (ARVN) forces.

As the buildup in U.S. forces continued, so, too, did U.S. combat operations against the Viet Cong guerrillas.

Up until the arrival of USNS *Card*, the ARVN forces had held the Viet Cong at bay with some support from American Special Forces advisors.

From the outset, air-assault tactics proved extremely valuable. Using aerial reconnaissance and intelligence to pinpoint enemy strongholds, commanders could now move large numbers of troops into remote areas—areas that had previously been completely inaccessible were now mere minutes away by airmobile insertion. These tactics helped neutralize the Viet Cong, but not without losses. As the size of the battles grew, so did the need for more aircraft. To bridge the gap, and to take advantage of the greater performance of the UH-1, a test unit of armed Hueys was sent to Vietnam in September 1962.

Designated as Utility Tactical Transport Helicopter Company (UTTCO), fifteen of the aircraft had jury-rigged weapons systems mounted in Okinawa before arrival at Tan Son Nhut. UTTCO showed the army the effectiveness of armed escort choppers by substantially reducing friendly casualties in the landing zones (LZ). Eventually known as gunships, the armed Huey was the basis of the future attack helicopter.

In 1962, Secretary of Defense Robert McNamara directed the army to take a bold, new look at its forces and needs, focusing on innovation and airmobility. As a result, the now-famous Howze Board was convened.[1] Named after the chairman, Lt. Gen. Hamilton H. Howze, this project was the watershed for forcing the army away from its traditional conservatism toward researching futuristic concepts using cutting-edge technology. The board would report directly to the secretary of defense. Very few times in history has a project enjoyed such leeway and discretion as the Howze Board.

For eleven weeks in 1962, the Howze Board used thirty-two hundred military personnel and over ninety civilians in war games, equipment testing, and unit training. Units of the army and air force were diverted from overseas deployment to participate in the project. More than forty different major tests, three week-long field exercises, and numerous live-fire demonstrations were conducted and evaluated by fifty officers and an advisory group of civilian scientists. Some even toured overseas combat operations for further evaluation data.

The Howze Board report was submitted to the secretary of defense on August 20, 1962. Included was the proposed design of the air assault division.

The board additionally recommended activation of a fully airborne air cavalry combat brigade to perform the classic cavalry functions of screening, recon, and delaying actions.

To effect such a reorganization within the army, the number

1. One of the Howze Board members, Brig. Gen. Edward L. Rowny, took a special research team to Vietnam in 1962. The Army Concept Team in Vietnam (ACTIV) evaluated a variety of nonstandard systems and doctrines for possible adoption by the army. ACTIV was a key element in the fielding of the Cobra, recommending prompt acquisition of the AH-1.

of pilots needed would jump from 8,900 in 1963 to 20,600 by 1968.

Finally, the board had a single, overriding conclusion: It is necessary and desirable for the army to adopt the airmobile concept.

As the Howze Board report was being studied, the war in Vietnam continued to grow. The Viet Cong grew in strength, and more and larger units of the North Vietnamese Army were being encountered as well.

January 7, 1963 marked the beginning of the 11th Air Assault Division and the 10th Air Transport Brigade when the deputy chief of staff for operations issued a plan for organizing, training, and testing them both. By February the units were activated with a skeleton-crew staff at Fort Benning, Georgia, and began the building-up process. Although both units were strictly experimental at the time, they'd be the vehicles the army would use to turn the Howze Board findings into reality.

It would take a year and a half to complete the design and testing process, and to bring the two units up to full strength.

The eighteen months of preparation were finally put to the test in a major certification exercise called AIR ASSAULT II, held from October 14 to November 12, 1964.

The exercise proved a success, with the 11th AAD troops meeting or exceeding the objectives of nearly every combat mission. Even the aggressor commander, Maj. Gen. Robert H. York, enthusiastically endorsed the new division and brigade. In March 1965, the decision was made to convert the 11th Air Assault Division (Test) and resources of the 2d Infantry Division into the 1st Cavalry Division (Airmobile). The new unit was then deployed to Vietnam by ship. An advance party reached Vietnam on August 25, 1965, and immediately began preparing the "Golf Course," soon to become the world's largest helipad, at An Khe.

By the beginning of October, the full division was settled in and began the serious business of conducting combat operations. The first airmobile division had finally arrived.

It was on the battlefields of Vietnam that the concept of airmobility was proven out in one successful operation after another, but after years of using converted scout and utility helicopters in the fire support role, the need for purpose-built attack helicopters finally became evident.

Chapter 1

DOOR GUNNER

When S. Sgt. Jerry R. Ballantyne was transferred to Vietnam, he could hardly have anticipated the assignment that awaited him. Coming from an armored cavalry unit in Germany, Jerry was well trained as a scout in M-114s, small armored personnel carriers used primarily for reconnaissance. Ballantyne was confident his expertise with a map and tracked vehicles would land him in armor cav. But it was not to be. He was destined to do his scouting from the air.

Coming in-country in June 1967, Jerry's flight from the States landed at Tan Son Nhut airbase near Saigon. From there, the troops on his flight went by bus to the "reppo-depot," Long Binh's 90th Replacement Detachment. While awaiting orders for his new unit, Ballantyne followed the routine training schedule that most "newbys" followed while processing through. He and his apprehensive hootch-mates were required to spend a week, a good part of it in the field, learning to set up defensive perimeters, night sentry skills, and planning fields of fire.

Through his previous years of experience in the army, Jerry was one of the few new troops who knew claymore mines, so he usually set most of them out. Most of the replacements had only handled claymores once or twice in training, but Jerry had trained subordinates in using the mines back in Europe. The others would string concertina barbed wire, fill sandbags, and dig foxholes. Then they would be assigned guard shifts and wait for dark.

7

Not realizing they were in a fairly secure area, the new troops would huddle together through those first nights in the field, nervously anticipating a major Viet Cong assault, which, of course, never came.

When Jerry's orders eventually showed up, he was pleased to learn he would soon be a scout with A Troop, 1st Squadron, 9th Cav in Phan Thiet. Though he didn't know it then, the 1/9 Cav was the unit that grew from the first Sky Cav troop of Colonel Vanderpool, back in the early sixties when airmobile was still in its infancy. Restructured and renamed several times in the previous few years, it had become a full-blown aeroscout squadron, the Headhunters, performing target acquisition duties by looking for enemy troops for the 1st Cavalry Division (Airmobile). The full division was stationed further north in Binh Dinh Province, with headquarters in An Khe, but the units in Phan Thiet were a battalion-size slice constituted under the aegis of Operation BYRD. The task force was the 2d Battalion, 7th Cavalry, configured like a mini-airmobile division and serving in the zone from late August 1966 until January 1968. Their mission was to protect the port city of Phan Thiet while working with the Army of the Republic of Vietnam (ARVN) in suppressing the Viet Cong.

Eagerly anticipating his new assignment, Ballantyne was transported by C-7 Caribou to Phan Thiet, a small coastal town where the Cav had set up a substantial fire base and landing zone on the ocean cliffs overlooking a beachhead landing. The road from there into town wandered through a graveyard and several miles along a slow downhill slope to a fertile valley just inland. Across the valley, lush, jungle-clad mountains rose up and continued into the interior of the country.

When the C-7 touched down at the Phan Thiet LZ, however, Ballantyne was a bit more than surprised to see helicopters everywhere instead of armored vehicles. Meeting his new platoon sergeant, he soon learned that, indeed, he would be a scout, and a section sergeant as well. The catch was that he wouldn't be in a track but, rather, in the funny looking "erector sets" that were officially called the OH-13 Sioux helicopter!

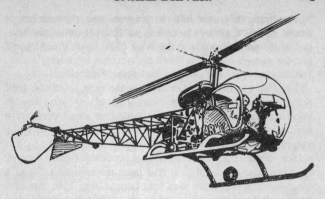

The OH-13 was the military version of Bell Helicopter's Model 47. Acquired by the army just before the Korean War, the Sioux was a leftover from an earlier era and was considered obsolete by the time of the Vietnam War. In spite of that, they served long and hard in the hands of dedicated crews. The entire airframe was skeletonized, without any skin, except for the prominent plastic bubble canopy. Its 260-horsepower piston engine, with an external fuel cell mounted above each side, allowed for a cruising speed of seventy knots with a maximum of eighty-seven knots. These ungainly contraptions took off "heavy" for every combat mission, since the rated payload was only four hundred pounds. Weapons, ammo, and armor generally exceeded that.

Jerry's new noncommissioned officer in charge asked if he had ever read a map from the air. He hadn't, but like all new aeroscout observers, he would soon be trained to navigate, call artillery fire, and serve as a door gunner in the OH-13.

The next day was his first mission. Jerry initially thought it would be a combat mission but soon found it was more of an orientation flight. As the aircraft lifted off from the perforated-steel-plank (PSP) runway, he looked down to see the rest of the crews laugh at him as they watched the launch.

The pilot, a seasoned veteran in his early twenties, asked Jerry if he'd ever been in a helicopter before. Again, the answer was no. No sooner had Ballantyne responded than the pilot began swaying his chopper from side to side, over and over, until Jerry became quite nauseous.

The pilot waited for Jerry to get sick, and when he had to heave, gave the aircraft some left pedal. That turned the helicopter to one side, making the wind blow in on the pilot and out the gunner side. The vomit sprayed out over Jerry's skid. Ballantyne could tell the guy had done this before.

The flight lasted about an hour, as the little helicopter took Sergeant Ballantyne on the worst ride of his life. Besides swaying and rocking, he was treated to rapid drops and climbs, sharp turns that had him looking straight down at the jungle below, and descending corkscrews.

The whole troop was waiting when they finally landed, laughing and applauding. It had been his initiation flight, a long-standing ritual that was now behind him. That was also his first taste of the crazy kind of air combat that would soon become routine. The initiation served an additional purpose of breaking in the cherry-boy and getting him ready for the serious business of aeroscout training.

He spent that night recovering. The following morning, he arose for an early first-light mission, feeling much better. As they departed the LZ at the crack of dawn, his pilot pointed out rising smoke columns all around in the neighboring jungle. Jerry was told those were campfires, one way of finding the enemy as the Viet Cong prepared their morning meals.

The first days in the air were spent learning to fire the M-60 machine gun. This involved flying over jungles, looking for wild pigs, then shooting the hell out of them. Using belts of all-tracer ammunition, it took little time for Jerry to learn how to target the running hog by firing ahead of it, then walking the hot tracers right into the frightened animals. The boars were a good deal smaller than men and certainly ran much faster, so by the time Jerry had "waxed" fourteen or fifteen pigs, his pilot was confident that he'd work out well as a gunner.

Though they would have made a great barbecue, the slain pigs were seldom retrieved, since no one wanted to sit down alone deep in VC country. It's probable that Charlie[2] himself enjoyed many a pork chop from the practice gunnery runs.

In addition to the M-60 machine gun, the observers carried

---

2. The Viet Cong, or VC, were often referred to by the phonetic alphabet words "Victor Charlie," "Charlie" for short.

an M-79 grenade launcher. The M-79, fondly known as Chunker from the dull thud of its low-pressure muzzle blast, fired a single 40mm grenade at a time. It was much more difficult to aim and fire accurately than the machine gun, and without the rapid fire and tracers of that weapon, several months of aiming at stumps and blowing them out of the ground went by before Jerry was satisfied with his M-79 skills. By then, he could put a 40mm round in a garbage pail while traveling at seventy knots. He also learned to throw smoke grenades, hand grenades, and white phosphorous grenades at all speeds and angles.

Throughout the gunnery training, to and from the field, he also learned aerial map reading. It was different from what he'd learned on the ground. The terrain was observed from new angles, requiring additional skills to determine positions, distances, sizes of objects, and heights. And he was moving at much greater speeds than his old M-114 ever traveled.

In those days, the door gunner carried the M-60 in his hands, attached to the aircraft by an elastic bungee cord with a hook at each end. One hook was fastened to the doorway and the other to the gun, leaving it free to move but still safely attached to the helicopter. Jerry didn't use the cord because he felt it was too restrictive when he had to fire under the aircraft, past the pilot while in tight banking turns, and even up through the rotor disc. He just didn't care for bungee cords as much as some of the men in his unit did.

The gunners liked to modify the machine guns to their personal preferences. Over time, a roughly standardized and completely unauthorized table of modifications was developed through trial and error. The oversized and overly heavy butt plate, designed to absorb recoil and contain the receiver parts, was the first to go, replaced by a small angle iron that held the gun's guts in against the recoil spring. The spring, in turn, was shimmed with washers to give it more tension and reduce the bolt travel. That increased the rate of fire. Next to come off were the bipod, sights, and carry handle, since they all got in the way. A little honing of the clockworks for that hair-trigger effect, and it was time to go hunting!

None of these alterations would have ever been allowed back in the States or in Germany, but in Vietnam, regulations took a backseat to survival. The OH-13 was never meant for attack, and the M-60 was designed for infantry.

There was another M-60 trick that most of the scouts did mostly for kicks. The weapon had a barrel that was easily replaced when it became too hot or too old. The gunners of the 1/9 Cav could tell by a drop in accuracy when a barrel was reaching the end of its service life, or "shot out." At that point, the barrel was good for about five hundred more rounds, or one mission.

The gunner would then remove the barrel and cut it with a hacksaw just ahead of the gas-piston housing, then square it off with a draw file. The result was awesome. The rate of fire slowed, and the sound of the muzzle report increased dramatically. And the muzzle, too, projected a huge finger of orange flame with each shot, making the gun appear to be a much larger and more powerful weapon.

To the surprise and delight of Ballantyne, the effect was so impressive that some VC, at the mere sight of it firing, would throw their hands in the air in surrender. It wasn't very accurate, but precision wasn't needed when they just gave up!

For self-protection, Ballantyne wore a flak jacket and several pieces of scrounged armor plating, one under his rear and the other at his back, tucked into the uniform. When a gunner left his aircraft at night, he'd take three things with him; his two pieces of armor plate and the M-60. Aircrews were also issued a chest and abdomen protector called a "chicken plate." Sometimes, between missions, the scouts just sat around and counted the bullet dents in their armor.

In front of each gunner was a box of machine-gun ammo belts of around five hundred rounds each, plus a variety of grenades: smoke, 40mm, and white phosphorous. Jerry also liked to carry a .45 automatic. It seemed a bit meager against the other firepower he had, but he didn't think one could ever be overarmed over VC territory. On the instrument panel was a hook used to pull grenade pins with one hand while the other was busy firing the machine gun. It was a big hook, since it had to pull a lot of pins.

The training could only last so long before it came time to put what he'd learned to use. By the end of his first month with the 1/9 Cav, Jerry found himself on a real combat mission, facing the real enemy instead a pack of hairy hogs.

Ballantyne would never forget his first KIA. He was on his first combat mission, flying with another OH-13. One was the lead ship, the other the chase ship. The objective of the lead ship was to find and make first contact with the enemy. The chase ship would fly to the rear and above, in order to call for help if the lead was shot down. Shoot-downs happened so fast there was no time to radio a Mayday. The chase bird was essential to call for help and to protect fallen comrades.

The instant contact was made with an enemy, the chase bird would kick out a situation report, or sitrep, alerting base of the action. An infantry platoon, or Blue team was always on alert to fly out to a contact, be inserted, and attack on the ground. The scouts were the White team.

Jerry was observer/gunner in the chase ship as the White team flew out at treetop level, seeking targets. Nervous, he really didn't know how he'd react in real combat. Although he was section sergeant, he was still a newby, riding in the chase ship because he lacked the experience needed to fly lead.

As they snapped along, doing about seventy knots through the trees, they soon spotted five Viet Cong soldiers running along a trail, weapons in hand. Caught without an escape, the VC turned and fired at the lead ship. One was quickly cut down by the lead gunner.

Spotting another VC beside a tree, Ballantyne shouted to his pilot to bank right as Charlie's AK-47[3] opened fire on his OH-13. Circling the tree, Jerry couldn't get a shot as the Cong kept moving behind the trunk. Round and round they went, the hovering chopper and the desperate soldier, each one looking for the right moment. Finally making a break, the frightened VC ran for a spider hole and dropped down into it out of sight.

Ballantyne watched the soldier's head just inside the previously hidden hole in the ground as the pilot brought them to a hover overhead. Leaning over the skid, Jerry fired straight down into the hole. He froze on the trigger, falling under the spell of buck fever, common to hunters and soldiers alike, and let the M-60 keep hammering away without a pause. Finally, over the rattle of the M-60, the pilot yelled "You got him; you got him! Stop firing!"

Jerry stopped. He had pumped nearly five hundred rounds into the spider hole.

The lead ship had killed the other four Viet Cong, and a Blue team was called in to search the area and clear it.

The infantry recovered the bodies and their weapons and they came over to the spider hole to get Jerry's first kill out. They reached down and pulled the body out, then *walked* him over to the lift ship. The guy hadn't been touched. The frightened Cong was a babbling idiot at that point, but he wasn't even scratched.

Jerry was harassed that night about his first "KIA." Embarrassed beyond words, Ballantyne swore it would never happen again.

Within weeks, though, the war caught up with him, and he learned the ropes faster than he ever wanted to. As mission mounted upon mission, Jerry soon had the experience to fly in the lead ship.

The 1/9 Cav's mission of scouting and recon for the division took them over vast expanses of their operations area as they sought targets for the grunts and artillery.

The scouts frequently came across an ambush set for the

---

3. The AK-47 assault rifle was the standard infantry weapon of both the VC and the NVA. It was a full or semiautomatic rifle, firing 7.62×39mm cartridges with a detachable thirty-round box magazine.

infantry. They would then turn the tables and fire up the ambushers, call in artillery to demolish the area, and report the site for Blue teams to attack.

They could also spot booby traps. Flying at an altitude twelve feet above the jungle canopy, scouts scanned a route of march for punji pits, mines, and any number of other unpleasant surprises. They marked suspicious spots with smoke so the ground troops could move up and neutralize the threat.

On the morning of October 22, 1967, the scouts received a distress call from a long-range reconnaissance patrol (LRRP). The LRRPs were small squads of four to six heavily armed soldiers, inserted by helicopter deep into the enemy's operational area. Moving undetected through the jungle, they'd report enemy concentrations, weapons emplacements, and other critical intelligence. LRRP actions included sniping at or ambushing choice targets and setting demolitions before melting back into the jungle.

This LRRP patrol, however, had been spotted by the enemy and was now surrounded and trapped on a hill by a company-size force of North Vietnamese Army regulars. The hill was about four hundred meters high and thoroughly forested with jungle. The LRRPs were at the top, holding out against nearly 150 attackers.

Sergeant Ballantyne was in the lead ship of the White team that responded to the call for help. They immediately flew out to relieve the pressure until a stronger force could arrive. As they rolled in, ground fire was immediate, and Jerry started blasting away with his M-60. The first five or six VC he engaged fell quickly, and the enemy began to disperse into the jungle, firing as they ran. A number of rounds found their way to the aircraft.

Ballantyne grabbed the M-79 and poured out as many explosives as he could while the enemy was still exposed. The jungle wasn't very thick just there, and he could spot them fairly well.

Jerry shouted directions to the pilot who was doing an incredible job of keeping trees between the chopper and the bulk of the enemy. Ballantyne chose and engaged his targets as fast as he could. At times it seemed he was firing his M-60, M-79, and throwing grenades all at the same time.

NVA troops began appearing everywhere, firing at the two OH-13s from all sides.

The pilots called for help—the NVA force was too much for a couple OH-13s. They had found the main enemy element and now needed artillery, gunships, and forward air control to call in an air strike. As the UH-1C Huey gunships came in to rake the area with rockets and automatic weapons, the scouts moved about a hundred meters out of the way, and there they found an NVA regimental headquarters.

The camp contained an immense force of soldiers that Ballantyne later learned was massing for a major operation in Binh Thuan Province. Those troops were soon greeted with heavy artillery fire, many more gunships, and everything else the Cav could bring to bear on them.

Back on the hilltop, the NVA were closing their circle around the LRRP patrol. Over the radio, Jerry could hear the Americans on the ground calling desperately for close-in, heavy automatic fire. A very real problem was that the top of the hill was covered with extremely thick triple-canopy jungle. Ballantyne could hardly distinguish between bad guys and good guys through the branches and vines. Seeming to know it, the NVA got as close as they could to the hard-fighting LRRPs and made it impossible for Ballantyne's M-60 to ferret them out without causing friendly casualties.

By then, Jerry and his pilot were doing a macabre sort of aerial ballet. Directed by radio from the ground, they hovered above the LRRP position, and as the pilot spun the chopper in circles, Ballantyne sprayed the surrounding area with machine-gun fire. But the NVA kept moving in closer.

Ballantyne grabbed the hand mike, shouting orders to the LRRPs to break out their Day-Glo orange spotter panels and stand on top of them. By doing that, they were now clearly marked, even through the foliage, and Ballantyne poured a blistering volume of fire into the surrounding trees within a few feet of the nervous patrol, breaking the back of the enemy unit and forcing them to withdraw.

With fresh confidence, the patrol renewed their defense, increasing the intensity of their own fire. They were soon able to break away and head for a nearby landing zone.

Even as the NVA retreated, Ballantyne continued firing and throwing grenades until he discovered that his right arm would no longer respond. Then he noticed the huge red stain spreading in his sleeve.

"I'm hit," he said, not believing it himself. He didn't feel any pain, but, unable to fire the machine gun anymore, he pulled the pins on some smoke grenades with the panel hook and his left hand, then dropped them on the NVA to mark an air strike.

The pilot broke off the contact and headed for help, as Jerry, suffering from blood loss, passed out on the way to the hospital.

The battle raged into the night, illuminated by flares and now engaged by infantry that had been lifted into the area. For three days, the Cav attacked until the NVA gave up and bolted into the hills, leaving hundreds of dead and tons of equipment behind.

The scouts worked around the clock, seeking and reporting targets, and attacking others. As one aircraft took off, another would land to refuel and rearm, then take off again.

The LRRP patrol had been successfully extracted by a flight of UH-1 Hueys shortly after Ballantyne's aircraft had left. The other OH-13 had remained on station to provide security until the LRRPs had been able to safely reach their LZ.

Sergeant Ballantyne spent several weeks convalescing from his wounds. He had taken an AK-47 round through the length of his upper arm. Shrapnel had entered his chest, striking a rib.

When Jerry had first returned to consciousness, he was lying in a rear-area field hospital, trying to peer through a hazy blur. He thought he was dead. All he could see were shiny stars, and his fuzzy thoughts imagined he was in heaven. When he at last grasped where he was, he also understood that the stars were real.

General William C. Westmoreland was standing beside his bed. Westy was the commander of all U.S. forces in Vietnam, and there he was visiting a lowly E-6 door gunner. He even pinned a Purple Heart on Jerry.

Ballantyne managed to produce a weak smile for the momentous event. Damn, he thought, Westy came here to see me!

As Jerry watched, the general moved to the next bunk, pinning another Purple Heart on, then another.

It was a routine walk-through that the general did wherever he went, and he was just passing through.

In a few weeks, Ballantyne's wounds were nearly healed. The boredom of the hospital finally aggravated Jerry to the point that he walked out, hopped a flight back to his unit, and went back to work.

He was soon deep into the war again. It seemed that no day went by without a combat mission for him, partly because there were so many operations going on and partly due to Jerry's soft heart. As a section sergeant, Ballantyne was responsible for dispatching door gunners on missions. He couldn't stand to send some of the young kids he had out on dangerous assignments. It broke his heart every time he lost one in action, and he often felt guilt for sending them. Jerry's solution was to go on the tougher missions himself. His experience gave him a better chance of surviving, and he would put them on simpler missions until they could build up a skill level that could keep them alive.

The 1/9 Cav was a constantly active combat unit, and at times it seemed everyone had a Purple Heart. It became so prevalent that some new troops didn't feel like they belonged unless they'd caught some lead. One young fellow, having a misguided sense of esprit, actually looked forward to it, and Jerry worried that the young fool would get killed doing something dumb. It was not long before the kid returned from a mission with one foot nearly shot off. Jerry had to help him out of the chopper. It was so bad, Ballantyne had to cut the boot off to avoid pulling off the remnants of the kid's shattered foot. Through it all, and between the shouts of pain, the guy was glad.

"I finally got it, Sarge," he said. "My Purple Heart. How about that shit!"

By December 1967, A Troop had moved from Phan Thiet to An Khe in the north, rejoining the 1st Cavalry Division for Operation PERSHING in Binh Dinh Province. From the sixth through the twentieth of December, they conducted sweeping combat operations in conjunction with the ARVN forces against NVA and VC strongholds in the area.

Sergeant Ballantyne and his pilot were returning from one of these battles in a single aircraft to rearm and refuel. The

OH-13 made it back to base, refueled, restocked with ammo, and took off again, alone, to return to the mission.

They were about thirty minutes out of An Khe, doing nearly seventy knots at ground level, racing back to battle, when a single shot rang out.

"We're hit!" the pilot exclaimed as they both looked at the instruments in time to see the oil gauge drop to zero.

The pilot instantly pulled hard on the controls, flaring the rotor-blade pitch for an emergency landing. This was an attempt at autorotation, a standard maneuver to softly land a disabled chopper by applying maximum lift at the last moment before crashing. In the next second, they hit the ground hard.

Both skids broke off as the chopper smacked into an open rice paddy, miles from any help.

Ballantyne grabbed the fire extinguisher and quickly put out an engine fire caused by the bullet that had brought them down. As he did that, the pilot got out of the aircraft and stood up on the floorboard to see where they were.

Jerry heard a dull thump and turned to see the pilot fall over into the paddy. The stabilizer bar of the still-turning rotor had whacked him in the head, crushing his flight helmet and leaving a horrific gash across the man's forehead.

Ballantyne rushed over and wrapped the wound with his fatigue shirt to stop the bleeding. Jerry then dragged the unconscious man over to the edge of the rice paddy, getting clear of the aircraft, which he feared might explode. He ran back, grabbed the M-60, and about two hundred rounds of ammo. As he returned to the pilot, he heard small-arms fire beginning to strike the downed chopper. Looking back, Jerry saw a Viet Cong coming toward him, raising an AK-47 to fire. With an incredibly lucky shot, Jerry dropped him with his .45.

Neither Jerry nor the pilot had thought of making a distress call. They had gone down too fast, and now Jerry realized that no one knew they were down, or where. He ran back to the wreck, grabbed the radio mike, and began shouting, "Mayday," without result.

A movement caught his eye, and he looked to see his pilot, who had regained consciousness, holding up his hand and flicking his wrist. It suddenly dawned on him that it was a hand signal. Turn on the ignition! Of course. Nothing worked without electrical power, so Jerry flipped the switch and, within seconds, reported his status and position. Within fifteen minutes, he heard the sound of choppers coming over the horizon.

That was the thing about the Cav; if one of their guys was in trouble, the whole unit came rolling in to the rescue.

By then, he was getting heavy automatic-weapons fire from nearby woods. Water sprayed all around him from impacting rounds. Reaching into the chopper for the M-79, he noticed his cigarette lighter, one he had earned from the NCO academy in Germany, drop out of his pocket and into the mud. As he was spattered with water from another burst of fire out of the wood line, he continued to search for the lighter until he found it, grabbed the grenade launcher, then ran back to the pilot.

Saying a silent prayer, he pulled the pilot to the other side of the dike for protection from the gunfire. Jerry fired some 40mm grenades into the woods as he heard the choppers coming closer. As they drew near, he realized he hadn't marked his position. He pulled the pin on a smoke grenade, but in his haste he threw it into the water too fast and it fizzled out. Grabbing another one, he set if off properly and hoped he'd be spotted. The flight was already past, but a crew chief sitting on the back ramp of a CH-47 spotted him.

As Jerry sat in the water watching, the massive formation of helicopters did a neat about-face in the sky and came screaming back. It seemed to Jerry as if six thousand aircraft had descended on the area. He tried using hand signals to indicate where the enemy was, but to no avail. He then picked up the M-60 and pumped all the ammo he had into the tree line, laying down a field of fire that left no doubt where the enemy was. Enemy fire suddenly increased dramatically as their position was exposed to the assault force.

A Huey gunship came directly overhead and let go with twenty rockets, twenty feet over Jerry's head, startling the hell out of him. VC were running everywhere, trying to escape the helicopters. Jerry had no idea there were so many Cong in the area. The Cav teams were making contacts all around him. An OH-13 came in overhead and hovered above, rotating on its axis and firing, just as Ballantyne's aircraft had done in the LRRP rescue.

As the battle moved away from the crash site, a UH-1 landed nearby to pick them up. The Huey pilot waved to Ballantyne to climb aboard.

"No way!" Jerry bellowed. "You take this wounded man first!"

He scooped up the pilot and deposited him on the Huey, then threw his M-60 and M-79 in after. He then waved the chopper off.

As he stood there and watched it go, it dawned on him that he should have been on it. Standing there, alone and armed only with his .45, he felt a little silly as a second Huey sat down near him. The pilot smiled and gestured to him to climb aboard.

In early February 1968, the 1/9 Cav moved to Quang Tri, toward the later part of Jerry's tour and during the buildup of NVA forces around Khe Sanh. The NVA hoped to embarrass the United States with a decisive victory similar to the 1954 defeat of the French at Dien Bien Phu. Toward that end, they were massing huge forces in the hills surrounding the Marine base camp there. The U.S. counter operation was called PEG-ASUS. As with most 1st Cavalry operations, the 1/9 Cav was right out in front throughout the battle. Ballantyne was there, too.

Looking for infiltrating NVA troops, Jerry was flying in the chase ship of a White team moving toward the Cambodian border. They were in a free-fire zone, an area where anything that moved was a target, when they came upon a major camp where no friendly base was supposed to be. He called the lead ship and talked to Sergeant First Class Sing (not his real name), who had become Jerry's closest and most trusted friend. Neither of them could identify the camp, which had an American type layout, M-151 jeeps, duece-and-a-half trucks, and which generally looked like a U.S. base.

They called back for guidance and were told there were no friendlies in the area. Deciding to get a closer look, they moved down, hovering above the camp and looking around. Suddenly, Sing yelled and fired.

"NVA," he reported as a soldier came out of an underground bunker, firing. Sing stitched him up with his M-60. Then NVA came pouring out of other bunkers and the surrounding jungle, firing at the two scouts.

The camp was later identified as the old Lang Vei Special Forces base, overrun earlier in a bloody battle and now occupied by the minions of Ho Chi Minh. The vehicles there had been captured.

A fifty-caliber machine gun opened up and started shooting at the choppers. It's throaty pounding echoed above the sounds of the smaller weapons, coughing huge tracers into the sky.

The lead ship, dodging and spinning as it went, moved into a hover over the big machine gun and its crew. Jerry watched in horror as Sergeant First Class Sing pulled the pin on a grenade and prepared to toss it out. As though frozen in time, Ballantyne saw a green tracer from another heavy machine gun, firing from farther away, come loping in and strike Sing square in the chest.

The impact threw him back into the OH-13, still holding the grenade. The chopper exploded and burst into flames as it fell to the ground.

Ballantyne screamed to his pilot to land by the wreck. Reluctantly doing so, he let Jerry out, and had to lift off immediately to avoid the heavy fire on all sides.

As Jerry approached the flaming aircraft, he saw the pilot lying to one side, thrown clear. Miraculously, the injured man raised an arm toward Jerry, still alive and needing help.

Even as he reached out to the pilot, Jerry saw the fifty caliber start firing again. The gunner riddled the pilot with bullets, cutting him to pieces with the big gun. As he stood, stunned, with his .45 dangling in his hand, a Huey gunship came out of nowhere and landed behind him. The crew chief leapt from the aircraft, grabbed Ballantyne, who was frozen with shock, and pulled him into the ship as they took off in a fusillade of fire.

Jerry was evacuated back to base camp. He went immediately to flight operations. Something had finally snapped, and he was thoroughly pissed that the crew of the downed chopper had been left on the ground, even though the area was crawling with NVA, and even though they were both dead.

Grabbing the microphone, he started shouting orders to the choppers in the area to get them out. He had to be dragged out of the room by his friends and calmed down.

After Jerry regained his composure, he walked away to a

quiet spot. Sitting on a tree stump, he put his head in his hands and cried until he couldn't cry any more.

Jerry Ballantyne finished his tour with the 1/9 Cav and went home. By then, he had been credited with over 250 KIAs, and he had been on combat missions nearly every day of his year in country.

Within two months of his return to the States, he was back in Vietnam, this time as a LRRP with the Rangers. For another six months, he battled the Viet Cong and NVA again, this time on the ground and deep inside the jungles he'd seen so often from the air.

Ballantyne still had his courage, but his luck ran out again. Jerry was medevac'd back to the States halfway into his tour, shot to pieces in an ambush. Perforated by a burst of fire from an AK-47, he had a bullet lodged in his spine that required lengthy and delicate surgery to remove.

It took years for Jerry to recover from his wounds, and he still carries scars. Once he was back on his feet, he became a hometown recruiter in Tacoma, Washington. He was proud of his uniform and wanted to stay in the army.

Sitting in his downtown Tacoma office, nearly two years since his 1/9 Cav service, Sergeant First Class Ballantyne received a large brown envelope in the mail. The return address indicated that it was from Headquarters, Department of the Army.

Opening the envelope, he pulled out a handful of certificates, all signed by Maj. Gen. John Tolson, commander of the 1st Cavalry Division during Jerry's first Vietnam tour. In another corner was the signature of Stanley R. Resor, secretary of the army. Each one was for S. Sgt. Jerry R. Ballantyne. They were citations for awards. One was for the Silver Star, awarded for an action on September 19, 1967. He wasn't really sure just which battle it was, since there were so many then. Another, the Bronze Star, was dated May 18, 1968, just as he was going home the first time. The Distinguished Flying Cross was there for the LRRP team rescue over that lonely hill outside of Phan Thiet. Eighteen awards of the Air Medal were in the envelope, too, hardly beginning to cover the number of combat missions Jerry actually flew.

And two Purple Hearts. The Purple Hearts were the only medals of the bunch that had been presented by a real person. Jerry eventually had to write to a private mail-order catalog and pay cash to get the actual medals.

Chapter 2

HUEY GUNSHIP

WO-1 Jim Kreutz was still a bit fresh out of flight school to be where he found himself. With only two months time in country, he was copiloting a UH-1C gunship, a heavily armed version of the Huey, into a hot LZ deep in Laos. The target area was called Hotel-9 and had a nasty reputation as an extremely dangerous area for any kind of operations. Beginning just west of Ben Het on the northwest border of South Vietnam, Hotel-9 stretched into Laos as far as the town of Ban Phiaha just above the point where Cambodia, Laos, and South Vietnam met. It was a hotbed of North Vietnamese bases and troops.

Even the mission was the kind that promised all the worst things that happen when aircraft are too far from help and home. A Special Forces Hatchet team, company-size strike force, subordinated to MACV's Studies and Observation Group ("SOG") had been inserted on September 26, 1967, the previous day. Its original mission had been to destroy an NVA truck and vehicle park along the Ho Chi Minh trail, then hightail it to an LZ for extraction by slicks.

Long before the mixed company of American and South Vietnamese troops reached its objective, some wizard had decided to prep the motor pool with CS gas, dropping canisters of the not-so-deadly riot-control agent from the air. By the time the Green Berets reached the target area, they were greeted by massed volumes of automatic-weapons fire from NVA regulars wearing protective masks.

Outnumbered and outgunned, the small force broke away and fled into the jungle, abandoning its objective and retreat-

25

ing to an impromptu extraction point. With the NVA hot on their trail, the planned LZ was no longer a viable option. The enemy pursued them vigorously and in great strength. By the time the men reached a suitable LZ and lift choppers from the 189th Assault Helicopter Company arrived, the intensive ground fire from the enemy made it impossible to land. Even an air strike by A-1E Skyraiders failed to clear the area of enemy enough to allow the extraction. The first flight had to settle for dropping supplies and equipment to the beleaguered defenders and fly back to base at Dak To as night approached.

Throughout the night, ground crews readied choppers for the dawn mission that they hoped wouldn't come. If the SOG force could break contact during the night, they might be able to sneak out to an area where the slicks could pick them up without a battle.

But radio frequencies monitored from the area indicated a steadily worsening situation. By sunup, an extra flight of slicks had been flown in from Pleiku to help pull the team out in a single lift. Jim Kreutz and the rest of the "guns" of the 189th Assault Helicopter Company were ready to go, too, by the time the order to launch came.

Jim was flying with his usual aircraft and AC (aircraft commander), CWO-4 William "Bull" Durham. Durham was a grizzled veteran who was short and stocky and got along with everybody except FNG (fucking new guy) copilots, like Kreutz, who had only been in country for fifty-eight days. Jim didn't mind because the aggravation was well worth the survival skills he absorbed by working with the curmudgeon.

The old Huey was another story, though, with crazed plastic in the windshields, a chattering fuel pump, sluggish throttle linear hydraulic actuator, and an intermittently inoperative fuel gauge. In spite of those and other deficiencies, there were no showstoppers to keep them on the ground, and the "Jesus nut" still held the whole ship to the rotor head. That particular part was so named because it was threaded onto the rotor mast and was the only thing keeping the rotor head and blades from separating from the complete helicopter. With equal panache, the army would term such an event a "catastrophic failure."

Jim had checked out all the weapons prior to the mission. On the nose was an M-5 40mm grenade launcher, often called a "Frog" or "Thumper." He didn't care much for it, since it jammed a lot, and the rounds flew only slightly faster than the aircraft. Great for static targets that weren't returning fire, but . . .

Kreutz greatly preferred what was mounted on either side, below the sliding side doors. Right and left were seven-tube, 2.75-inch rocket launchers, for a total of fourteen rounds, plus four stripped-down 7.62 mm machine guns, aimed and fired by a scissors-and-pivot-type contraption called a pantographic sight. These were augmented by a door gunner with a "free 60," M-60 machine gun, out of each side. They were free because only a bungee cord and the gunner held them to the aircraft.

Just for good measure, Kreutz had tossed a couple extra cans of machine-gun ammo inside and grabbed an M-79 Blooper that fired single 40mm grenade rounds.

All these weapons, added to the UH-1C by the army in Vietnam, turned it into a surrogate attack helicopter, commonly called a gunship. The troop-lift Hueys, on the other hand, were called slicks because they lacked weapons other than a door gun on either side.

While the Huey slicks and gunships made their way to the site, air force A1-E Skyraiders known locally as Spads, had been hammering the area around the Hatchet team. It was essential to not only relieve the pressure on the friendlies on the ground but to suppress the huge volume of antiaircraft fire that could destroy the rescue mission.

As Jim absentmindedly fingered his lucky tiger tooth, a gift from a friend who was later killed, he thought about the pre-flight briefing. The NVA in Hotel-9 were armed with .50-caliber machine guns, 23mm and 57mm antiaircraft ("AA") guns, and plenty of small arms. It would all be triangulated into kill zones in the LZ.

"What the hell am I doing here?" he mused.

Kreutz knew they were in the area when he spotted a command-and-control (C & C) Huey hovering overhead near smoke from the Spad strikes. As the gun platoon leader, Avenger Six, led them into the area, Bull armed the guns and rockets, putting them on hot, and reminded the door gunners to identify targets before shooting. The team on the ground was receiving fire from all quadrants, and the aircrews had to know what their perimeter was.

The gunships dropped to the very tops of the 120-foot trees and made a high-speed 120-knot pass over the LZ without firing. From the jungles all around, twinkling muzzle flashes from literally hundreds of weapons of all calibers lit the morning.

Kreutz spotted the Special Forces team using a bomb crater as a defensive perimeter, huddled in the center and partially obscured by smoke, haze, and mist.

Rolling back around for another pass, Bull fired off a pair of 2.75-inch rockets as Jim let rip with the M-5, plunking out a few rounds just to see if it still worked.

The longer the extraction took them, the situation could only get worse, so Avenger Six started working the slicks down to the LZ, one at a time, to pick up the soldiers on the ground. It was a difficult task, since there was only a small hover-hole for one bird at a time to drop into, load up, and move clear for the next. This small break in the jungle was made by the bomb that made the crater the Hatchet team was now using as a fortification. The helicopters' rotors cleared the edges by only a few feet, and the tail rotor had to be maneuvered between branches on the way down and up again.

As the team was slowly extracted, one Huey at a time, the gunships had to make continuous runs on the NVA, keeping them occupied to protect the almost defenseless slicks.

They set up a racetrack of firing runs, preplanned attack patterns based on the slick's flight paths, so they could deliver maximum fire without interrupting the lift.

At one end of the track, Jim kept hearing what sounded like an old SKS carbine firing at them each pass. It stood out above the din of battle because its report was so different from the staccato chattering of AK-47s and the hammering of 12mm heavy machine guns. It was also quite close to the LZ.

Well, it seemed a bit ridiculous to focus one's attention on such a low-level threat in this dangerous airspace, but Chief, one of the door gunners, began to take the one-shot Charlie very personal. On every pass, as they approached the area where this guy would fire from, Chief would hang all the way out, restrained only by his monkey harness, a rigging that kept crew members from falling out of the helicopter, and fire the M-60 at the sound of the shots. He'd begin firing to the front, swing around as they passed and then shoot down along the tail boom. By the time they turned away, Chief was nearly inverted and firing under the Huey, between the skids.

He never did get the guy, because they still heard the old SKS as they left the area later.

The slicks had been rolling in and out like clockwork, and every gun run meant another batch of grunts was in the air. With each run down the racetrack, the muzzle flashes would decrease. Kreutz could see concentrations in some areas, but laying down overall suppressive fire was more important than hitting point positions, especially when the slicks were the most vulnerable.

As Bull jockeyed into position, setting up a beautiful firing run alongside the next slick, Kreutz sensed, felt, and heard it happen.

"Oh shit! We're hit!"

He felt a searing heat in the back of his neck as the master-caution light flashed on, indicating an electrical failure some-where, along with the hydraulic-segment light, which meant flight-control problems. Letting go of the sight, Jim grabbed the back of his neck, but could feel no blood, just a piece of hot brass ejected by the door gunner's M-60.

Kreutz looked at Bull and saw beads of sweat forming on his face and forehead.

Their UH-1C was in reality a hybrid B/540, an older

UH-1B with the newer 540 rotor system added on, which had only one hydraulic system and no backup. If they had a total hydraulic failure this far from home, they stood little chance of surviving.

Expecting the worst, Bull tried the controls and told Jim to do the same. They felt normal to both men.

Bull simply shrugged and went in for the next gun run.

By the time the last flight had dropped in to load the last of the Hatchet team, the Avengers were worried that the NVA might try a full-blown assault to finish off the last lift.

The aircraft in the hover-hole was partially obscured by smoke from the battle and smoke grenades used to mark the LZ and mask fire. Drifting dust from exploding rockets and ripping fire from the guns crisscrossing the area around the LZ made it difficult to place fires without hitting the slick. In spite of the reduced visibility, the aircraft commander of the Huey in the hole kept telling the guns to bring fire in closer.

"Come on, Avengers, get it closer, get it closer," he repeated calmly as his ship came under ever more intensive enemy fire.

As the Huey hovered up and out of the tiny clearing, then sped away, Kreutz swore that he'd never rag a slick pilot again. He'd kidded them before with jabs like "slicks are for kids," preferring the macho image of shoot-'em-up Huey gunships, but he wouldn't bother them again. He had new respect for their courage under fire and cool-headed flying in a tight spot.

On the way out, the FAC (forward air controller) spotted an NVA company massing for an attack on the LZ. Kreutz and Bull wanted to use up their remaining ammo, but Avenger VI canceled the idea. The air force was on the way back to clean up the mess.

On the trip back to their base at Kontum, the two pilots wondered about the warning lights. They were sure they'd been hit, but the aircraft was doing fine.

Inspecting the ship after they landed, it was discovered that a round had creased a hydraulic line on the 40mm pod on the nose. It wasn't leaking, only pinched, causing a constriction in the flow that made the lights flicker.

The final verdict was that if the M-5 could stop bullets that would otherwise enter the cockpit, it wasn't completely useless after all.

The seven aircrews of the 189th AHC, plus the Alligator ship from 119th AHC, who flew into the hover-hole on Hotel-9 that day had more balls than a bearing factory. They had flown into massed, intensive antiaircraft fire, dropped into a tiny hole in the trees hardly large enough for the aircraft, and held an above-ground hover while loading troops. All while surrounded by explosions, incoming automatic-weapons fire, and nearly complete visual obscurity. The gunships had done such an effective job of suppressing and drawing enemy fire that not one slick was shot down or suffered any casualties. As a result, Cap. John J. Holland, the Hatchet team commander, recommended the entire flight for Air Medals, aircraft commanders for the Distinguished Flying Cross, and the Silver Star for the mission commander.

The 189th Assault Helicopter Company was part of the 52d Aviation Battalion, 17th Group, 1st Aviation Brigade. The unit's home base was Camp Holloway, near Pleiku. Jim had come in country in mid-September 1967, starting his tour with the 189th AHB lift company, Ghost Riders. As a slick pilot, he flew UH-1Bs and then H-models, but soon moved to the Avengers, who flew the UH-1C Huey gunships.

Besides support of the Special Forces, the 189th had additional missions of flying support in the II Corps area from Kontum to Binh Thuan provinces and, on an as-needed basis, support for the 4th Infantry Division.

The majority of Jim's missions were cross-border missions into Laos and Cambodia, again, in support of the Studies and Observations Group in operational areas called Prairie Fire and Daniel Boone, all highly classified at the time.

Jim's expertise as a gunship pilot grew with each additional mission he flew, and as his skills improved, so did his chances of surviving the war. But, because of the classified nature of the unit's mission, they were often called upon to test new equipment and weapons. Sometimes, that was a real bonus. Other times, it seemed something much less. One such item of new equipment Kreutz was involved with testing was something called the people sniffer. The people-sniffer was a device that would scoop atmospheric samples and, by the presence of certain chemicals in the air, determine if large numbers of people, most likely enemy troops, were in the area. An earlier version of the device was a huge console that dominated the interior of an aircraft and required a specially trained operator to be at all effective.

The mission began with Kreutz on standby while two Studies and Observation Group (SOG) teams were out in the field. The aircraft would be ready to launch if any of the Green Berets or their Vietnamese counterparts got into a tight spot. The SOG teams would generally be comprised of U.S. advisors with a mixture of Nung tribesmen, Chinese mercenaries, Laotians, and Cambodians recruited in the area, and whoever else wanted to fight against the North.

While idly waiting for a mission to be called, they noticed a civilian, dressed in unmarked fatigues, sitting in on the morning briefing. There were rumors that the man was from a laboratory back in the States. That was not cause for concern, since they were used to people coming in from the States with new gadgets to try out. Sure enough, Bull was called into a meeting that same afternoon to talk to the civilian about the new gadget.

This new people sniffer was modest in size, with an external sensor and simple indicator gauge on the panel. Kreutz and Bull watched curiously as the civilian began working on their aircraft. He put in a gauge about the size of an automobile tachometer, ran a wire out the door, and mounted a little antennalike device on the skid. It struck them that it was quite small, especially in comparison to the previous device.

Having installed it, the man then gave them a short briefing on how to operate it. He explained that they needed to enter a target area at about fifty feet AGL (above ground level) and then zero in the adjustable dial. Having done that, they would only need to watch the needle for movement to indicate when they were over large groups of people. However, the device wouldn't tell them if a group was friendly or enemy, just human.

To the chagrin of Jim and Bull, the major in charge said they would make the test in the Hotel-9 area. As Kreutz and Durham knew, the NVA had division-size elements and training camps throughout the area, making it one of the hottest pieces of real estate in Southeast Asia.

Jim leaned over to Bull and said, "Hey, this doesn't make

a lot of sense. Why don't we just fly over the compound or Kontum City? If it picks up people, it'll spot friendlies just as easy as bad guys." Bull agreed, but they were vetoed by the major. It seems that an important part of the success of the test was a body count. The civilian wanted to return Stateside to his lab with not only the number of enemy detected by his device but also with a laundry list of those killed after being found.

Against their better judgment, Jim and Bull launched with one other UH-1C about 3:30 that afternoon and headed for an area at the southern end of Hotel-9 called the old French fort, after some ruins there. About thirty-five minutes later, they dropped just over a road flanked on either side by tall elephant grass, with their wingman flying overhead cover, to zero in the people sniffer.

Jim turned the knob back and forth and the needle jumped around, but it would not calibrate to zero. Bull reached over to try his hand at it, while hovering at about fifty feet in the middle of enemy territory.

About that time, hostile troops on the ground became rather nervous, and all at once, the whole area lit up with muzzle flashes. The bird overhead reported on the radio that it appeared to be an area equal to four grid squares, all firing at the hovering Huey. They didn't know whether they had found a battalion, a division, or a major camp, but it was big.

Jim's ship took hits immediately as Bull pulled up and made a break for the east to head back home.

As they gained altitude, Jim saw guns firing at them as far as the eye could see in every direction. Bull just said, "Piss on it," and turned back around to make some gun runs. That many targets deserved to take a few rounds before they turned tail and ran. Identifying a particularly heavy concentration, Bull made a run with the rockets and door guns while Jim pounded away with the M-5.

One soldier was firing his AK from a small rise that Jim tried to hit several times. The rounds from the 40mm were so slow that he could see them in flight all the way to the target as he walked them into it. The soldier on the hill could see them coming, too, and would jump out of the way just before they reached his position. Then he'd hop back into place and begin firing again.

After a few passes, Jim was frustrated by his inability to hit the target, but the door gunner spotted what was going on, and as the NVA jumped back up when the Huey went by, he nailed him cold with the M-60 machine gun.

Remarkably, this was the only mission Kreutz had ever flown that the M-5 didn't jam right away. They carried about 300 rounds, and he had expended nearly 275 of those by that time.

But the action was costly; their wingman started taking too many hits, both door gunners were injured, and the hydraulic warning light illuminated, so they broke off the mission and headed home again.

They swore all the way back that they'd never fly an experimental mission again. They dropped the wounded off at the medevac pad in Dak To, one with a chest wound and the other with a shot through the foot, and returned to base.

The civilian was waiting for their report when they arrived. Between the heated words that Jim and Bull threw at him, the technician realized that his device had not functioned properly. An inspection of the aircraft made the reason clear. When they boarded for the mission and the door closed, it had clipped one of the leads between the gauge and the sensor unit. "No problem," said the man. He'd simply splice it, and they could try again. Jim and Bull both had the same response.

"Not just no, but hell no!" This guy was just a civilian, and they didn't have to follow his orders. And no one in charge cared to send them back out for a second test.

But that was not the end of experimental equipment. Before long, the army began sending them new types of 2.75 FFARs, or folding-fin aerial rockets. The Avengers had started out with the pure high-explosive (HE) rounds, but they soon began to receive new types. One of the early versions had a nineteen-pound warhead. They weren't too successful, since they tended to lose speed and drop off faster than the 40mm rounds out of the M-5. Jim thought they just rolled out of the tube and fell on the target.

Next came proximity-fuzed rounds that were expected to provide an air burst for a wider kill radius. Sometimes, however, if improperly torqued when they were assembled and loaded, the rockets would explode on or near the aircraft with uncomfortable results. Jim, fortunately, never had the bad luck to use any.

White phosphorous was another story, however, being very effective when properly employed. The extremely high temperature incendiary caused monstrous damage and horrible burn wounds that scared the living daylights out of NVA and Viet Cong alike. Avenger crews learned quickly that they could saturate the area around an LZ with WP rockets, and the enemy would not walk through it for any reason. It created a very handy protective zone of burning chemicals and vegetation that shielded the troops on the ground.

Of all the rockets they tried, Jim liked "nails" the best. Officially called flechettes, they were particularly well suited to the 189th's missions. The gunship crews liked to prep an LZ with a few rockets before inserting infantry on slicks. This served to draw enemy fire, if any were in the area, and expose their positions, but also raised a lot of dust and smoke, obscuring vision.

The nails, on the other hand, had a relatively clean burst that spread several thousand steel darts showering over the area. Frequently finding a lot of dead bad guys in the area when they used them, flight crews always made sure to pack a few nails for each mission. Soon, everybody wanted them, and they were in short supply in no time.

The nails came in very handy on one particular mission in July 1968. The NVA would build huge caves along the Ho Chi Minh trail to hide in when spotted from the air, or as rest and maintenance stops along the way.

Following the insertion of an SOG team along the Laotian-Cambodian border, Jim and Bull were flying along when they caught a large number of people on the trail. All of them immediately bolted into a particularly large cave, just off the road.

Lining up for a firing pass, they sped in and fired a salvo of flechette rockets straight into the entrance. The rockets burst inside, killing most of the occupants. The remaining unfortunates ran out again, only to be policed up by the miniguns on the wingman's ship.

The flechettes were later taken out of the inventory after some poorly placed shots caused some friendly casualties in other units. They weren't a good close-support weapon, due to the large bursting radius, and improper use made them dangerous to friend and foe alike.

The 189th pilots still liked to have their nails handy, though, and managed to get a few from the air force for those special occasions.

As Jim's tour wore on, he eventually became a short-timer, having served nearly a full year in Vietnam and fast approaching rotation back to the World, as the States were referred to.

He was eventually sent to the Mang Yang Pass on Highway 19, which ran from Qui Nhon, to fly convoy cover. Mang Yang Pass was infamous for a brutal ambush the Viet Minh had sprung on the French Mobile Group 100 in June 1954. The sides of the road were liberally covered with the clearly marked graves of hundreds of Frenchmen.

When Jim was there, though, he felt somewhat secure, since convoy cover was considered to be easy duty, a soft mission. The Viet Minh were long gone, and the Viet Cong didn't care to attack when air cover was around.

Stationed at An Khe, Jim and his aircrew would get up each morning, launch, and fly cover for a convoy going through. Ambushes were usually set for the first or last convoy of the day, so the ship would fly ahead to try and locate and neutralize the enemy's planned attack.

Most of the convoy's problems involved road mines and booby traps, though, which the choppers couldn't help with.

Jim's ship was tasked on September 1 for a mission outside of their usual routine. Another unit had a ship down and needed cover for a LRRP insertion, so Jim filled in. Putting in a LRRP team was just like inserting SOG teams. The difference was in the recon mission of the LRRPs, while SOG performed a variety of specialized tasks.

As a secondary mission, Kreutz was also giving an aircraft-commander check ride to another pilot for his AC certification. Aircraft commanders were needed as experienced leaders for combat missions. The next level after AC was fire team leader, requiring the highest degree of skill and judgment under fire. Most of the current ACs, like Jim, were getting short, and the unit needed to certify more of their pilots while the older pilots were still around.

The other pilot, CWO-2 Joe Olson, had already made AC twice, but had gotten into trouble with his CO. Joe was an excellent pilot with plenty of time flying gunships, but he had made the mistake of trading his .38 revolver for a Swedish K (M-45) submachine gun. Most of the pilots considered the .38 to be woefully inadequate if they were ever shot down in Charlie's backyard. So Joe made a swap of his issue weapon with a Green Beret who could easily get another one of the 9mm submachine guns for himself.

Shortly thereafter, the .38 came up missing in a company-level arms inventory. When the commander found out that it had been traded away, he went ballistic and required Olson to track down the Green Beret and get his sidearm back. Joe had to give the Swedish K and a bit of cash to reclaim the pistol, and the CO also pulled his AC rating as a punishment.

When a new CO arrived later, Joe was rescheduled for his second AC checkout, since the unit was short of aircraft commanders again. Unfortunately, his check ride was also a mission deep into Laos at a time that he was suffering from Ho Chi Minh's revenge, a virulent strain of dysentery characterized by uncontrolled vomiting and diarrhea.

On the return flight, after completing the mission, Joe's problem reached a point that can only be described as unbearable, so he unstrapped himself from his seat, dropped his trousers, and poked his buttocks out of the aircraft window.

So immediate was his need that he didn't have a chance to inform the door gunner on his side of the aircraft, and the unsightly mess was blown by the rotor wash at force into the poor gunner.

Joe was lucky that he only lost his AC orders again. He was more than a little worried on the remainder of the flight as he noticed the unfortunate gunner angrily swinging his M-60 forward and caressing the trigger.

With Jim Kreutz, a CW0-2 himself since August 29, as pilot in charge, Joe was on his third AC check flight, this time into the Mang Yang Pass. The LRRP team was to be inserted into a fairly secure area near the road so they could monitor any sabotage or ambush operations.

Kreutz and his crew, lulled into a sense of complacency since leaving the SOG support missions behind, were a little too careless and inattentive lately, which would cause them some problems soon. Jim had only two weeks to go on his tour, and his mind was on the good old USA instead of the mission.

They also planned on doing a little showing off to show the slick pilots what guns were all about. They thought it would be a kick to give them what they called "extremely close" coverage when the LRRP team was inserted.

The LZ was a small bald hill that they had flown past a thousand times on convoy escort missions. The surrounding area was peppered with rolling hills covered in elephant grass and patches of jungle. Jim had never seen any NVA, Viet Cong, or anyone else in the area, so no one expected anything to happen on this routine insertion.

As the slick approached, Jim and Joe put their ship in position to go down right into the LZ with the slick. As the slick set down, the gunship began a steep climb to clear a second bald hill, slightly higher, just beyond the first, and straight ahead.

They began the climb with the guns armed, and just as they reached the top, spider holes started popping open all over the hilltop, exposing Viet Cong troops who leapt out with their weapons. One soldier was so close that he almost stuck his AK into the greenhouse chin bubble as he stood up. At least ten to twelve troops opened up on the Huey from all sides, and Jim's bird took a number of hits, mostly in the tail boom. The wingman behind him opened up with all his weapons and started saturating the hilltop with fire the moment Kreutz was clear.

At the LZ, the slick had been hovering while the LRRPs disembarked and was instantly fired upon from all quadrants. As soon as the soldiers were clear, it did an immediate 180-degree turn and fled the area.

Both of the gunships began a racetrack circuit of gun and rocket runs on the spider holes and the surrounding area, laying down suppressive fire that effectively quelled the ambush. Since the LRRP team was now clearly compromised, the slick came back to pick them up and abort the mission.

Jim and his wingman began to prep the area again with rocket and minigun fire. On the third run, Jim's ship shuddered as it took a huge hit from an unknown type of weapon. The windscreen shattered, and Joe dropped the controls as Jim pulled up and cleared the area. Jim looked at Joe and saw blood spurting from his leg. Curiously quiet, Olson simply said he was okay, and sat there holding his foot. Kreutz radioed that they'd been hit, made one more pass on the target and left the remainder of the mission to the other gunship.

An Khe was only ten minutes away, so he had Joe at the medevac pad in no time flat. Fortunately, Joe had taken a bullet through the foot and nothing more. He would be all right.

Examining the aircraft, Jim found holes in the tail boom and saw that the clear plastic chin bubble had been blown out. It would suck wind, but the chopper would still fly. Picking up another pilot, Jim put him in the gunner's seat and returned to the LRRP extraction. By then, he was one of three gunships on-site supporting the lift mission. They suppressed the fire, got the slick in, and the LRRPs out.

Returning to An Khe to top off fuel and rearm, Kreutz was standing by the aircraft when his door gunner walked up with tears in his eyes. "Sir," he said, "I'm sorry. I'm so sorry."

"What are you talking about?" Jim said. "You did fine."

"I shot Mr. Olson!"

Jim looked at him in shock.

"You did what?"

"I'm sorry, sir, I shot him."

Sure enough, when they went around to look at the door, the bullet entry holes coming into it were from the back side and up high; the gunner had misjudged his aim while hanging out of the Huey, firing forward during the gun run, and several rounds went through the door. Although they had been hit by enemy fire at that same moment, the round that struck Joe's foot came from their own gunner! Not one to make a bad situation worse, Jim told the soldier not to tell anyone else. It was an understandable, though tragic, error, but Joe would be fine, and he was even going home.

Olson had also just received his Purple Heart at the hospital, and if the incident was reported, he would lose the medal. No one would profit by making a case of it, so the whole story was better left untold.

That mission was one that Jim Kreutz couldn't forget, because too many things had gone wrong. After surviving for so long in the Hotel-9 area, he was mad at himself for letting his guard down, for being careless, and for showing off at the wrong time. It almost cost some lives, and he didn't like that thought.

Jim left Vietnam on September 16, 1968, and was transferred to Fort Eustis, Virginia. About four months later, in the mail one day came a big envelope. Opening it, he took out a citation for another Distinguished Flying Cross and a small box containing the medal.

It was for the mission where Joe had been shot in the foot. Kreutz couldn't quite accept the idea that he'd been cited for his worst mission, but he sat and thought about it for a while. All of the secret missions into Laos and Cambodia had been infinitely more harrowing and dangerous, but due to their classified nature, not many citations were made for those actions. He pinned the ribbon on his uniform and smiled. Sure, he had earned the DFC. They just hadn't done the paperwork right!

Chapter 3

BIRTH OF THE SNAKE

While the war in Vietnam raged on, the debate over close air support and transport aircraft heated up in the Pentagon. Still concerned about erosion of the air force mission, USAF brass watched with increasing anxiety as army C-7 Caribous moved troops around Vietnam and OV-1 Mohawk surveillance aircraft mounted .50-caliber machine guns to exploit targets they might develop.

The army, in turn, found an increasing need for better armed and faster escort aircraft for troop insertions. In the early years of the war, OH-23 Ravens and OH-13 Sioux augmented the firepower of the lift ships' door gunners.[4] Even when the UH-1s were modified into gunships, they were found to be slow and underpowered, struggling at 140 knots maximum airspeed to keep up with the 165 knot cruise speed of CH-47 Chinooks. The gunships ran out of fuel, ammunition, and rockets quickly as well. Despite these inadequacies, they continued to fight on for lack of alternatives.

Meanwhile, the debate between army and air force aviation advocates had reached a peak, resulting in a formal agreement between the army and air force chiefs of staff in an attempt to put the issue to rest.

The accord, signed on April 6, 1966, laid out several basic rules.

4. The use of OH-13 and OH-23 observation helicopters, armed with door gunners, constitutes the earliest version of a surrogate attack helicopter in Vietnam. The latest example, prior to the Cobra, was the arming of UH-1s with rockets, machine-gun and grenade-launcher systems, and door gunners.

First, the army would transfer all of its Caribous to the air force and release any claim to future purchases of fixed-wing troop-transport aircraft. The air force would then relinquish any right to armed helicopters other than self-defense systems for search-and-rescue and administrative aircraft. They would also refrain from purchasing or employing rotary-wing aircraft for troop movement or tactical logistics.

The rest of the agreement dealt with joint consultations on the design and use of aircraft to support the army and other details concerning the Caribou transfer. A key point in the agreement, that the army would have the only fire-support helicopters, advanced the possibility of a dedicated attack helicopter's being fielded.

Although a series of programs was already underway toward that end, the time had become right to acquire such an aircraft. The army itself visualized attack helicopters as modifications to utility types. Neither the Rogers Board nor the Howze Board had recommended acquiring a purposely built, rotary-wing strike aircraft.

True, a few officers had foreseen the eventual need for such an aircraft, but their numbers were few, as were budget dollars. Most of the planners deemed it more prudent to squeeze a variety of capabilities into a single airframe.

Bell Helicopter, on the other hand, anticipated that the army would someday need a "killer chopper," since any modern battlefield would likely be populated with an unlimited number of threats. In such a hostile environment, part-time gunships would be eaten alive. The Vietnam War ultimately proved Bell correct.

As early as 1958, with its own corporate funding, Bell had built a mock-up helicopter to demonstrate the concept of a combat reconnaissance helicopter. This first version was the D245. The next version, again only a mock-up, was put together in 1962 to show the Howze Board what an attack helicopter might look like. This more ambitious design, called the D255 Iroquois Warrior, looked like a manned rifle bullet. It had smooth lines that put many jets to shame. Though it was projected to be built from UH-1 components (hence the Iroquois name), the D255 was a radical departure from any previous helicopter planform.

The pilot and gunner were seated in tandem, with the forward seat staggered below the rear seat. Enclosed in a long and rounded canopy, both crew members would have a wide and uninterrupted field of vision in all directions.

The tandem placement enabled the fuselage to be narrow and long, reducing the head-on size of the aircraft, presenting a smaller target, and allowing for improved aerodynamics.

Streamlining the chopper would reduce drag, while increasing payload, performance, and range. A nose gun, set in a small turret, was augmented by a ventral belly gun, set in an aerodynamic integral pod with room for a large caliber automatic cannon.

As the mock-up went through design refinements, small wings were added—to increase lift as aircraft speed increased and for mounting weapons. A smooth cowling was added around the rotor mast as well. Only the tail boom remained unchanged from the parent UH-1 design.

Advanced as the D255 was, and it certainly was admired by the army officers who inspected it, it was simply too early. One problem was that the old guard of conservative officers in the army was taken aback at such a radical departure from conventional helicopter design. Still smarting from recommendations made by the Howze Board that would likely be forced on them, the old armor/infantry/artillery boys were still trying to digest the whole sky cav concept. No one could make them eat this "supersonic whirlybird," so it was an idea whose time hadn't come, and it never went beyond the mock-up stage. Many of its features would be seen again.

Bell Helicopter didn't give up on the idea and, in December 1962, began work on a flying demonstrator.

Since the project was still coming out of Bell's pocket, the company's management decided to modify an existing aircraft to an attack configuration rather than build a D255 prototype. While the demonstrator was helping the designers to iron out bugs, Bell engineers busied themselves with design work on a full-production version. By keeping development costs down, the plan could take as long as needed to mature.

The demonstrator was built around an OH-13S Sioux of the type then being used as a scout in Vietnam. The new model was named the Bell Model 207 Sioux Scout.

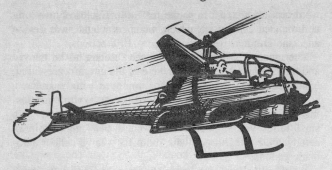

First flown on June 26, 1963, it included a fully enclosed cabin, with the pilot and gunner once again seated in tandem. The teardrop-shape plastic body tapered into the tail boom and back to the tail rotor. Under the nose was a new Emerson Electric TAT-101 "chin" gun turret with two 7.62mm machine guns remotely fired from the cockpit. The gunner aimed and fired the turret, using a floor-mounted pantographic gunsight.

Both crew members had flight controls, but the cyclic stick attitude-and-roll control for the gunner was mounted on the right side on a small console, leaving the usual between-the-knees location for the gunsight apparatus.

Small wings mounted just aft of the canopy added lift and decreased vibration during flight, and plans were discussed to use them as hard points for weapons.

The supercharged piston engine provided little more performance than the OH-13 could muster, but that was a moot point since the entire aircraft was a surrogate. It was understood that a full-scale attack helicopter would be impossible without a turbine engine, such as the TL-53-11 used in the Huey.

After more than four months of exhaustive testing and modifications, the Sioux Scout was taken to most major army bases in the country and demonstrated to the army aviation community before being handed over to Troop B, 3d Squadron, 17th Cavalry (AIR) of the 11th Air Assault Division.

After putting the little ship in every conceivable training situation, the army pilots sang its praises. They recommended that, with the addition of turbine power, a dedicated attack helicopter could be of great value to the army in general and the air assault division in particular. Bell immediately went to work on such an aircraft, which, when completed, was designated the D262.

In the second half of 1964, convinced at long last of the viability of an attack helicopter, the army began a competition to develop a prototype for what they termed the Advanced Aerial Fire Support System (AAFSS). From its inception the program was an overblown attempt to get too much aircraft in too short a time for too much money. The draft specifications alone bore requirements that exceeded existing technology (such as a speed of 200 knots [230 mph]).[5] The powerful twin-engine, twin-rotor CH-47 Chinook fell thirty-five knots short of that at maximum power.

Bell entered its D262 into the competition, but the aircraft had been designed prior to the writing of the specification requirements and, subsequently, did not meet a number of them. Lockheed Aircraft Corporation ultimately got the nod from the army with their AH-56A Cheyenne prototype.

The Cheyenne, amazingly, seemed to actually be nearly everything the army had asked for. In level flight, it went close to 215 knots (245 mph) due to a pusher propeller mounted just behind the tail rotor.

The damn thing was a mixture of airplane and helicopter, with a four-bladed rotor augmented by a 26.7-foot-wide set of wings for lift, and it incorporated every manner of high-tech whiz-bangery available at the time. It had a centralized integrated computer system, infrared night vision, hingeless rotor, advanced control systems, and much more. And it had a twenty-four hundred mile range! That would give the craft the ability to hit distant targets or remain over a target for a long time.

It's anyone's guess how it may have served the army, since it never did; the Vietnam War interceded again, and Bell was ready. When the D262 was dropped from the AAFSS compe-

---

5. Helicopters are limited in their forward speed by a phenomenon known as retreating-blade stall. As the revolving blade moves from the back to the front on the aircraft, lift and thrust are generated, moving the machine forward. On the other side, however, the forward speed of the aircraft joins with the backward swing of the the blade, causing an increasing loss of lift, or blade stall, to that side. The effect generally occurs somewhere above 200 knots.

tition, Bell Helicopter's chief experimental projects engineer, Charlie Seibel, convinced the company that the army would need their new attack helicopter sooner than AAFSS could deliver it.

With American combat divisions already in Vietnam, the need for helicopter fire support was more critical than ever, and AH-56 wouldn't be available until 1970. An interim aircraft was needed to fill the gap.

This scenario had been discussed by Bell's management as early as 1964, and now they were ready with their project Model 209. Bell dipped into the company kitty yet again and decided that the Model 209 had to be in the air within six months. They also decided that a million-dollar cap should be placed on the project.

The deadline was met, and the project went only forty thousand dollars over budget. But now they were ready to talk to the army.

The first prototype was registered with the tail number N209J. It was a thing of beauty. Never had there been a helicopter with such smooth, clean lines, such style and aerodynamics.

In evidence again was the tandem seating arrangement. The pilot, in the rear seat, was elevated above the front-seat gunner for the panoramic view needed in combat. The rounded canopy followed a long, even curve from the shark-style nose back to the vane-style rotor cowling. The fuselage tapered in slowly narrowing angles from the chin-mounted turret, back along the slender tail boom and into the sharply angled tail fin. Unique to N209J was a ventral fin, later removed, that enhanced the sharklike appearance.

A T53-L-13 Lycoming turboshaft engine was faired into the design just behind and below the rotor cowling with a ram-air intake on each side. A narrow thirty-six-inch-wide fuselage carried stubby wings under each intake.

In another departure from convention, N209J had retractable landing skids. A considerable amount of discussion and engineering tests went into the final decision to use fixed landing gear on the production models. It was thought that retracting the skids would reduce drag and, so, improve performance. Without the landing gear being in the way, there would be a greater firing radius for the chin turret. Finally, in an emergency, jettisoned weapons couldn't strike skids enclosed in the fuselage. These arguments were compelling enough that retracting gear was installed on the prototype. Testing, however, changed the equation.

The mechanical limits of the turret left the skids untouched by gunfire, and a simple jettison charge could blow the stores away at an angle clear of the skids. As well, skid drag could be reduced greatly with streamlined fairing tubes. And, of course, while landing, pilots might forget to extend retracted skids. Also the increased complexity and maintenance requirements of retractable skids, coupled with the other factors, outweighed their small advantage.

In the chin turret was a single, 7.62mm General Electric Gatling gun capable of firing thirteen hundred or four thousand rounds per minute, depending on trigger travel from one detent stop to the next on the pantographic sighting system. This was the TAT-102A turret, again, from Emerson Electric.

The main rotor was of the same type employed on the Huey, the famous 540 "door-hinge" system, but with a big difference. The Huey rotor had a set of weights on posts mounted at ninety degrees to the rotor head. These harmonic dampers reduced vibrations and helped counterbalance the many forces that effect a rotor.

Model 209, on the other hand, employed a stability control augmentation system (SCAS) integrated into the fore-and-aft directional and lateral flight controls. The SCAS sensed external disturbances and provided compensating control inputs, assisting the pilot in maintaining aircraft attitude and stabilizing the ship for more accurate weapons firing.

Bell named the new aircraft Cobra. It was the only army helicopter that ever had other than an Indian name. A variety of stories have sprung up as to why, but the most widely believed explanation was that the UH-1 gunships in Vietnam were frequently referred to as Cobras, and the name simply carried over.

A number of important people are frequently given credit for the name, but in the end, soldiers will name things whatever the hell they please. On a trip in Vietnam, a Bell executive noticed the pilots and crews called their Huey gunships Cobras or Snakes, so, when the time came for the factory to tack a moniker on Model 209, the two most commonly used colloquialisms were slapped together into HueyCobra. The aircraft was dubbed Cobra by the men who flew it and maintained it, and by those whose asses it saved again and again through the course of the war.

From its first flight on September 7, 1965, until it was retired to the Patton Museum at Fort Knox, Kentucky, in 1971, N209J flew 1,090 hours—none in combat, but as a demonstrator and test-bed airframe.

In August 1965, Bell made a presentation to the army, discussing the need for a faster and more heavily armed escort helicopter in Vietnam. AAFSS, they pointed out, wouldn't arrive soon enough, and their Model 209 could be put into production right away with UH-1 parts.

The army agreed, but with a condition. Bell's new attack helicopter would be reviewed for adoption by the army against a group of aircraft offered by other helicopter companies.

N209J was tested against four other contenders as an interim attack helicopter. The contenders were the navy's Kaman UH-2 Seasprite, the Boeing-Vertol CH-47 Chinook, Piasecki's Model 16H Pathfinder, the Sikorsky S-61 Sea King, and the Cobra. All the aircraft except the Cobra were converted utility craft rather than being designed for attack. The Chinook and Pathfinder were eliminated right away, but it took a two-month fly-off at Edwards Air Force Base in California to finally narrow the choice to Model 209. Moving at glacial speed, the army finally awarded Bell a contract on April 4, 1966 for two preproduction prototypes. On April 13, the order was placed for 110 HueyCobras.

By this time, the army had settled on the aircraft designator AH-1G, for the new attack helicopter. By October 1968, 838 AH-1G HueyCobras had been ordered by the army. By the end of the production run in February 1973, 1,126 Cobras had been sold to the army and Marine Corps through army contracts.[6]

6. Cobras remain in service throughout the world today, both in the U.S. Army and with foreign nations like Israel, Pakistan, Jordan, South Korea, Japan, and others. The latest and most impressive version is the Marine Corps AH-1W+ SuperCobra. This is a twin-engine model with a four-bladed rotor system that outperforms the new AH-64 Apache.

N209J was so well designed that only a few modifications were needed to put the AH-1G into full-scale production. The retracting skids were replaced with fixed gear, the ammo bay behind the turret was enlarged, the wing pylons were modified and reinforced, and the ventral strake on the tail, an unneeded lower fin, was eliminated. Another detail that didn't make it into the production model was a distinctive collective-lever handle in the shape of a cobra snake's head.

Within eighteen months of the initial contract awards, the AH-1G Cobra was deployed in strength to Vietnam and was actively engaged in combat. This rapid turnaround was due to several factors. The Cobra was constructed of primary components of the UH-1B, reducing tooling time and expense. In fact, the purchase of the HueyCobra was based on an engineering change proposal of the Huey, rather than a contract for a new aircraft. The extensive use of Huey components also reduced the time needed to train flight and maintenance crews and for the stockpiling of spares.

Of course, Bell Helicopter deserves most of the credit. Their foresight about the need for an interim attack helicopter kept the design process alive without benefit of government funding (or interference). By the time reality caught up with army planning, Bell had the right answer ready to go. Taking an enormous gamble with their funds in an unsure and unstable market, Bell's careful planning had hit pay dirt for them and for the GIs fighting in Vietnam.

The production model Cobra was powered by a fourteen hundred horsepower Lycoming T-53-L-13 turboshaft engine mated to a transmission rated at eleven hundred shaft horsepower. The reason for the difference between the ratings of the engine and transmission was the hot-and-high effect of the Vietnamese climate, which degraded engine horsepower in tropical environments. The loss in power in Vietnam made for an effective 1100-1100 match of power and drive.

The Cobra had a maximum cruise speed of more than 150 knots (171 mph), 190 knots (216 mph) in a shallow dive. This was more than adequate to keep up with Hueys and Chinooks. Even though the aircraft weighed nearly the same as a Huey, its performance was greater due to the streamlined body, a crew of two instead of four, and the uprated turbine.

The armament of the Cobra was the biggest payoff of all.

Early versions had the TAT-102A turret with a single General Electric M-134 7.62mm Gatling-style machine gun, called a minigun because of its compact size. This was soon replaced on production models with the M-28 turret, which mounted a minigun and an M-129 40mm grenade machine gun (GMG) with a cyclic rate of fire of 450 rounds per minute. At the discretion of the gunner, this dual turret could be reconfigured to mount two miniguns or two 40mm GMGs.

The turret was controlled and fired by a pantographic sighting apparatus in the forward cockpit. For the minigun, the firing trigger had two detent positions, which provided varied rates of fire from 1,300 to 4,000 rounds per minute. The internal ammo bay behind the turret carried 8,000 rounds for the minigun and 231 rounds for the M-129.

The turret had an azimuth travel of 115 degrees to either side, 60 degrees depression, and 25 degrees elevation. The pilot in the rear seat could fire the turret when the guns were in the stowed position, using a trigger switch on the cyclic stick and aiming with his panel sights. He couldn't rotate the turret, but aimed the entire aircraft like a fighter plane.

The aircraft commander (AC) flew the helicopter most of the time from his higher rear seat, and it was he who delivered the many kinds of ordnance that could be mounted under the stubby wings. In various combinations, configured to specific missions, the four pylons on the wings could mount rocket pods, minigun pods, or 20mm cannon.

The pilot aimed and fired these weapons by means of an Mk-18 adjustable rocket sight mounted on the top of his instrument panel. He selected the desired ordnance and ripple-fire rate for rockets on an intervalometer selection panel. In an emergency, the gunner was able to fire wing stores with his pantographic sight.

The rocket pods made it possible for Cobra to carry as many as seventy-six 2.75-inch rockets at a time. The pods were available in nineteen-round or seven-round versions and could be mixed and matched with each other or the gun pods, depending on mission needs.

Crew protection had been added, with armor shielding around the cockpit area and critical flight components. The windscreen was made of bulletproof glass, and the fuel tanks were self-sealing with foam fire retardation. Coupled with the

Cobra's speed and maneuverability, these improvements made it much more survivable in combat.

On August 31, 1967, the army and Bell established the New Equipment Training Team (NETT) at Bien Hoa near Saigon to train pilots to use the Cobra. Only four days passed before the first Cobra kill was made.

Maj. Gen. George P. "Phip" Seneff, commander of the giant 25,000-man 1st Aviation Brigade, was on a Cobra indoctrination flight with NETT instructor CWO J. D. Thompson northeast of Can Tho. Encountering a sampan with four Viet Cong aboard in the Mekong Delta, they destroyed it with rockets and minigun.

The first unit to use the Cobra in an operation was the 334th Armed Helicopter Company, the Playboys. Flying escort for the 118th Assault Helicopter Company, two Cobras fired up an LZ so effectively that ten Huey slicks dropped troops without any casualties. The Cobras then proceeded to destroy four VC bunkers and fourteen sampans.

During the infamous Tet Offensive of February 1968, the 334th and the NETT were credited with breaking the back of communist attacks at Tan Son Nhut Airbase, Bien Hoa, and around the Saigon area. So awesome was the firepower Cobras could direct against pinpoint targets that no Viet Cong formation could stand up to them. When supported by Cobras, air-assault operations against the Viet Cong successfully inserted troops where they could best block and destroy VC before they reached their objectives. In the Saigon area, the Cobra was a key element of the Communists' defeat during Tet.

The Marine Corps wanted Cobras, too, but it wasn't until February 1969 that it received the first thirty-eight AH-1G models. Before shipping out for Vietnam in April, the Leatherneck pilots were trained at Hunter Army Airfield in Georgia by the army.

The Marines liked the Cobra, too, but after evaluation in combat, the Corps decided to have Bell make a twin-engine version for greater safety in flights over water. At the same time, the chin gun was upgraded to a single, three-barrel, 20mm Gatling gun. The resulting aircraft was the AH-1J Sea Cobra. Because the Marines had actually been pushing for such an aircraft since 1967, the conversion process was already well under way. The first of forty-nine Sea Cobras was delivered in October 1969 and included Marine Corps avionics and a rotor brake for shipboard operations.

So successful was the Cobra as an interim attack helicopter that the AAFSS program was ultimately canceled. The AH-1G had become the army's primary aerial fire-support system.

One of the first things many pilots did was to paint fearsome looking shark mouths on their Cobras, adding to the Snake's already ferocious appearance. The sleek lines were just right for the snarling teeth made famous by the Flying Tigers of World War II. The practice of putting fangs on aircraft came to Vietnam before the Cobra, when former Flying Tiger Brig. Gen. Robert L. Scott, Jr. wrote the following letter in June 1966.

I consider it the appropriate time to acknowledge your letter of June 14th—requesting permission to adapt the shark-mouth used on our P-40s back in World War II—to the "faces" of your organization's 540 Huey 'copters. . . . So—you have my immediate permission. As the Commander of the 23rd Fighter Group as well as General Claire Chennault's Fighter Commander for the CATF—I pass it on to you because I know that if he were still alive he would give it to your organization. He and his Tigers gave me that permission long ago—and they would want any group of American fighting men to aid in its continuance of use—for the purpose of winning against the enemies of the United States. . . .

Therefore, authority is hereby granted . . .

Throughout the Vietnam War, a variety of fanged visages could be found on jets, props, and helicopters of all the services, but none so prevalent as on the AH-1G Cobras.

By the close of 1967, the army was fully geared up for the AH-1G, with a Cobra transition school in Georgia and another one permanently sited in Vung Tau, on the Vietnam coast. The Vung Tau school took over in-country Cobra transition from the NETT in Bien Hoa.

The Stateside transition school site was Hunter Army Airfield, part of Fort Stewart, Georgia, near Savannah. The school itself, called Cobra Hall, was converted from an old Strategic Air Command base no longer used by the air force.

The school consisted of two separate courses, transition and instructor, and required the already experienced student pilot to complete twenty-five hours in the Cobra for the transition segment. Transition students arrived only after completing the primary and turbine helicopter schools, while instructor pilot students needed five hundred hours under their belts, preferably in gunships.

Much of the course involved introducing the student pilots to the effects on flight characteristics of more power and the stability control augmentation system. Forced landings required a modified sequence of flight control inputs, since the SCAS might violently overcorrect and cause severe "mast bumping," the tendency of the rotor head to score the mast shaft, eventually causing it to separate from the aircraft.

The powerful engine could cause the pilot to overtorque the power train, particularly during maneuvers, and cause every manner of severe damage to the aircraft and the crew. This extra power was to be "pilot derated," meaning each operator had to know and compensate for the limits of the machinery.

For instance, in a left turn, the advancing blade encounters more resistance to the air, adding forward speed to blade speed plus turning speed, so more power is needed. In a right turn, just the opposite happens, and less power is needed since the advancing blade is, in effect, moving slower relative to ground speed. The result is a tendency to overtorque to the left during extreme maneuvers, breaking pieces of airplane. That's just one of the many intricacies that came with flying the Cobra. Students were instructed to "fly ahead" of the aircraft, anticipating and correcting for its performance extremes.

The four-week course was divided into two phases, transition and gunnery, and included sixty hours of academics in addition to required flight hours. Ninety students a month were graduated at the peak of the Vietnam War.

In the first week, students learned preflight, aircraft equipment, and emergency procedures. Week two focused on electrical, hydraulic, and engine systems. The second week additionally demonstrated the Cobra aerodynamics that had to be experienced to be understood. The third and fourth weeks gave the new Cobra pilots comprehensive training in the design, maintenance, use, and tactics of the many weapons at their disposal.

By the end of the course, the student understood and knew how to use the most powerful helicopter in history.

They had become Snake drivers.

Chapter 4

A DEADLY NEW TOY

CW0-2 Tom Meeks was one of the lucky pilots selected to attend the new Cobra transition school at Bien Hoa in May 1968. He had been flying a UH-1C Huey gunship with the 3/4 Cavalry of the 25th Infantry Division in Cu Chi since his tour began in September of 1967. Meeks was anxious to find how much better the new ships would be.

Things got off to a bad start for Tom. He arrived a day late, and when he did start training, his first two flights went poorly. Being a day behind the other students and having two pink slips noting inadequate performance, he was concerned and nervous when the third flight came around.

His instructor pilot for this was CW0-4 Trim Johnson, an old veteran who knew what was right and wrong with a student pilot through years of experience. Trim watched Meeks go through the flight routine and had some words of wisdom when they landed.

"You don't have any problems; you just don't know what the hell you're doing," he said. As a result of that dubious appraisal, Tom stayed in the school, with a permanent instructor named 2d Lt. Jim Lee.

Lee had been a warrant officer and had just converted to commissioned rank, so he wasn't the typical naive "butter bar" one might expect. Lieutenant Lee took Tom through the transition phase of the course, where he learned the flight controls and characteristics of the Cobra. He also studied the avionics and operator maintenance procedures.

Next came the gunnery phase. This part of the course was down-and-dirty. It was assumed that the student was familiar with the weapons, having flown UH-1Cs in combat already, so the instructors concentrated on the "switchology"—the science of pushing the right button and throwing the right switch to energize and employ the different weapons systems. Having mastered the electronics, the pilots tested their skills in gun and rocket attacks on various targets, some set up for practice, others very real and firing back.

Mr. Meeks graduated and returned to his unit to await delivery of their first Cobras. The first ones arrived at Vung Tau on the coast, so he and his fellow Snake drivers flew down and picked them up.

It was the best time of his life; the United States Army had just entrusted him with the wildest toy in the world. It made plenty of noise, went real fast, and carried the most firepower of any helicopter on earth. And it looked neat as hell: long and lean and only thirty-six inches wide, his new Cobra was like a giant wasp ready to sting the life out of anything.

Tom and the other pilots were convinced that they would be invincible. Everyone that flew the Cobra thought so. Occasionally, a pilot became so overconfident that he'd neglect to wear his body armor or carry a personal weapon. While such instances weren't recommended practice, they weren't uncommon. Tom learned later the importance of being prepared, that the Cobra couldn't do everything.

Since few Cobras had arrived in Vietnam by then, his squadron was issued only five. Their strength was rounded out by retaining five of the UH-1C gunships to operate alongside the new Snakes. The new AH-1Gs were equipped with blue Plexiglas canopies, intended to limit sunlight glare but really more efficient at limiting visibility, especially in low-light conditions. For that reason, the Cobras weren't allowed to fly night missions, which were parceled out to the Charlie models. That meant the Cobra pilots had to switch back and forth between the two types for day and night missions, which was like going from a Model A Ford to a Cadillac Eldorado.

The Cobra had more power than Tom knew what to do with. He could load it to the hilt and fly all day. The old Charlie models would take seven or eight hundred pounds of fuel and fly an hour or an hour and a half, depending on loads. Cobras had bigger fuel cells and weighed less than Hueys, so they were able to sustain more than three and a half hours of flight and still carry a full combat load. The UH-1 also had limited ammunition capabilities. Tom's old Huey had 7.62mm miniguns and two seven-shot rocket pods. The Cobras, on the other hand, had a minigun and a 40mm grenade launcher in a flexible turret. The wing stores could be mission-configured with a variety of systems. On the inboard pylons might be the M-18 pod-mounted minigun. Seven-round rocket pods could be mounted, but the most popular load was four nineteen-round rocket pods, for a total of seventy-six 2.75 inch rockets. They sometimes called that configuration "Seventy-six Trombones." It was a wealth of firepower compared to what the Huey could carry.

The first chance Tom had to use the new aircraft in combat came just outside of Saigon, and he discovered right away that some changes in tactics were in order. Before the Cobras arrived, Tom and his gunner, Bruce Powell, had previously come in at around twelve hundred feet in Hueys to begin a gun run on a target. By the time they had fired all their ordnance, they'd be at eight hundred feet or more and then break away. A very short run. Now in his AH-1G, Tom began this target run at two thousand feet, nearly out of sight it seemed. Firing as they dived, the pilots found plenty of rockets and ammunition remaining as they pulled away at the bottom.

With the Huey, in a heavy firefight, ammunition would generally be expended within the first fifteen minutes of action. The aircraft would then need to return to base for reload and, often, refueling. Now, with two Cobras on station, Meeks found that forty-five minutes had elapsed, and they still had ammo left.

The only drawback was the time required to reload all that ordnance for the next strike.

Yet, in spite of the extra reloading time, the multiple weapons available were a distinct advantage. Only a few Hueys had a 40mm grenade launcher, and those versions were prone to jamming. Other versions had miniguns mounted on the pylons, fixed in a forward-firing position with only a small degree of elevation and deflection available. Cobras had a minigun in the TAT-102 chin turret, with an improved 40mm mounted beside it. The turret was fully articulated, with a full range of traverse, elevation, and deflection. A flick of a finger gave the gunner his choice of weapons.

The new Cobra pilots soon became the envy of chopper pilots in Vietnam. Tom felt like the only kid in school with a new Corvette. Early on, a lot of calls for missions were from units with marginal targets to engage, but who really just wanted to see the new attack choppers in action.

Meeks and his fellow pilots frequently held dog and pony shows, where they would show their aircraft to visiting brass, setting up static displays with all the weapons and ammunition laid out. They also spent considerable time taking VIPs on check rides, showing the aircraft's capabilities and letting their guests fire the weapons.

Air force pilots were particularly excited about the AH-1. They would promise nearly anything to "get down and gravel with the grunts" in a Cobra.

After flying at Mach speeds and extreme altitudes, the bomber and fighter jockeys seldom saw their targets as anything but explosions far below or bleeps on a radar screen. When they flew in a Cobra, on the other hand, Tom would show them a whole 'nother meaning of seat-of-the-pants flying. They'd go snapping through the jungles, below the tree level, at one hundred knots and then rotate on the aircraft's own axis, heading 180 degrees back where they came from.

Live missions were appreciated most. The blue-suiters seemed to enjoy counting the bullet holes around their canopy when they'd returned.

Every unit in the war zone wanted Cobras, so the 3/4 Cav managed to have only nine by the time they were fully reequipped. By that time, the Cobras had been refitted with clear canopy plastic and could be flown on night missions.

There was also an interesting piece of reverse engineering done to correct a minor design flaw.

The clear canopies led to another alteration to compensate for the problem the blue canopies were meant to alleviate. The fully enclosed canopy made it difficult to hear weapons firing below, and the heat often became unbearable inside. For that reason, an air-conditioning unit was installed in all production Cobras, just behind the rear seat with an intake vent at the front base of the rotor cowling. It was called the climate control unit, or CCU, and was indispensable in the tropical heat.

Tom Meeks was more than pleased with his Cobra. After

flying the overweight, undergunned, worn-out Hueys, he felt his confidence in the Cobra growing more with every mission. But he was to have a rude awakening, one that almost killed him and his gunner.

Two aircraft had been on standby, waiting for a mission request. The ships would sit on the apron, loaded with fuel and armaments and ready to go if needed. Early in the morning, well before dawn, a call for help came from a fire base on Nui Ba Den, north of Saigon.

The two ships on standby were a Cobra and a UH-1C Huey, so the response team was a mix of the two helicopter types. The launch was at about 3:00 A.M., and the two aircraft immediately went to eight hundred feet AGL (above ground level).

The weather was rain and fog, reducing visibility to only seven hundred feet. Coupled with the darkness, and the cloud ceiling dropping the farther they went, the aircraft had to return to base.

In spite of the conditions, the call for help persisted and they decided to try again. This time, a Huey slick loaded with an infantry Blue team went along, hoping to reinforce the fire base, under increasing pressure from NVA attack.

Halfway out, the team was called to divert the mission to another base also under attack. Tom called for coordinates to the new target area and turned the flight.

Traveling at eight hundred feet again, their speed was limited to seventy knots by the slower Charlie model. Tom told his gunner to take the controls while he read the map and oriented himself better. He directed the gunner to maintain his current heading and altitude while he reached for the map and spread it out before him against the instrument panel. Reading the map by the light in the cockpit, Tom plotted his course, making mental notes as he followed the grids, then folded the map and put it and the light away.

Looking back to the panel, he instantly sensed something wrong. The airspeed indicator was reading over 150 knots, and the altimeter showed 150 feet!

In a split second he realized he was in a dive.

The gunner had inadvertently run away from the slower Hueys. The lack of visibility had disoriented him to the extent that he had overcompensated the nose-down flight attitude common to helicopters. The result was a rapid loss of altitude and an increase in forward speed. The Cobra was so smooth, though, that neither of the pilots had felt vibrations or changes that would alert them to the condition.

Fortunately for both aviators, Tom was fully instrument rated and spotted what was happening the second he looked at the gauges. He quickly grabbed the cyclic stick and pulled it straight back into his chest to bring the nose up, simultaneously making a stout pull on the collective to gain altitude. Just as the big chopper's rotor blades bit into the air harder, the aircraft hit the ground, just outside a rubber plantation. The Cobra bounced up, rising through the trees, and actually climbing again, until the tail rotor struck a branch, and they lost countertorque.

Knowing he would crash as the ship started to spin, Tom lowered the collective and rolled the power off, allowing the rotor to freewheel a moment and gain blade speed. Cutting the power reduced the helicopter's spinning against the engine torque.

Then, just before the second impact, Tom pulled hard on the collective again, restoring full pitch and lift, and cushioned the crash with a perfect autorotation. Except for the shattering of the blades as they struck trees. And the breakup of the canopy as it smashed into branches. And the shearing of the transmission mounting bolts against the crashing rotor.

After the branches and other debris had settled, a deathly quiet fell upon the crash site, except for the drizzle of rainfall and the hissing of water against hot metal. Tom decided he was okay, since he could feel all his parts throbbing with his pounding pulse.

The gunner, on the other hand, had been blinded by the breaking canopy, suffering a scratched cornea. The man had dismounted the aircraft from his left-front canopy door and fumbled his way around to Tom's side of the ship, then tried to drag Meeks out even though he was still strapped in.

Tom was unhurt when the Cobra had settled, but the man-handling he received as the gunner jerked him out of his seat bruised his ribs. He was afraid they might be fractured. After unsuccessfully trying to radio the other helicopters, Meeks unbuckled his seat harness and climbed out of the aircraft to assess the damage. Locating his flashlight, he flicked it on to discover that the batteries were nearly dead.

Meeks realized then that he had no weapon. He had been on standby as a favor to a friend who was sick, so he had neglected to put his gear in the aircraft when he went on duty. Nor did he have a survival radio. Just a broken Cobra with a blind gunner.

Tom searched his memory for details of the area, trying to remember it from previous flights when the air was clear. He scanned the map under the dim glow of the flashlight, deciding they were in a rubber tree plantation he'd passed before.

By dead reckoning, they wandered off in a direction that he thought would lead them to a nearby field where search aircraft might spot them.

It was nearly half an hour before they reached the field and encountered deep elephant grass. It hadn't looked so high from the air.

Tom led the gunner along the trails as the unfortunate man followed trustingly, more on hope than anything else.

Standing in the middle of the grass, they heard the other helicopters flying just out of sight in the fog, looking for them.

Tom directed the gunner to sit at the base of a large tree that dominated the field. He hoped he could see, and be seen, better from higher up.

Curiously, the gunner grabbed his arm and said, "Vertis! Don't leave me. Don't leave me."

Vertis is Tom's middle name, one he hadn't told anyone, so he found it strange at this time and place to have it pop up.

"You sit right here," Tom said as dawn was just beginning. Climbing the tree, he thought he might get some pilot's attention with the dim flashlight. Halfway up, he stopped and noticed that they'd left a huge path of flattened grass right up to the tree he was in.

Holy shit, he thought, if anyone comes after us, they can follow that right to us! Scrambling back down the tree, he went back and tried to stand the grass back up, to no avail, so back he went up the tree to try the flashlight signal.

To his surprise and amazement, the dim flashlight did the trick. One of the Hueys did a quick left and moved right over to them, descended and came to a hover. They were taking a bit of a chance that the two men were friendlies, since no radio contact had been made and visibility was still low.

Meeks came right out of the tree, picked up the injured gunner, and they were on the Huey without it ever touching ground. He kissed both the pilots.

The two Cobra pilots were airlifted back to a hospital where doctors determined that the gunner had indeed scratched his eyes. The vision loss would be temporary but would require a great deal of treatment to overcome. That meant a trip home for him.

Tom's ribs were only bruised, and he was released. The gunner had been rough with Meeks only because he thought the chopper was going to explode. It was certainly an act of courage, even if unnecessary.

From the hospital, Tom went back to flight operations to ride a Chinook leading a light fire team to the crash sight to retrieve the Cobra.

By the time they reached the wreck, the North Vietnamese were there, too, trying to remove the weapons systems.

The aeroscouts had a field day with the miniguns on their little OH-6 helicopters, firing up the NVA as they broke and ran for cover. Once the area was clear, the big CH-47 sling-loaded the stricken Cobra and hauled it back to the airfield.

Although it had crashed and been subsequently shot up by friendly scouts, it hadn't been captured or stripped by the enemy. And CW0 Meeks had learned some important lessons about flying Cobras. They could bite you if you dropped your guard.

The 3/4 Cav would often run convoy cover over Highway 1 out of Saigon. The road, which ran to Cu Chi and then on to Tay Ninh, was a favorite for the Viet Cong to mine and set booby traps.

On an average day, a mine would be set in the morning, a truck would blow up, and that would be it for the day.

After the Tet Offensive, later in the summer, a series of convoys had been frequenting an area near where Tom had crashed.

On one morning, the Cobras were flying ahead of the convoys, clearing the roads as they scouted at treetop level for ambushes and other hazards, then covering the convoy as it passed through. This went on from tree line to tree line as the convoy advanced until, at one wooded area, the first truck going in simply blew to pieces.

Unfortunately for the enemy troops who had sprung this trap, they were in an area small enough for the Cav pilots to bottle them up. Enough aviation resources were available to completely seal off the area and then systematically destroy the entire team.

It was like shooting fish in a barrel. The enemy force was a small one, however, and a total of about twelve were eliminated.

The action served the purpose of warning the enemy to avoid that piece of road, so a period of relative security began for subsequent convoys. The Viet Cong went to hunt somewhere else where the Snakes weren't so deadly.

Chapter 5

VUNG TAU TRANSITION

Flight Candidate Chuck Nole watched in awe as the three Cobras roared overhead in formation. Their sleek lines and high speed show of performance and maneuver made an impression on him that would change his life. Turning to his buddies watching the same Bell Helicopter AH-1G demonstration, he made an announcement to no one in particular and the whole in general. "That's what I'm going to fly. Eventually, some way, somehow, I'll be a Cobra pilot!"

It was at the height of the training buildup of army pilots for Vietnam, and Hunter Army Airfield in Georgia was augmenting the schools at Fort Rucker, Alabama.

Given a choice between the two, Nole chose Hunter to be near the new Cobra transition school upon graduation from primary rotary-wing flight school. He'd stand a better chance of being selected after turbine transition if he was close to the Cobra school.

During his stay at Hunter, Chuck spent his off-duty time at Cobra Hall, as the transition school was known. He often took his girl and a six-pack out to park beside the runway, spending Sunday afternoons staring at the deadly Snakes lining the runway apron.

He knew it was his destiny, but fate had some tricks to play on him first. Instead of Cobra Hall, WO-1 Nole was sent straight to Vietnam, much to his chagrin. He wasn't alone in his dismay because his entire class was dealt the same hand. Each of them was ordered to different aviation units scattered around Vietnam.

When Chuck showed up at his new assignment, D Troop,

3d Squadron, 5th Cavalry located in LZ Bearcat, his new CO gave him an in-brief and billet assignment. He was Maj. Dwayne Brofer, a man Chuck would learn to respect as an ass-kickin', commanding son of a gun.

"I'm putting you up with another new pilot who came in a week ago." Brofer said. "Fella named Newkirk."

The name rang a bell.

"Dave Newkirk?"

"Yup."

Dave Newkirk was his old roommate from flight school. They'd been really tight buddies, even jointly buying a little MGB-GT to get around in. In all of Vietnam, it was a hell of a coincidence. They reunited when Newkirk came back from that day's mission. A small but happy reunion ensued, with the two men laughing and slapping each other on the back. This war might work out okay after all. It was August 1968.

Their new unit, D Troop, had just received some other new items besides the two warrant officers.

The scout platoon had just turned in all of their OH-23 Ravens and reequipped with the OH-6 Cayuse, an egg-shaped light observation helicopter (LOH) the pilots called Loach. The gun platoons just traded in their UH-1C Hueys. For Cobras.

The OH-6s were all parked along the airstrip and simply weren't ready for use. With much of the hardware still in packing crates and no one to train the scouts how to fly them, all the Loaches sat idle for days. A training and maintenance team was scheduled to come and set everything up and get the ball rolling, but the scout platoon leader had other plans. His name was Ace Cazzolio. Grabbing a handful of manuals, Ace set about checking the shit out.

"All right!" was his first reaction as he began inspecting crates.

"A minigun."

That first discovery was a real icebreaker as Cazzolio and his team of wrenches figured how to mount the wicked little machine gun on the Loach. Next came all the on-board tools and accessories as he supervised opening of boxes, researching of manuals and scratching of heads and scrotums.

Just a day later, the platoon of Loaches was doing run-ups and systems checks, fully assembled and ready for the next phase.

Ace was the first to solo. His instructor pilot was the operator's manual that came with the ship. In about an hour and a half Ace learned to fly the Loach and declared himself IP—instructor pilot!

To add to the minigun's firepower, door gunners were designated to sit on the right side with an M-60 machine gun, suspended by an elastic bungee cord hooked to the gun and the doorframe, respectively. The self-anointed instructor pilot then trained the rest of his pilots to fly the OH-6s, completing the transition from OH-23s.

Ready to go at last, Ace changed the name of his platoon from Spooks to War Wagons.

Just before Nole had his first in-country check ride, he was witness to a horrendous accident that cost lives and equipment and nearly destroyed their base. A leak in the refuel area had spilled fuel on the ground around two UH-1Cs waiting for takeoff clearance. Fully loaded and ready to launch, the older gunships had been scrambled for a mission. But they couldn't take off yet. A monsoon rolled through the area, saturating everything with rain and blowing sheets of high wind across the compound. Then a bolt of lightning flashed down from a cloud, striking the rear Huey and firing all seven rockets on each side. Into the forward Huey.

The rockets hit on the AC side and blew the pilot to pieces. Some went through the windscreen and impacted the berm beyond.

The aircraft and crew were totally destroyed. Chuck, who was twenty-three at the time, had never seen people die. Now he was witness to human meat scraps around a pool of flaming wreckage. That was the point where he realized, this shit is for real!

Chuck Nole was ultimately assigned to the scout platoon. When he first arrived in country, he and Newkirk both flew slicks. Bored and disappointed in that, Chuck asked for a switch and wound up in a Loach. Ace, the IP, gave Chuck his official one-hour OH-6 transition school, and Chuck was set to go hunting. First mission in his new steed began with a test-fire of the minigun. Flying at low level, doing nearly ninety knots, Chuck fired up the little Gatling and scared the crap out of himself.

Startled by the loud chainsaw rasp of the muzzle report, he was equally amazed at the huge mud splash it threw in the air when the rounds impacted.

Anxious to try the little chopper in actual combat, Chuck was soon on a mission flying "trail," i.e., behind another Loach as they headed to My Phuoc Tay, about twenty miles south of Saigon. The two scouts located a camouflaged sampan hidden in a canal feeding the Ma Be River and began strafing it with their weapons.

In short order, the two little choppers eliminated the enemy crew without taking a single round of return fire.

After that, they were heroes, because it took six Huey slicks to carry out all the grenades, explosives, weapons, and ammunition that were found on board.

Next day, a second scout team in the same area located an enemy force. The scouts warned the infantry commander not to insert his troops, but they went in anyway. As a result, the troop commander was shot down, and five Hueys were lost. The grunts managed to low crawl out under intensive fire and were finally evacuated by more slicks.

On the third day, Chuck's scout team was flying down a man-made canal in the same area, looking for those pesky bad guys again. Suddenly, the lead bird shot off to the right and headed for the middle of an immense rice paddy. He was following a small irrigation ditch, which soon converged with another small canal.

"We're going to make a minigun run," he suddenly announced, and proceeded to strafe a flotilla of camouflaged sampans covered with broad leaves.

The two Loaches wheeled around, then headed down for another attack. The lead ship completed its run and broke away. Chuck's minigun jammed. The Viet Cong stood up in the boats and peppered his ship with rifle fire.

Luckily, they didn't hit him or his gunner who was busy stitching up every Communist in range of his M-60.

The second Loach came around again and used the minigun to its best advantage, while both door gunners pumped thousands of rounds into the enemy below. They killed 138 Viet Cong before they were done. With nowhere to hide, they were meat on the table for the Loaches.

When it was over, the scouts sat down and loaded mortars, weapons, pistols, and documents onto their choppers.

Chuck, while searching bodies for military documents, found a diary. Looking through it later, he was impressed that the man was an artist and a poet. The diary had careful sketches of U.S. jets being shot down. There was a portrait of his girlfriend, or possibly his wife. Of course, that sentiment was overwhelmed by his knowledge that these were the same men who had shot down the helicopters the day before. The scouts knew these were the same VC because they had some helmets and gear from the wrecked Hueys stashed on their sampans.

Once again heroes, Chuck and his colleagues triumphantly returned the merchandise to the previous owners back at Bearcat.

"Hey, you dumb fucks! Is this your shit or what?"

Chuck enjoyed flying scouts, but he still had his eye on the deadly Cobras he frequently operated with. His first Cobra flight, though, was entirely accidental. It was during a combat operation in the Plain of Reeds, with Nole flying his Loach into a beehive of Viet Cong activity. He and another scout had spent the day firing up Charlie and eventually expended all their ammo.

Returning to refuel and rearm, Chuck examined his Loach and found it was too shot up to continue flying. Stuck at the forward aircraft refueling point (FARP), he watched as the gun platoon Cobras moved out to the area to continue the attack.

They, too, expended their ammunition and began hovering around the target area, shooting .45 and .38 pistols from the canopy doors to keep the enemy contained. One of the Cobra pilots, a captain, accidentally discharged his .45 through his own hand, rendering him somewhat useless as a pilot.

When the Snake came back to the FARP again, Nole was drafted as an instant impromptu Snake driver, flying front seat. It was his first Cobra flight. And it was a great day. Chuck burned up ammo with the mini and forty, felt the power of the big ship as it rolled in and out of the target area, and generally had a hot-shit time of it.

The AC pilot was a pro, too, showing him a few tight turns and hammerhead stalls. Chuck loved it. He made up his mind to double his efforts to get Cobra transition.

Nole flew scouts for about eight months before he finally got the break he'd waited for. Pilots who agreed to extend their tour in country were allowed to go to the Vung Tau Cobra Transition School, so Chuck extended and was accepted. Ace Cazzolio had already taken advantage of the option when the New Equipment Training Team had an interim school set up. The NETT had operated from Long Thanh to the south until the AH-1Gs came in, then set up the Bien Hoa Cobra Transition School.

Meanwhile, a larger and more comprehensive course was established in Vung Tau, a coastal seaport town that poked like a finger into the South China Sea southeast of Saigon. Ace was two classes ahead of Chuck, and the school had moved to Vung Tau when Nole finally started the course.

It was a long time and many miles since he'd dreamed about Snakes in Cobra Hall, but Chuck Nole had finally reached his goal. He was ready and eager. But fate wasn't through with him yet, because Vung Tau was Party City.

It was an in-country rest and relaxation (R & R) center that was loaded with bars, clubs, and beautiful women looking for GI bucks. In the center of town were a myriad of flesh pots, sin bins, liquor lockers, and card clubs to keep the weary warriors smiling and happy after a hard day in the cockpit.

Most notable, and popular, was a glorious den of decadence named the Pink Panther, where the discriminating partygoer could see to any number of physical needs and bodily functions.

It was also the hotel where the NETT lived. Chuck was already familiar with some of the brighter spots in town from previous stops at the air base while flying scouts. He settled in for four weeks of Cobra transition training. And a little celebrating on the side.

The IPs at Vung Tau were among the best in the army. Chuck had the benefit of training from men like Bobby Miller and Pete Rawls, pilots who had flown Cobras from the earliest days of army fielding. Ace Cazzolio had already told them to look after Chuck when he came through.

"Here comes another crazy bastard who's wilder than me," was the glowing report they'd been given about Chuck Nole.

Ground school was taught by a Bell tech rep named Bob Gustafson, who also flew with the IPs. The transitioning pilots were evaluated through the duration of the course by a go/no-go system at certain milestone points. A no-go was on a pink slip following an unsatisfactory check ride. Three pinks and you were out.

It was a system carried over from flight school. Chuck had never been issued a pink slip in any training he'd had. Hell, everyone had at least one pink somewhere along the way, but Chuck always seemed to excel and hadn't had one. Until now.

He was flying from the front seat and lost the balance of the airplane. It was a common thing that happened to many pilots flying front seat in the Cobra. Well ahead of the center of gravity, with a short cyclic mounted to the right and a big gunsight crammed into his crotch, he became disoriented just enough to earn a bad check ride. Then he lost confidence and screwed up the flight. No-go. Pink slip.

Chuck was scheduled to fly with a different IP the next day. This new instructor talked with him before the flight and helped calm Chuck down. Nervous as a cat and worried he'd wash out, Chuck needed the reassurance the veteran pilot gave him to restore confidence in his abilities. Chuck did fine after that and never had another pink slip. Chuck realized his problem with flying front seat went beyond a mental block or unfamiliarity with the aircraft. He had been, in fact, worn-out up to that point. And not by overwork.

Soon after his earlier arrival at Vung Tau, he had checked into his room at the Pink Panther and immediately set about greeting some of the friendlier natives in town. In no time at all, he had a French-Vietnamese girlfriend who was stunningly gorgeous, from her inviting smile down to the dress that soon dropped around her ankles.

Chuck spent most of the first week at her apartment, doing what lonely soldiers do best. The only breaks in the most extensive sexual marathon of his life were to go to class and to shower and change.

Finally, fatigued from days of training and nights of romance, Chuck got the pink slip and realized he had to stop seeing her. He bid the smiling lady farewell and returned to the Pink Panther. Nole was soon totally involved in the Cobra School again, and his performance improved dramatically.

Chuck learned a lot about the AH-1G at Vung Tau. It was a strong and agile aircraft that a good pilot could do almost anything with, even turn it upside down. Some of the training done there included maneuvers that would never be allowed Stateside at Cobra Hall. Low-level, high-speed autorotations for example. They'd shut the throttle off, pop up to five hundred feet, do a 180, and come back down and land.

Much of this kind of training was done in a zone to the southwest of Vung Tau. Called Rung Sat by the Vietnamese, it was about one hundred square miles of salt-water marshes, laced with channels and mud flats. The pilots called it the Sperm Pits.

On this planet, there are fewer places less suited to human habitation or more worthless to any but inedible scaled things. It was a fine place, though, to hot-rod choppers through. The students would carry a half-turret of ammo just for self-defense, since the VC often wandered by.

The Sperm Pits were ideal for practicing diving fire, high-speed dives, engine failures during extreme maneuvers, tail-rotor failure, and autorotations. It was a hell of a transition school.

Bob Gustafson explained the systems of the airplane, and Chuck tried them all out. He became the definitive systems man, learning the mechanical capabilities and limitations of the Snake in a wide range of conditions. Nole had thoroughly overcome his pink-slip paranoia by then and was as comfortable in the front seat as he was in back. The students even scrambled for an alert one night during the school and picked up twelve kills in the Sperm Pits.

After graduation, Chuck wound down with a little fun time before he went back to Bearcat. He was sitting at a table with a Vietnamese girl, smokin' and jokin', when his ex-IP, Bobby, came rolling up in a jeep.

"Hey, Chuck," he shouted. "Let's head to the beach. I have a real beauty waitin' on me to pick her up!"

"Well, I'm with this little gem, so let's go!" With that, Chuck and the girl jumped into the jeep, and off they went. As they headed to pick up Bobby's date, the guy raved on and on about what a beauty she was and how Chuck would really be impressed.

He was.

Pulling up in front of a familiar building, Chuck saw a very familiar French-Vietnamese beauty come walking out. With a wink at Chuck, she climbed in, and they were on their way.

"Hey, man," Chuck said to Bobby, with a big, toothy grin.

"Yeah, what?"

"Guess who that is!" Bobby's date was none other than the French-Vietnamese lover Chuck had been romancing. The curious foursome had a hearty laugh and plenty of good times for the rest of the afternoon and into the night.

Having passed the course with flying colors, Chuck finally returned to the 3/5 Cav. He was a CW0-2 by then, so Ace Cazzolio gave him an AC check ride and certified him as a Cobra aircraft commander. After eighteen months in combat, CW0 Chuck Nole had finally become the Snake driver he always knew he would.

Ahead of him was the rest of the war, but Chuck would still be flying Cobras twenty years after April 19, 1969, when he graduated from Vung Tau Cobra Transition School.

Chapter 6

AIR CAVALRY SQUADRON

There was a running joke in army flight school during the war. The question and answer were both punch lines.

"Where are you going when you get your wings?"

"Germany."

Each man knew few of them would go anywhere other than Vietnam, especially in January 1967 when WO-1 Thomas R. Wie pinned his shiny new wings on. The U.S. Army was approaching the peak of its wartime troop strength, so pilots were desperately needed in every zone in country.

Tom was scheduled for direct assignment to the 12th Combat Aviation Group in the Delta region, so it surprised him when he was cut orders for Germany. About fifty pilots were diverted to fill a shortage caused by putting most pilots into Southeast Asia. That added a new twist to the old flight-school joke.

Tom served a year in Augsburg, Germany with a brigade aviation section of the 24th Infantry Division. That is; he *was* the aviation section. The army in Europe was so short of pilots that Tom served as maintenance officer, troop supervisor, training officer, and plenty other assorted tasks. He was also pilot for the brigade commander, a full colonel who wasn't too sure he liked being toted around by a teenage warrant officer. Tom was careful not to scare him too often, so the commander tried not to scare nineteen-year-old Tom more than he needed to.

Tom was lucky to gain experience in Europe before going to Vietnam, increasing his chances for survival when he did go. That eventually happened as a result of his interest in the

AH-1 Cobra. The men in his unit were talking about a new kind of helicopter, an attack aircraft that would soon be fielded in Vietnam to kick Charlie's ass all over the war zone. The *U.S. Army Aviation Digest* had run an article on the prototype aircraft in May 1966.[7] The article, simply titled "HueyCobra," showed a photograph of the N209J prototype, with retracting landing gear in the extended position. Flight controls and panels were displayed in the magazine, including a custom touch unique to the prototype aircraft—the collective lever was made in the shape of a Cobra snake's head. The text of the article elaborated on advanced capabilities of this new ship, built mostly from UH-1B components.

Later articles described upgrades in the production models, establishment of Cobra transition schools in Vietnam and Georgia. Pilots army-wide watched with interest as the type progressed.

Tom's interest was such that he applied for Cobra school. Other pilots in his unit were interested in Chinook transition, but Tom's shot at Cobras began as a joke. He was sure that a WO-1 in Germany didn't have a snowball's chance in hell of getting the school. The radical new helicopter would likely be reserved for senior aviators, captains, majors, and light colonels. So he applied for laughs. And because he didn't want Chinooks.

He was one surprised and happy aviator when he received orders for Stateside Cobra transition en route to Vietnam. Tom was ecstatic. He just couldn't believe he'd be flying the Ferrari of the skies. Tom was promoted to CWO-2 en route to the school, making his time there all the more satisfying. For four weeks at Hunter Army Airfield, he trained to be what he'd never dreamed luck would allow. A Snake driver.

After transition, Tom continued to his hometown of Portland, Oregon, relaxing on leave before heading to the war. Unlike his parents, Tom wasn't overly concerned about going to Vietnam. It was just another assignment to him, though it promised more excitement than Germany. His folks, on the

7. This article ran so early in the development of the Cobra that the helicopter was even referred to as the UH-1H. Only the N209J prototype had been built, but that single aircraft was so radical for its day that shock waves of anticipation ran throughout the army.

other hand, tried to put a happy face on what Tom knew was worry and fear over his safety. During his combat tour, he wrote to set their minds at ease, but a few hairy news stories that made it back to Portland sort of blew that plan.

When he finally hit Vietnam in May 1968, Tom's new unit was his original assignment from 1967, the 12th Combat Aviation Group, located at Long Binh. The 12th CAG belonged to the 1st Aviation Brigade, a unit with more soldiers than a full division, and spread throughout the country. Comprising four huge aviation groups, the brigade boasted three air cavalry squadrons and fifteen aviation and aviation support battalions. Salted in were a mixture of specialized aerial surveillance, electronic warfare, and air-traffic control units. The 1st Avn Bde was activated as an aviation support organization, providing an airmobile capability for every unit in Vietnam. The big 1st Cavalry and 101st Airmobile divisions had their own aviation assets, but other divisions needed aircraft to conduct airmobile operations. So the 1st provided the lift, firepower, transport, and supply by air that was essential in jungle warfare.

Tom's assignment to the 12th Group was just the jumping-off point to his final assignment. He spent that first night at Long Binh, because he missed the flight to his final unit of assignment, the 3/17 Air Cavalry Squadron in Tay Ninh to the northwest. That evening, while waiting for another slick to pick him up, some acquaintances told him how Tay Ninh had just been mortared, and filled his ears with scary stories about his new home. The rest of the night was uneventful, but Tom was worried, now.

Next day brought his Huey. When he arrived in Tay Ninh, Tom was assigned to Alpha Troop, the Silver Spurs. The 3/17 Air Cavalry Squadron had five troops, as cavalry companies are called, and a headquarters element. In Tay Ninh were the headquarters, Headquarters Troop, and Alpha Troop. Another troop was stationed forward at a base known variously as Redcatcher and Plantation. Two other troops called Long Binh home.

Tom was with Alpha troop for two months before he saw a Cobra. The Silver Spurs were still flying Charlie model Huey gunships, and the Snakes began arriving in July. The first Cobras into the unit had the single minigun TAT-102 chin turret. Soon, however, deliveries were equipped with the XM-28 turret with a dual weapon mounting. The early Snakes suffered jamming problems with their miniguns, often launching with a gun seized up just so the pilots could get a ship in the air. The front-seater on these trips was often referred to as the "forward-bullet-stopper" and given an extra chicken plate, the euphemism for standard chest armor.

When dual turrets arrived, the pilots experimented with different arrangements, like dual miniguns or double-forties, but the most versatile arrangement was a minigun on the right and the forty-mike-mike to the left. They also determined part of the jamming problem was related to the dual-speed gun trigger. When a gunner moved back and forth from low to high speed on the rate of fire, ammo belts jumped and snagged in the feed chutes. It was best, therefore, to stop firing before moving to a faster or slower speed. The worst jammer seemed to be the dual-minigun setup. Only careful loading and an experienced shooter could ensure jam-free operation. Many jamming problems were later solved when the removable ammunition drums were redesigned to feed better.

Tom liked the forty. He called it the fun gun. He learned early to carry just the right tools around. When they rearmed and refueled at a forward base, there might not be all the magic goodies they needed, like a big screwdriver to run the gear that moved the firing pin away from the cartridge primers. Or duckbill pliers to crimp links together on belts of grenades.

As Alpha troop put in plenty of hours flying and learning about their new Snakes, one particular aircraft became known as the "gun-shy Cobra." It was the oldest Snake they had and rife with maintenance problems, a "hangar queen" that spent as much time deadlined as it was operational. They used the old single-gun ship for practice and training, or just to run for parts. As an instructor pilot, Tom put many hours on that airframe, too, usually coming away impressed at its performance. Remarkably, it was the fastest and smoothest aircraft in the unit. But whenever it went into real combat action, some kind of major malfunction would occur, whether it was hit or not. Total hydraulic failure. Electrical power loss. With monotonous regularity, Tom and his colleagues watched it break down whenever the game was real. There was even an unconfirmed legend about the gun-shy ship, which had tail number 525. The story went that it was one of the very first AH-1Gs in country and had been used in the Tet Offensive around Saigon. A major and a warrant officer with the famous 334th Playboys were flying 525 against Viet Cong insurgents when a .50-caliber round killed one of the crew. After that, it was used for parts until the 3/17th had a Cobra shot up and needed a replacement. Not wanting to give up a good aircraft, the 334th reassembled ol' 525 and shipped it off to Tay Ninh. It was a jinx.

Alpha troop eventually unloaded 525 in much the same way it was acquired. Another aircraft suffered a massive overtorque, requiring a new transmission, turbine engine, rotor mast and head, and numerous other parts. To remedy two problems at once, 525's entire drive train was removed, with a similar operation performed on the damaged Snake. The mechanical guts were then switched between the two patients, resulting in one very sound and airworthy Cobra. Of course, it was not 525. The old gun-shy hanger queen was returned to the World for complete remanufacture. It's probably sitting in some National Guard hanger today as a rehab S model.

The 3/17 Cav's mission was to support the 9th Infantry division in the Mekong Delta and surrounding areas. Each day, whichever battalion had airlift assets committed for support also had Cobra fire teams to escort the missions. The duties involved hunter-killer Pink teams, which included Cobras ("Red") for firepower, following an OH-6 Cayuse (White) scouting for targets. They'd fly to suspected hot spots reported by intelligence, using preplanned LZs for infantry insertions by Slicks. If the Pinks found the enemy, infantry Blue teams were called in as Cobras developed the target.

Recon by fire and H & I by the Pink teams drew return fire from the NVA hidden in the jungles, which exposed them to direct attack. The Cobras softened up and destroyed enemy troops and emplacements as much as possible before the Blues came in. Once on the ground, the infantry then did a deliberate and detailed search-and-destroy operation in the area. Throughout that phase, the ground commander directed Snakes to individual and area targets, as needed.

The Loach, meanwhile, orbited the area to ferret out fleeing enemy troops, containing the battle, or spotting NVA tactical maneuvers against the Blues. Such a battle was busy and confusing, so much so that Tom once unintentionally shot down a Loach. Not just any Loach, either. If Wie were going to screw up, he'd do it in real style. Tom knocked off what was almost the first Loach to fly one thousand combat hours in Vietnam. Almost.

The aircraft in question was assigned to Alpha troop and was coming up on high time. Because of the hazardous nature of aeroscout operations, it was uncommon for an OH-6 to remain flying for so long. They'd usually need a complete rebuild back in the States because of battle damage, or just be blown to pieces by ground fire. Everyone was watching this Loach, since it seemed to be the first to beat the odds. On the fateful day, Tom was following the OH-6 as it flew along a river, working the nipa palm forest for contacts. Before long, bad guys in the trees began firing at the scout. Dumb bad guys. In a monumental act of stupidity, the NVA troops left the cover they had in the nipa palms and tried to swim across the river, a fairly wide river, right in front of the scout and two Cobras.

Riding front seat, Tom instantly brought the turret around to engage them while his pilot positioned the chopper for a rocket attack. The first burst of minigun fire was short as the gun jammed, so he switched to 40mm with the fire buttons on top of the grips. Watching the slow-moving grenades go *thunk-thunk-thunking* out from the nose, Tom suddenly noticed the Loach moving into the sight picture below his Cobra. Tom let go of everything, missing the Loach.

When the grenades began hitting the river, though, shrapnel hit the little chopper and damaged it severely. The Loach barely made it back to Tay Ninh, and it took more than three days to patch it up. Hundreds of holes had punctured windshields, sheet metal, hydraulics, instruments and a myriad of other parts on the tiny helicopter. Tom wasn't very popular with scouts for a while, but he'd just been doing his job. It was plain dumb luck.

Eventually, the scout platoon took their sacred Loach and began flying it in shifts, just around the base in traffic patterns, to build up the hours without exposing it to any more combat. Or to Tom. They eventually put the one thousand hours on and won their record.

Most of the 3/17th's support operations for the 9th Infantry Division were around Tan An, but they'd occasionally be vectored to Ben Tre to support a different brigade of the 9th. Ben Tre was a little strange in that it was reputed to be the location of a Viet Cong R & R center (rest and relaxation). Whenever Tom's Snakes went there, they'd usually kick plenty of ass on the first day. They'd have a good time shootin' up bad guys in every direction. Day two was always rough. Charlie would be recovered and waiting for them when they came back, so it was touch and go with the massive ground fire they encountered. Tom tried to find some other mission if they scheduled more than one day in Ben Tre.

Sometimes luck was the single element determining life or death. Wie watched one day as a VC lined up a Cobra with an RPG-7. It was a long shot, but the other Snake was just loafing around the area. The guy on the ground took a one-in-a-thousand chance and nailed the chopper right above the wing in the transmission area. In yet another twist of fate, the rocket didn't explode. It was either too close and hadn't armed or the angle was too oblique to detonate the fuze. It bounced right off. The pilot flew the ship home, and he and his gunner promptly got blitzed to celebrate their untimely survival.

Because helicopters needed no runways, open fields often served as impromptu airfields. In order to stay near the battlefield and be on station within minutes, Alpha Troop conserved fuel by locating a safe place to land between support missions. Scouts cruised the surrounding terrain to ensure security of the ships on the ground. They'd pop in and out, moving between the Blues locked in combat elsewhere and the landing field.

Tom was waiting on such a field with a group of other Snakes when a single Loach zoomed in and hovered down to ground. The pilots wandered over to the little chopper while its pilot cooled down the turbine. He might have a progress report on the action going on. The pilot was Tom's good friend, Brian.

Frequently, while elements of Alpha Troop were staging out of a field, Vietnamese children came to see the helicopters and jockey for handouts. Their big, pleading brown eyes and cherubic faces melted even the hardest hearts, and lots of C rations and candy were passed out. Brian was always glad to see the kids. A large and husky but kindly fellow, he loved every child he met and always played with them as much as possible. The kids instinctively knew he was an easy touch for goodies and flocked around him every time.

On this particular day, Brian had befriended a tiny little Oriental girl who was giggling and laughing as he tickled and tossed her in the air. Tom talked to another pilot as they walked back from the Loach when he heard a queer sound. *Thunka-bump!* He turned to see Brian, with a look of shock and horror etched into his face, gently laying the tiny figure onto the grass beside the chopper. He had lifted her too high, too close to the rotor blades.

Calling for medics, the men put the girl on a chopper with her mother and headed for a hospital. But it was simply too late. The child died long before they got to help. Brian was depressed about it for a very long time. In combat, friends are lost to enemy fire, and tragic as it is, those deaths are anticipated. Even accidents are expected from time to time, but this was something much harder to swallow. He eventually worked out of the depression, but remained subdued for quite some time.

Tom flew front seat for a while with a fellow named John Knox as his PIC (pilot in charge) in the backseat. The two of them managed to prove to the world that Cobras' taillights were designed incorrectly. The single light was first mounted on a fairing extending from the top of the tail fin. This caused the fin to vibrate in flight, and the light would eventually separate from the aircraft.

Tom's taillight took its leave via the tail rotor, striking a blade and degrading flight control. Having just refueled at a forward refuel-and-rearming point, they just launched and were preparing to hover into a takeoff position out of the small base. Around and below them were huge, rubber blivet, fuel cells, full of JP-4 aviation fuel. Rockets and ammunition were stacked in each revetment. It was that moment the light flipped off. The Cobra, losing tail rotor countertorque, began spinning in circles over the explosives and flammables, nearly out of control. But not completely.

Knox managed to work the aircraft over to one side and, as soon as they were clear, plop it rudely down onto the ground.

He didn't consider a ten thousand-gallon fuel bladder as an optional landing pad, so he wasted no effort screwing around with technique or finesse. The skids spread, and the turret was dented, but pilots and aircraft would fly again. Cobras were later modified to mount the taillight in a safer spot.

Hunter-killer teams were a specialty of Alpha troop. Like a regular Pink team, they were comprised of Loach and Cobra working together. The difference was that two Snakes and two Loaches headed out then broke into two teams to work over a large area. With the OH-6 as terrier and AH-1 as Doberman, they'd ferret out the enemy and put the bite on them. As time passed, one pair returned to reload and refuel, then return while the second couple restocked. This tactic provided unbroken coverage of an area over an extended period of time.

Brigade and battalion designated areas to check out, based on intelligence reports of enemy activity. The scouts hovered in along the treetops, blowing the bushes around with rotor wash, looking for trails and sign of the enemy. They were pros at it, too. Tom knew that if a scout told him he saw a blond-haired, blue-eyed NVA general, he could even expect a surfboard with stars on it. But he also thought they must be insane to be a good scout and survive the war.

If a pilot tried to do the job safely, keeping up airspeed breaking away quickly, and so on, he was dead meat. The careful pilots never seemed to make it with Loaches. The bold and aggressive madmen, on the other hand, were the ones that did a good job and lasted the longest.

One wild man, in fact, caused a lot of problems by taking on the whole war himself, firing up companies of VC and NVA with his minigun and door gunner. He wouldn't get out of the Cobras' way.

Between seven hundred feet and ground was often called the dead-man zone, since it was optimum range for small-arms fire. Tom's unit frequently operated there to draw fire and thus spot the enemy. They were told to remain above fifteen hundred feet, but with the scouts hanging out front, the Snakes wanted to be close on their tail. If a Loach was fired on, Daddy Cobra was right behind to ripple-fire a salvo of 2.75 rockets into Charlie's lap.

The 2.75-inch folding-fin aerial rocket (FFAR) was a

weapon that gave the AH-1G a real Sunday punch, but the Snake driver needed to understand the effects of airspeed and aircraft attitude when firing rockets. Because the 2.75s were fin-stabilized, the direction of flight they took when launched was affected by relative airflow over the launch tube. If the Cobra had too much nose-down attitude, the rocket would rise before reaching trim. Nose-up firing positions would make the rocket drop off too much. Tom sometimes used this effect to advantage, single-firing rockets down a tree line with a little pedal to one side. The result was a row of hits, one after the other for a long distance, without the need for repeated diving attacks. The rockets angled out to the side against the offset airflow. On the second run, he'd come from the other direction and use a pod on the other side.

Occasionally, though, it was Charlie's game played by VC rules. A slick, disabled by sniper fire, had been trapped in an LZ and needed cover fire while a rescue was being mounted. The aircraft had taken numerous crippling hits, and the covering aircraft felt the heat of ground fire, too.

It seemed an eternity and required more aircraft and strikes before they finally got the people out. By then, a couple of them were dead. Tom learned later it was one sniper in a tree who had held them at bay for so long. The wrecked slick they pulled out had an eight-ball painted on it. The eight had a bullet hole in the center of each circle on the number. The men on the ground knew it was a single soldier pinning them down, but the survival radios were out, and they couldn't vector the Snakes to him. They never did get the guy.

Tom took his share of hits on missions, so many once, that he had to land away from the fight and have his ship sling-loaded back to base. But that was nothing compared to the Tet Offensive of 1969. That night, Tom shot down his second aircraft, a Huey, and also won the Silver Star.

Alpha Troop was in the Tan An area, expecting some problems since the previous Tet holiday was a major battle. The unit was undergoing a program of limiting flying hours, or "blade time," so many aircraft were only in the air for half a day. Tom was inside the tactical operations center (TOC) at brigade headquarters, monitoring radio traffic. On the radio tower outside the TOC sat a spotter with a Starlight night-vision scope, watching the surrounding terrain for signs of in-filtration.

It wasn't long before the guard reported suspicious activity outside the perimeter of the base. Soon, riflemen were taking pot shots at fleeting figures in the dark, but no hits were confirmed. The figures would lie low for a while, then begin activities again.

The decision was soon made to launch the Firefly, a UH-1 with a spotlight cluster mounted to one side. Sitting in the TOC, Tom heard the Huey wind up and launch. Then, over the same FM frequency as the Huey, they heard a long stream of invective. It was the Firefly reporting a very large number of enemy troops setting rockets up to hit the base. Aimed point-blank at the perimeter, propped up on bamboo supports, were dozens of 106mm rockets ready to launch.

Firefly began attacking with M-60 door guns while Snake drivers sprinted for their gunships. The first rockets began slamming into the base. Tom jumped off the PSP runway and over some sandbags, landing between them and the barracks. A pause in the bombardment gave pilots a chance to reach the Cobras, only to be fired on by their own nervous troops. Fortunately, they hit no one as the pilots dove into bunkers for cover. Before long, someone passed the word around not to shoot anyone inside the perimeter. Not yet, anyway.

Tom finally reached the Cobra, so he and his front-seater launched to relieve the Huey, now out of ammunition and firing with a .38 revolver out the aircraft window. The Cobra gunner was a captain with a French surname. Not particularly popular with the other pilots, he was nicknamed Fifi. One could say he was less than brilliant, with a twenty-watt personality to match.

Their ship had a dual minigun turret, requiring a light touch and a bit of finesse to operate. Captain Fifi immediately began jerking the triggers in and out to hose the enemy with lead. He jammed both guns in a matter of seconds. For the rest of the fight, Fifi was just ballast. Tom was mad about that as the FM radios started going crazy with people on the ground calling for fire missions. Some of the transmissions were encoded, so Fifi asked Tom, "You want to decode those?"

"Sure," Tom responded, "pass 'em back." Nothing came

back to him, since the captain hadn't bothered to take the messages down. He must have figured Tom could fly the aircraft, fire rockets, and take dictation all at once.

Tom returned to base to reload after expending all his rockets on the enemy launchers. In the rush, little attention was paid to the kinds of warheads being shoved into the tubes. They just wanted to get back in the air in a hurry.

Back out over the perimeter, Firefly was illuminating targets for the Snakes, so Tom moved in and began guiding the slick.

"Move up a little." The slick went a bit higher and Tom launched a pair of 2.75s. He came back around for a second pass. The first pair of rockets were ten-pounders, with a fast and flat trajectory. Firefly kept drifting down, so Tom instructed him to move up again. Next pair were ten-pounders again. Once again the Huey came in closer. The third pair of rockets were seventeen-pounders with proximity fuzes that exploded before they hit the ground, showering the slick with shrapnel. Seventy-six holes punctured the skin, fuel cell, and doors. One piece scratched the pilot's leg, for which he was later awarded a Purple Heart. Firefly crippled back onto base, done for the night. Tom had shot down his second friendly aircraft.

The strikes continued into the night until all the enemy were gone or dead. Next morning, Tom had the unique experience of walking through the area he attacked all night. He'd never had the opportunity to see up close what a Cobra could do. It was a real eyepopper, with trees ripped into splinters, torn and twisted rockets and launchers thrown around, and blood trails everywhere, where enemy dead had been dragged away.

That same day, the 3/17th held an award ceremony. Tom received the Silver Star for his part in stopping the NVA rocket attack. Captain Fifi got a Distinguished Flying Cross for warming the cushion in the front seat. It galled Tom more than a little. A Silver Star was a step higher than the DFC, but as an aviator, the Distinguished Flying Cross was near and dear to his heart. He had sixty-nine Air Medals to go with his Silver Star, though, from 2,174 combat flight hours over two tours in Vietnam.

Medals were sometimes an item of contention with pilots.

They thought it inappropriate that infantry types could get Air Medals for simply riding in the back of a Huey. After all, air-crew didn't get Combat Infantry Badges for the same missions.

One time Tom was instructed to write up a citation for a captain who was getting short and ready to return Stateside.

"Well," Tom asked his commander, "what did he do?"

Tom couldn't recall the man's participating in any missions while he was around; the officer had stayed in Operations the whole time, and now he was getting a DFC?

"He must have done something, Tom," came the reply. "You find out then write it up." Mr. Tom Wie didn't feel particularly imaginative, so he developed the narrative for the citation from an action he had done himself. The medal was presented to the captain but Tom had actually earned the damn thing.

Although most medals awarded were truly earned by the pilots who wore them, all too frequently a citation was hung on a commissioned officer to enhance his career. The perception was that lieutenants, captains, majors, and lieutenant colonels had a career to build and would devote their life to the army. These folks were often referred to as "RLOs," for real live officers.

A warrant officer, on the other hand, supposedly only cared about jerking up the collective and swinging the cyclic around. Since they only wanted to fly, why waste medals on them? As a result, the threshold of awards varied between ranks. An I-showed-up-for-the-war medal for a warrant officer was an Army Commendation Medal with *V* for valor, while an RLO would rate a Bronze Star for the same service. Just because they were there. That's not to say that most medals weren't earned. Most were. But a lot of career enhancement went on through the good-ol'-boy network, too.

Tom could tell an RLO from a serious leader by the way they used a bogus kind of code language on the radio.

"Put a little redleg over there," one would transmit, as if the enemy didn't know artillery were nicknamed redlegs.

"I'm coming up the red ball to the green ball," even though the bad guys likely had the same map with the same road signs on it.

"We got slicks coming down blue," (Hueys on the river) "and buckets on the hardball" (tanks on the road). They just made the shit up as they went along. Tom saw a few other examples of plain stupidity in other ways, ways that got good men killed.

When slicks dropped Blues off in rice paddies, the grunts would drop into the water and lie low as they moved toward the enemy. Scouts flew ahead and reported enemy positions to the ground commanders so they could plot their attacks. Too often, though, men would get up on the dikes between paddies to walk easier. And get shot easier. Sure enough, it sometimes required a couple of dead buddies to return them to cover. Dumb, thought Tom.

Alpha Troop had its morons, too. One was a major, who we'll simply call Barney Fife to protect his family's fond memories. Besides, that's who he looked and acted like, and that's what his men called him. Barney was the new scout platoon commander and was flying with a lieutenant on a simple administrative flight. Well, he wanted to see the infamous Iron Triangle, which was pretty flat from air strikes by then. Around Cu Chi and Xeon, they radioed over troop frequency that they were heading out to take a look around. All by themselves deep into VC country. They never came back.

When the Loach was reported overdue, a search party flew out and found the wreckage. And the bodies. Both the men survived the crash after they were shot down, but the enemy greased them both where they stood, then stripped the bodies and the aircraft for whatever they could use. Tragic, but also dumb. They were foolish to go alone and doubly foolish to fly low enough to be hit by ground fire. And the flight was completely unnecessary.

Tom had more of a tendency toward survival and was much more cautious when it was possible. He learned maneuvers that would enhance his ability to survive against dangerous targets like gun emplacements or massed troops. Some of the maneuvers were even fun. Like the high-speed, low-level, pop-up, 180-degree autorotation. This was a low-G maneuver that enabled a Cobra to return to its target without having to fly in a circle and come back for an additional run. Frequently called a hammerhead stall, the Snake would actually turn on its own axis, positioned to fall right into an extra pass at the back side of the target.

This not only surprised Charlie, but caught him with his head still down and guns pointed the other way, totally exposed to minigun and 40mm fire. It had to be done just right, though, or the Cobra would encounter a phenomenon called divergent roll, flip upside down, and drop like a rock. Just another of the curious flight characteristics unique to the Cobra. Engineers back in the States discovered this unrecoverable stall condition in flight tests and published warning orders that eventually reached the pilots in Nam.

The hammerhead continued to be used, since it was safer than exposure to enemy fire, but the report explained a mystery crash that had occurred previously.

Tom's roommate, a fellow named Walt Koslosky, had a mission to a pineapple plantation southwest of Saigon one night. The aircraft had crashed without any evidence of enemy fire. Examination of the wreckage next day indicated a catastrophic in-flight breakup, so they surmised that it had taken some rounds in the main rotor and shook itself to pieces on the way to the ground. After the divergent roll reports came in, Tom was sure that Walt had gotten into a low-G condition, unloading the critical balances of the rotor, and it had snapped off, destroying the aircraft. Walt was listed as a combat loss, but there was no doubt in Tom's mind that he died from the aerodynamic quirks of the AH-1G.

The carefully engineered stress factors on the Cobra's rotor components were maintained and controlled by the cyclic, collective, and foot pedals, augmented by SCAS. When a maneuver out of the normal flight envelope changed the balance of load ratios beyond the limits, the Snake went its own way and usually couldn't be recovered. To be a Snake driver required a high skill level and constant attention. The best pilots in the army were those who flew the AH-1G safely over a long period of time. Which defined CW0 Tom Wie.

As an instructor pilot, Tom flew many hours training the junior aviators in the aerodynamic semantics of Cobra flight. On those occasions, since they mostly did traffic-pattern work and limited maneuvers near base, Tom flew without his chicken-plate body armor or his sidearm. Training flights were usually done with a ship fresh out of maintenance, one which hadn't been rearmed yet. The IP would do the instruction flight, then have the student land the Cobra at the FARP (forward armaments and refuel point) and load up to mission-ready status before parking it.

It was at this point of a training flight, near the end of Tom's tour, another pilot ran up to Tom before they shut down the turbine. Tom was riding front seat, since he was IP. The other pilot said one of their aircraft had been shot up near Xuan Loc, an area Tom had never been to. Tom switched seats with the junior pilot, and they launched on the mission, even before the alert team could respond. When the team took off and caught up, they lined up on Tom's ship, heading for the stricken chopper. Nearly three-quarters of the way to Xuan Loc, they monitored radio traffic saying that the damaged ship was a Loach. It was shot up pretty bad, but managed to make it home.

Well, the Cobras were in the area anyway, they were loaded up, and there was still fighting on the ground, so they decided to deliver some ordnance to Charles before going home. Rolling in on the bad guys, Tom let rip with a salvo of 2.75s while the front-seater stitched them with turret weapons. A huge volume of tracers rose to meet them. As Tom broke away to the left, the pilot in the Snake behind him came over their frequency.

"They're shootin' at you! They're shootin' at you!"

"Don't tell me that," Tom responded angrily. "Shoot them!"

"You're takin' fire!"

"I know that. Shoot them!"

Irritated at the green pilot's comments, Tom watched thousands of red and green tracers rising up like upside-down rainfall. It suddenly dawned on him.

Here I am, he thought, with just a couple weeks left in country, no chicken plate, no sidearm and the whole commie army trying to blow me away. This is dumb. He made another trip around the pattern, then broke to the right so he couldn't see the tracers as easily. It made him feel a little better, anyway. They expended the rest of their ammo and headed home.

Tom stuck to training junior pilots after that mission. It was just about time to go home, and he didn't want to miss his flight.

Chapter 7

AERIAL ROCKET ARTILLERY

CWO-2 Rex Swartz was an ex-navy man. He served a tour as a sailor, then left the service and went to college. As it turned out, though, it was flying that pushed Rex's buttons, so he dropped his books for army flight school at Fort Wolters, Texas. From there, as a newly appointed warrant officer and pilot, he continued flight training at Fort Rucker, then went on to Fort Bragg, North Carolina.

The army was forming a new unit there, the 4/77 Aerial Rocket Artillery Battalion. This new organization was scheduled to transfer to the 101st Airmobile Division (previously Airborne) and ship out to Vietnam.

The 4/77 ARA was spread across two states before the deployment. Alpha Battery was stationed at Fort Sill, Oklahoma, and Bravo and Charlie batteries were at Bragg. All of them had UH-1B Huey gunships.

It would take six months for the pilots to familiarize themselves with the equipment, the tactics, and each other. Then came the day to ship the whole unit to the West Coast for deployment. Pilots and aircrews worked long and hard to ensure their Hueys were perfect before being hoisted aboard an aircraft carrier for shipment across the Pacific. Every fastener and bushing was checked and rechecked to ensure they'd be ready for Nam.

Whoever received them on the other end had some mighty tight Hueys, but it wasn't the 4/77. To their surprise, but not their dismay, they were issued new AH-1G Cobras upon arrival.

A Battery had arrived in country three months prior and already had the jump on the other batteries. B and C batteries languished for some time at Pope Air Force Base, near Bragg, waiting for a C-141 Starlifter jet flight to Vietnam. The entire unit packed all its equipment and supplies into steel conex shipping containers weeks earlier, and so had little to do but play cards and watch flight manifests being posted.

Once they were finally flown into Vietnam, they landed at Da Nang and were then flown, again as a unit, to Phu Bai in C-130s. The final leg of their long odyssey was a dusty truck ride about ten miles out to Camp Eagle, their new home. Phu Bai sat along a marshy strip of land next to the South China Sea. The base was located about forty miles north of Da Nang and ten south of Hue, ideal for aircraft defending both cities. To the west lay rolling hills and mountains covered with dense, triple-canopy jungle. It was March 1969.

Rex was soon transferred into A Battery to train with battalion pilots and aircrews with combat experience. Some of the new pilots were even sent south to other divisions in country, rounding out gunship crews theater-wide.

At the time, Swartz had never flown a Cobra, but was nonetheless assigned to front-seat combat missions right away. He was told he would attend the new Cobra transition school in Vung Tau when a space was available. Rex had over three hundred combat hours before that happened.

The mission of the ARA was exactly what the name implied, aerial rocket artillery. Although the battalion flew gunships, every battery was organized and employed like artillery, placing "steel on target" on demand. Exactly when and where it was required. For that, the minigun and grenade launcher were considered to be supplemental weapons. The real meat of the 4/77's Cobras were the seventy-six 2.75-inch folding-fin aerial rockets (FFAR) that each carried on nearly every mission.

Those rockets were placed on point or area targets under the direction of a ground controller or a forward air controller (FAC) just like a howitzer salvo. Certainly, the semantics of calling an ARA strike varied a bit from spotting cannon fire, but the purpose and result remained identical.

The pilots and their aircraft maintained graduated levels of standby readiness to respond to missions. The first, and most rapid response level, was the two-minute "hot section," backed up by a five-minute and a fifteen-minute section. If an infantry unit, or someone else in a bind, needed support, they would call for assistance over artillery radio channels.

The artillery officer then determined if it was appropriate to "lay some tubes" (howitzers) on the target, or to call in an ARA strike. Not all target areas were covered by the overlapping fires of artillery bases. Some areas were out of range and had no coverage at all, and frequently, the precision of direct rocket fire was needed.

Communist forces had developed a tactic called "hugging"—once their position was known, they moved as close to the U.S. or ARVN troops as possible, making it difficult to hit them without causing friendly casualties. Cobras were the best bet in those situations. The decision might even be made to use both ARA and howitzers, placing each where they would be most effective. Besides, the grunts on the ground liked all the help they could get.

Each aircraft underwent a preflight inspection and was given a full tank and ammo upload as soon as a section went on hot. This enabled them to launch within the two-minutes allocated. A hot section would remain on first status for a six-hour stretch, then revert to fifteen-minute status. The other two sections would then move up to the next quicker status. Whenever the hot section launched, the next section would go on two-minute status and the fifteen went to five. Nights were covered by a single hot section.

With A and B batteries located at Camp Eagle, and C Battery located at Camp Evans north of Hue, the 4/77 ARA could provide fire support to most of the part of South Vietnam above Da Nang, including the hotly contested A Shau Valley. Added to its fire support missions, the ARA also performed LZ preps, saturating landing zone sites with massed firepower ahead of troop insertions. Visual reconnaissance, or scout missions were also on the 4/77's attack menu, with the Cobras covering OH-6 Loaches poking around in Charlie's backyard.

Rex's unit shared Camp Eagle with a Special Forces unit whose troops were frequently inserted deep into Laos and Cambodia on classified operations. It was a time when such activities were little known to the public and highly controversial. The public mood Stateside was swinging well away from support of the war effort, so revelation of clandestine activities could only make political hay for vote-conscious politicians. The 4/77 had a Cobra section committed to the Green Beret's operations every day. They didn't have a mission every day, but when they did, their firepower was critical.

During early May that year, the U.S. Forces in Vietnam were engaged in a series of sweeps of suspected and known Viet Cong and NVA strongholds. Since the stinging defeat of the 1968 Tet Offensive, the Communists had avoided decisive battles with American troops. Most of their large units were in sanctuaries in Laos and Cambodia, while forces in South Vietnam were broken down to small units, harder to find and easier to move. The U.S. command wanted to ferret them out to keep them from consolidating, so it initiated a series of selected search-and-destroy operations in key areas. One such area was the A Shau Valley.

It was here that South Vietnamese and American troops of the 101st Division bottled up an NVA force dug in on Dong Ap Bia, Hill 937. What ensued was one of the most controversial actions of the entire war, Operation APACHE SNOW. For six days, troops repeatedly assaulted the hill, nine times in all, before finally driving the enemy off. From an estimated force of two thousand enemy soldiers, more than fifteen hundred were killed on the hill or slaughtered by artillery fire trying to run into Laos. The Americans lost 56 killed and 420 wounded.

Despite this lopsided victory, the battle became known as "Hamburger Hill" and was trumpeted in the American press as another example of a failed war strategy. Within days of taking the hill, it was simply abandoned since it no longer had any strategic value. There were also reports that American troops had been killed by American helicopters.

The first incident occurred on May 14, stalling an attack when command elements were fired on by their own Huey gunships. The second incident occurred later the same day. This time, rockets were fired at a command group, killing two soldiers and wounding fourteen. Among them were a company commander, forward observer, and first sergeant. The enemy exploited that incident with a counterattack, pushing the Americans back again. The third incident involved a Cobra. The pilot fired on an ammunition-carrying platoon, killing one man. Four were injured. Subsequently, the infantry commander ordered all gunships out of the area.

Rex was one of the pilots flying support for the Hill 937 battle. He, and A Battery, were employed in anti-aircraft suppression of the surrounding area. B and C batteries were flying fire support on the hill itself. Rex had just returned from a mission when he heard about the friendly-fire incidents. The 4/77 battalion commander called all the pilots together in a meeting and chewed them all out. Obviously, no one had wanted to shoot their own troops, and certainly, all possible caution had been exercised in spite of the heat of battle.

The incidents exposed several basic problems the pilots faced when supporting troops in the jungle. The heavy jungle in this area was called triple-canopy jungle because no less than three layers of thick green foliage lay between the aircraft and the ground. At Dong Ap Bia, the peak of the hill had been denuded by successive air and artillery bombardment, but the rest of the hill remained shrouded in vegetation.

As positions or targets were marked by smoke grenades to guide air strikes, the smoke drifted some distance, sometimes several hundred yards, before penetrating through the top where a pilot might see it. This threw off the placement of strikes by a considerable distance.

Another problem was the positioning of the radio operator and commander. More often than not, the man calling in air strikes couldn't physically see most of his troops. As they dashed about on the battlefield, attacking and moving up, the commander might not realize how far ahead his forward elements were and inadvertently call the strike on his own people.

There was also the massive firepower of the Cobra to consider. An inexperienced pilot couldn't place his rockets as precisely as an old hand, causing collateral damage to friendly forces.

No one can explain away the tragedy that friendly-fire casualties certainly are, tragedies like those in the battle that came to be called Hamburger Hill. But a clarification of the circumstances that caused them can help set the record straight and prevent similar deaths in the future.

But there were some genuine screwups, too. In a curious reversal of the situation, Rex almost became the victim of friendly fire. He was flying support for some Hueys whose mission was extracting a team of Vietnamese Rangers from a hilltop position. As the Snakes arrived, the ARVNs were under heavy attack, so Rex and his gunner went to work on the enemy while the Hueys dropped MacGuire rigs to the beleaguered defenders.

MacGuire rigs were simply harnesses at the ends of long ropes fastened to the inside of the aircraft. When there was no place to land, the soldiers below were lifted out, dangling below the chopper and carried out of harm's way like so many yo-yos.

As this was being done uphill, Swartz's Cobra saturated the downhill side with rockets to keep the VC at bay. Suddenly, Rex starting feeling flak bursts all around his ship. Looking around, he saw no gun positions firing, nor any of the green tracers common to big commie guns. But he did see hand grenades.

The ARVNs, hanging on ropes under the Hueys, were dropping frags down the hillside onto Charlie. Some exploded much too close to the Cobra, accounting for the flak! Rex continued his attacks from a safer distance until the mission was completed.

Early June found Swartz and A Battery on their way south to Chu Lai, fifty-six miles south of Da Nang on the sandy coastline. They were called upon to support the Americal 23d Infantry Division, desperate for additional firepower to support infantry operations in the Chu Lai–Tam Ky area. Unlike the 101st or 1st Cavalry divisions, airmobile and heavy with aviation assets, the Americal was a "straight-leg" i.e., infantry division, depending on other folks for a good part of its lift capability.

The Americal also had morale problems. It was this division from which the infamous My Lai massacre arose, an episode of the war only beginning to gather momentum at the time Rex Swartz and his colleagues in A Battery arrived, accompanied by a full brigade of the 101st Division's airmobile infantry.

The Americal Division had recently lost numerous sectors of its area of operations. Many positions had been overrun, and the enemy soldiers had to be dislodged before they could consolidate their gains. Rex and his colleagues were pretty

ragged when A Battery flew into Chu Lai. They had just
come off Operation APACHE SNOW and had no time to do laundry or shower. They were showing the wear and tear of several weeks of uninterrupted combat.

As the Cobras came in over the South China Sea, Swartz
was impressed with the white sandy beaches under the airfield approach. The helipads were on windy cliffs overlooking
the sparkling ocean, a view that made Rex forget the war for
a moment. Another surprise was the bus that arrived to transport them off the airfield; at Camp Eagle, they hoofed it or
rode trucks back to their hootches. Here, they were greeted by
an officer who welcomed them heartily, inviting them to hop
on for a briefing at the officers club.

The weary pilots dragged their gear aboard, soon finding
themselves in a luxurious restaurant/bar, atop the cliffs, with
an ocean view. Waiters served trays of coffee and doughnuts,
offering them to the tired pilots. No sooner were they settled
and comfy, than their hosts began assembling maps on the
floor to bring them "up to speed" on the current battle situation.

"We have troops out there we don't even know the location
of," they began, "and we lost control of the AO." As the
briefing proceeded, the officers painted an ever-more-grim
picture of a deteriorating situation. Through it all, they contin-
uously thanked the Cobras for coming down to help out.

The Snake drivers took it all in stride, basking in the adu-
lation.

"No sweat," one of them responded to the anxious briefers.
"We'll have it all cleared up in a few weeks!"

Their hosts offered them some nice hootches, but the pilots
declined in favor of their own tents, which could be pitched
closer to the flight line to respond to fire missions faster.

The first mission there was flown out of Tam Ky, twenty-
two miles to the north, a free-fire zone that was mostly rice
paddies and low hills. It was different from the triple-canopy
jungle and mountainous terrain up north. Swartz found the
area more to his liking, though, since targets were easier to
spot and mark, and to engage. The first day, however, they
found nothing at all.

Following maps to the precise coordinates given them, the

Snake drivers scoured the zone until they were sure a mistake had been made, then returned to base to double check.

"That's the right place," the operations officer told them. "We haven't been able to put any troops in there without an ambush on the LZ!"

The fire team returned to check again. This time, they'd do some priming and see what turned up under some hot guns. The recon by fire started with rolling in on some houses and villages, firing a few rounds to stimulate a response. What a response! They instantly drew massed small-arms fire from every quarter, as if every person down there had an automatic weapon. Which was what Rex and his mates were after.

The Cobras lined up and started their methodical and deadly attacks, firing rockets into where fire was concentrated and suppressing fire with miniguns and 40mm. It was good shootin' for the Snakes that day. The pilots and gunners liked how they could see the enemy, instead of spraying into blank treetops by radio direction. They followed the rocket trails straight into the huts where they could see muzzle flashes and watch the "target effect," erupting into a fireball.

Rex fired a few rounds at a hut with his 40mm, not to blow it up, but rather to set it afire. He was sure he'd seen some VC there firing at passing choppers. The Cobra moved away, but Swartz kept his eye on the structure. Sure enough, he saw enemy troops with weapons removing equipment from the now-flaming hut, so the pilot kicked the Snake around and shoved some rockets up their collective asses.

As it turned out, that valley was revisited many times by the Snakes, and became an extremely bloody battlefield. Many more VC and NVA would fall to the Snake guns and rockets in the weeks to come.

The Americal had a gunship company of their own, called the Blue Ghosts. Their commander just couldn't figure out, though, how the 4/77 managed to respond to a fire mission so fast. Swartz knew the answer after watching the Blue Ghosts in action. Since they were parked next to A Battery on the flight line, Rex had ample opportunity to view their unique techniques. When their operations received a call for air support, the message went down to the hootch where the pilots bunked. The pilots would then get dressed, if they weren't already, and walk up to operations for a briefing on the mission.

After the briefing, they went to the flight line and began the preflight inspection of the aircraft. Having completed that, the choppers were started, warmed up, and they eventually launched for the mission. All in all, the response averaged around thirty minutes from call to launch. Compared to 4/77's two minutes.

The ARA pilots could only laugh and shake their heads. Neither could they understand why the Blue Ghosts didn't take the cue from them and change their policies.

There were other things about Americal that Rex just didn't accept. After the brutal struggle to take Hill 937 back at Dong Ap Bia, he was surprised to see a similar fight on a hill north of Tam Ky. From his Cobra, flying fire missions in support of the infantry, Rex could clearly see the full scope of the battle as men died and rolled down the hillside. There were troops slugging it out from foxholes and bomb craters, clawing their way to the top of a worthless piece of dirt, a life at a time. It wasn't like Hamburger Hill, where most of the action was under triple-canopy jungle. He could see artillery landing over here, flamethrowers over there, and heroes take ground and lose ground.

He also saw the duds. There was a group of soldiers who were supposed to cover the rear from counterattack and sapper probes. Their collective attention was diverted, however. Rex called his air controller on the ground.

"Hey, you got guys down there just sitting around playing cards!"

A lot of soldiers died there. Not all of them had to.

While still operating from Chu Lai, Rex one day found his fire team diverted to the south to assist in a visual recon mission. Another Cobra company had some North Vietnamese regulars trapped on a sandbar in the middle of a river. It was a large island with numerous trees where the Redskins trapped the NVA troops just as their Snakes ran out of ammo.

As A Battery came upon the scene, the Redskins said to "keep 'em holed up while we go reload." Certainly.

The 4/77 Cobras began orbiting the island, firing short bursts at anything that moved, sizing up the encircled force. Rex watched as a single NVA soldier jumped up and started running out in the open. He swung the minigun around to fire, but the traverse hit its stop before reaching the target.

"Gimme some pedal!" Rex shouted to the pilot, who promptly brought the Cobra dead-on to the man on the ground. The sight centered on the doomed man just as he turned to fire at the big Snake. As he squeezed off a burst of fire, Rex thought that this was the closest he'd ever shot a man from. At the same instant, the Cobra hovered past a tree, masking the soldier from sight.

"Kick around," he said, and the Cobra moved back over.

There was only a blood trail where the man had been. The soldier had either pulled himself into the trees or been dragged in dead. Rex thought the latter, since he'd seen a burst of tracers meet the man's chest before they lost sight. A game of cat and mouse followed, with the harassed troops on the sandbar looking for a break; the Cobras allowed none. But it wasn't clear how many NVA they'd killed, or even how many were there.

They never found out, either. Gentlemen that they were, they stayed on until the Redskins were back, then returned to base to refuel. They were certain the Redskins would take care of business.

Things weren't always so easy. Often, pilots experienced frustration with decisions made by troops on the ground. One officer had his infantry company pinned down by a single sniper on a hill while advancing through the jungle. The Cobras were called in at a point where one man had been killed and one wounded. It would be a simple solution to have the Snakes take out the sniper, but emotions and machismo prevailed as the men below opted to "get that guy" themselves.

Swartz could hear the commander on the radio ordering his men off the hill so the Cobras could strip it with rockets. The sniper had killed a couple more of their buddies, and they wanted him bad. By the time the officer got them to back off, he was screaming bloody murder at his own men. In the end, the Cobras and massed artillery fire decapitated the hilltop, sniper and all. So much time was wasted on the sniper that the wounded man bled to death, waiting for his people to call a medevac.

A Battery's original boast of cleaning up the area in two-weeks time had somehow stretched out to three months. Not that they weren't doing a hell of a job. There was simply so much more to do. With no shortage of VC or NVA throughout

South Vietnam, their sector was no exception. The enemy wasn't the only threat, as Rex found out one afternoon. And a person couldn't ever have enough luck.

The battery's tents were pitched along an edge of the Chu Lai airfield, facing on one side towards the ocean and the other to the taxiway. On the other side of the strip were sandbagged L-shaped revetments where the Cobras were parked. There the Cobras were refueled and rearmed, each protected from incoming rockets and mortars by its own revetment.

The pilots liked to roll up the sides of their tents, letting the offshore breeze roll through and cool them while they talked, slept, played cards, or wrote letters home. One afternoon while he was off duty, Rex was sitting at a small table, playing cards, when another Snake driver brought his ship back early from a mission. The gunner was having trouble getting the reticle in the gunsight to illuminate, so they returned to check it out. The chopper settled into the revetment across from the tent as the armaments crew came out to repair the sight. Meanwhile, they'd upload ammo and refuel the ship.

About the time this was well underway, a Huey came hovering down the airstrip, taxiing to a revetment. The rotor blade on the Cobra hadn't been tied down and began to turn in the Huey's rotor wash. The mechanic in the Cobra quickly reached for the cyclic stick to stabilize the blade so someone could get a hook on it and tie it down. That's when it happened.

The weapons system was still energized while he was working on the sight. As he grasped the cyclic, he inadvertently hit the rocket firing button. Two rockets, one from each side, launched at just the right angle to clear the revetment to the front. They shot over the tail boom of the Huey, now hovering directly in front of the revetment, just missing the rotor blades. Then straight through the tent. In one side and out the other without touching a thing. They continued out to sea, exploding in a small fleet of fishing boats without hitting any. The boats promptly left.

At the air base, sirens were screaming and people were jumping into bunkers, most of them not knowing what had happened. Miraculously, no one had so much as a singed

The first of the Cobras was this unique prototype with the tail number N209J. It differed from all the Cobras that followed it by having retractable landing skids and a ventral fin at the tip of the tail boom, removed by the time this photo was taken. *Photo courtesy of The Patton Museum, Ft. Knox, KY.*

One of the first production AH-1Gs. Note the single minigun in the chin turret and the nose-mounted landing lights. Later variants had no tint in the canopy plastic, and the tail rotor was moved to the right side for better counter-torque control. Also discarded was the "Chinese hat" disk at the base of the main rotor to allow transmission cooling. *Photo courtesy of Bell Helicopter/Textron.*

An OH-13S of the 1-9 Cavalry gets a preflight maintenance check at the "golf course" helipad in An Khe. This is one of the aircraft SSG Jerry Ballantyne flew in during his many aero-scout door gunner missions. *Photo by Jerry Ballantyne.*

The same aircraft after being shot down by massed small-arms fire. Combat losses like this were airlifted out of the crash site and cannibalized for parts to keep other choppers airborne. *Photo by Jerry Ballantyne.*

Lieutenant Roger Fox and the "Magical Mystery Tour." The small logo, designed by Walt Disney Productions, signifies the "Smiling Tigers" of the 229th Assault Helicopter Company. *Photo courtesy of Roger Fox.*

Fox's Cobra sits loaded and ready for a mission. This ship shows how the Cobra had changed in five years, with the remounted tail rotor, twin-weapon turret, clear canopy, and removal of the landing lights in the nose. *Photo by Roger Fox.*

Still going strong and none the worse for wear, Roger Fox is currently the chief helicopter pilot for Seattle's KOMO-TV, an ABC affiliate. He's shown here with Chopper Four, a modified Bell Model 206 Jet Ranger set up for news-coverage missions. *Photo by Bob Rosenburgh.*

Gear down, a Vietnam Air Force A-1 enters the glide path on Pleiku approach. Officially called "Skyraider," the army chopper jocks dubbed the old piston-engine fighter "SPAD" after a noted aircraft from WWI. *Photo by John Cole.*

This is WO1 Jim Kreutz's UH-1C of the 189th Assault Helicopter Company. "Avenger-Eight" flew countless missions out of FOB II into Laos and Cambodia, striking the Ho Chi Minh Trail and Communist base camps. *Photo by Jim Kreutz.*

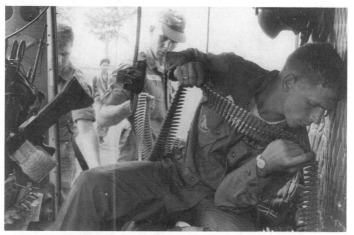

Sp4. Forrest French, crew chief of the UH-1C, loads 7.62mm ammo belts for the gunship's external weapons as pilot CW2 Christopher G. Hunt assists. Both served in the 197th Aviation Company. *U.S. Army photo.*

Twenty-two years late, Jerry Ballantyne is formally presented the twenty-three combat medals he earned in Vietnam. Making the presentation is Lieutenant General William H. Harrison, commander of I Corps and Fort Lewis, Washington. *Photo by Jennifer Weiner Jones.*

Capt. Lou Bouault, commander of the Rebels (part of the 1st Infantry Division), stands beside his office, the back seat of "Executioner." Seen clearly are the armored shields, the flight control instruments, and the primary sight for firing the rockets.

This Snake of the 229th AHC wasn't shot down by the enemy, but fell instead to the careless hands of a novice pilot performing a faulty autorotation drill.

CW2 Tom Wie of the Silver Spurs takes a break and a few notes while resting on a weapons pylon. To his left is the engine air intake with a filtration screen to keep particulate out of the turbine.

Today's AH-1S Cobra is extensively modified for anti-tank warfare with the addition of TOW missile systems. The once-graceful canopy has been replaced by a low-glare flat plate greenhouse. Upgraded avionics, infrared suppression devices on the exhaust, and nose-mounted articulated sights have robbed the Snake of its good looks but make it deadlier. *Photo courtesy of Bell Helicopter/Textron.*

The Marine Corps has upgraded their Cobra fleet to the AH-1W+ configuration, the SuperCobra. This twin-engine modernization with an all-new, four-bladed 680 rotor system makes the Marine Cobra the deadliest attack helicopter in the world. Not a bad showing for a design started over two decades ago! *Photo courtesy of Bell Helicopter/Textron.*

whisker. Except Rex, who laughed so hard he almost split a gut.

He had a few other good laughs while sitting in the tent playing cards. It was there he sat on the day one of his buddies looked up and absentmindedly noticed a curious sight.

"Say, man," the fellow said, "is that some new version of the Cobra or what?" Following the direction of a gesturing hand, Rex looked up at the aircraft approaching their base.

"Got no skids," Rex replied. "Can't be ours."

But it was a 4/77 ARA bird, and as it drew closer, they saw the skids had been snapped clean off the fuselage. Apparently, a new pilot was practicing autorotations and failed to pull the collective fast enough, causing the aircraft to hit the ground hard. The impact was insufficient to disable the aircraft but adequate to bust off the only means of landing a Cobra had.

As the broken chopper came over the field, shopping for a nest of some sort, a crowd gathered to watch the peculiar sight. Rex ran for his camera, returning with a fresh load of color slide film.

This oughta be good, he figured.

The Cobra found a patch of clear ground, and the IP set it gently down on the belly. What soon became obvious, however, was that he couldn't shut it off. If he lost the lift of the main rotor, the narrow body of the Cobra would tip over, allowing the blades to strike the ground. That, as any chopper pilot knows, would make the helicopter beat itself into scrap. So there they sat, waiting for a good idea or to run out of fuel. The group of observers, or possibly hecklers, soon came to a logical consensus on how to solve the problem.

Each of them ran to the ammo dump and came back with a couple of empty rocket crates. They began stacking boxes under the rocket pods until both sides were equally and fully supported. The pilot began to slowly and carefully back off the throttle, decreasing rotor speed slowly, with a minimum of vibration, until everything was settled and stable. Two embarrassed Snake drivers endured wisecracks and snickering for some time afterward. As for the otherwise-intact Cobra, it was hoisted up and fitted with a new set of skids. Rex put his camera away, and he and his buddies went back to their card game.

A Battery's six Cobras had been attached to the Americal

division since May 16, 1969, expecting to spend only ten days on the operation. By the time they were ordered back to Camp Eagle, it was July 24th. The day they left, Chu Lai began taking incoming mortar and rocket fire and tried to no avail to call the Cobras back.

Back at Eagle, it was like they'd never been gone. B and C batteries had been doing a brisk business in their absence and quickly fit A Battery right back into the schedule. Each battery had twelve AH-1Gs for a total of thirty-six aircraft. When an entire battery conducted a fire mission, referred to as an ARA Raid, the firepower was tremendous. The impact of 912 rockets plus twelve miniguns and 40mm-grenade machine guns made for awesome destruction. Just such a mission was planned for an attack on a mountain headquarters near Da Nang. Reputed to be the stronghold of an NVA general, G2 wanted it hit, very soon and very hard. A Battery got the nod for the assault, a first-light mission. The plan called for Cobras attacking from different angles to throw off enemy gunners.

The strike went off without a hitch. Ground fire was light, and the Cobras were accurate, ripple-firing salvo after salvo of rockets and stitching the area with tracer and grenade fire. It looked good, real good. Rex figured most of the enemy went underground when they first rolled in, since return fire was minimal. A flock of Snakes could run anyone off.

Did they get the general? Who knows, but Swartz was sure they disrupted the shit out of his whole day. One result of the raid was the desire of everyone to do it again. Only bigger. The sight of a mountain in flames triggered a plan for a full battalion ARA raid with all thirty-six Cobras. It was a sight to see.

The 4/77 started up Highway 1, headed north along the coast, flying in formation as a show of strength. When they reached Quang Tri, the battalion turned inland and headed for a road complex in the northern A Shau Valley. Aerial recon had photographed the area extensively, revealing massive NVA traffic, suggesting a major buildup. Not one to miss the significance of the moment, the battalion commander invited a reporter and photographer from *Stars and Stripes* to see the show. They were high above the massive formation in the C & C Huey.

The moment finally arrived as the Snake fleet sailed into the target area. On signal, all the Cobras moved on-line abreast, spanning several miles of road. Each aircraft was loaded with white phosphorous and flechette rockets. The choppers picked up speed as they approached, drawing very little ground fire, then began firing simultaneously, on cue. The rockets were ripple-fired again, for maximum area saturation, and nose guns blazed away.

Passing over the roads and completing their runs, every aircraft did a synchronous 180-degree pedal-turn and headed straight back. They immediately executed a second assault, on line again, and ripple-firing. In a few minutes, thirty-six aircraft had pumped 2,736 rockets and hundreds of thousands of grenades and bullets into the enemy stronghold. Hundreds of acres were in flames, with secondary explosions from hidden storage sites erupting all over.

When the battalion returned to Eagle, jubilant and elated at the fireworks, Rex was instructed to refuel and rearm and take his hot section back into the area for damage assessment. A couple of Loaches would lead them in and locate mop-up targets for the Snakes. The Cobras married up with the Loaches and headed for the target. The moment they arrived they started taking fire.

Now, Cobra pilots weren't always aware of just how much fire was being directed at their own aircraft. The enclosed canopy cut down on a lot of external noise, such as muzzle blasts and bullets snapping by. Rex's Snake had recently been fitted with a magnetic-anomaly detector dreamed up by some think-tank wizard to register the passing of metal objects, like bullets, within a given distance from the helicopter. The gizmo was called a bullet counter and would click off a number and sound a beep for each hostile shot entering the chopper's personal space.

Moving back into the target area, the scouts found lots of targets for the Snakes. There were military supplies scattered here and there, as though dropped as the owners fled, so the Cobras went about destroying them. Each time they'd attack, Rex's counter sounded off, and the number went up. He began to wonder if it was working right.

Pretty soon, he was really worried because the beeper was going crazy, and the numbers were off the gauge. The NVA probably figured that when thirty-six Cobras hit them, the biggest combat assault in history must be on the way behind the strike. They were everywhere, grabbing supplies and trying to pack them out before the imagined attack.

The Cobras and the Loaches had a field day, blowing up huge piles of munitions and weapons that had been dragged into the open by the nervous communist soldiers. One pile alone, found tucked under a group of trees, produced secondary explosions for hours afterwards.

The other pilots figured Rex was gun-shy, since he insisted he was taking heavy fire every time. But he was the only one with a bullet counter, so Rex figured the others were getting their share and didn't know it.

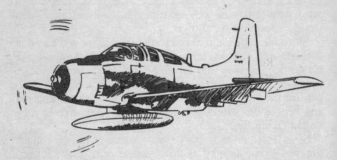

By then, a team of A-1 Skyraiders from Thailand, nicknamed Spads, was on station with wings full of ordnance, eager for targets.

"Where are you taking fire from?" one of the Spads queried Rex.

"Hold on and I'll mark it for you," he responded, then wheeled around and hauled across an open field. The bullet counter went ape-shit, beeping like crazy, as he felt several stout thumps shake the Snake.

"Mark, mark," he transmitted.

Then he stood the Cobra on its tail, rotated 180 degrees, and dove away. Once clear, the Spad screamed in and dumped napalm on the field, incinerating everything and triggering massive secondary explosions.

Rex and his copilot flew back to Camp Eagle to inspect

their aircraft. It had been hit in the nose by God-knows-what, leaving the turret chewed-up and inoperative. Otherwise, the ship was airworthy. They could still fire rockets, so they reloaded and headed back out.

Any unit that could launch a gunship had a piece of the action that day. The Spads returned for additional helpings, and the Redskins came by for a piece of the pie, too. Swartz spent more than nine hours in the air before they called it quits for the night. It was a very good day. A day he won the Distinguished Flying Cross.

But things didn't always work out as well.

Sometimes, everything went wrong, like the time he was flying in to relieve another Cobra on station near Chu Lai. The other Snake, piloted by a captain named Anderson, had been engaging a .51-caliber heavy machine gun and was just pulling out when Swartz and his fire team arrived to relieve them.

Just as Rex's team picked up the target and began their attack, Anderson's wingman called the captain over their frequency.

"Was that your tail rotor I just saw fly off?"

"I think so," Anderson replied. "We're starting to spin."

Then the big aircraft began a slow corkscrew down to the ground as the pilot fought to control the descent. He and his gunner talked to each other on the broadcast channel instead of intercom, so every pilot in both fire teams was hanging on every word. The voices of the men going down quickened as the ground rushed ever faster up to greet them.

Rex made several passes at the enemy machine gun, but was so engrossed in the crash sequence that he forgot to fire. When the Cobra finally hit, the impact was controlled enough that the Snake didn't disintegrate or burst into flame. It was still a horror to learn later that the main rotor had struck the ground and flexed into the canopy, decapitating Anderson.

The lieutenant in the back seat was in pretty good shape until he saw the captain.

"Get a medevac out here," called the other Cobra pilot, "We got a Snake down!"

While the Huey came to pick up the downed flyers, Rex and his shocked colleagues busied themselves finishing off the .51 caliber and everything else in the area that moved. It was a bitter finish to a thoroughly rotten day.

Another time, Rex's hot section was scrambled on a mission to Quang Tri that was unlike anything Rex had flown before. Someone thought a North Vietnamese airmobile assault was about to launch from the north. The bad guys did have a few Russian-made choppers on their side of the DMZ, but no one ever heard of their mounting any kind of airmobile operation, of any size.

But Swartz's section launched on the call and headed north to Quang Tri. From there, ground controllers vectored them by radar to a point just south of the DMZ. It was near Highway 1, close to a huge North Vietnamese flag just over the border. He knew right where he was, since everyone wanted to knock that goddamn flag down.

"Let's go knock that fucker down!" his gunner gloated.

"No way," Rex replied, "Every gun and missile in North Vietnam is probably waiting for anyone dumb enough to try it."

Meanwhile, the radar operator who'd sent them there began to describe what he saw on radar in their current location.

He told them it was a racetrack pattern of aircraft similar to a combat assault with gunships, and could they see it?

No. Nothing.

They were then vectored up to five hundred feet and sent in another direction to check it out. Rex figured this would be it, the first helicopter dogfight, him and his gunner against the NVA air force.

"He's on your tail!" yelled the controller.

"He's on your tail!" Spinning the Snake around, they saw nothing.

"He's right over you now!"

They looked up at the blank sky.

"He's under your ship!"

Not a thing below.

By now they had maneuvered down to the deck, chasing shadows. Rex called the operator.

"Is he under me?" he asked.

"Yes, he's right beneath you. Can you see it?" The controller was really hot for it now.

"Well, I'm fifty feet over a graveyard, and all I see is a

campfire on a hill." With that, they headed back to Camp Eagle. When they landed, everyone gathered around to find out about the NVA invasion.

"Whadja see, whadja see?" they asked eagerly.

"A fire on a grave." That's all he said and walked off, leaving a confused and disappointed group to scratch their heads.

One group that depended on pilots for its very existence was the Special Forces, whose teams were secretly airlifted by Hueys deep into Laos and Cambodia to gather intelligence, capture enemy troops on the Ho Chi Minh trail, or sabotage key targets. Generally made up of five men, the teams operated while surrounded by the enemy. Frequently their presence became known, and on such occasions it was critical to extract them before they were killed or captured. The emergency extractions were code-named Prairie Fire. And Cobras were critical parts of the teams that flew in to withdraw the Green Berets.

Rex flew one Prairie Fire mission deep into a part of Laos that was particularly hazardous. Spotted and chased by the enemy, the members of the team were separated while fleeing their NVA pursuers. The main body of the team was located by slicks and lifted out of the jungle on MacGuire rig hoists, under the protective guns and rockets of the Cobras. While orbiting the LZ, however, Rex caught some movement out of the corner of his eye. It was a single soldier, high up in a tree atop a hill several miles away, flashing him with a small mirror. It was sheer luck that Swartz had spotted him, but a lot more luck would be needed to get him out.

Rex reported the sighting, and a second Huey came around to drop a MacGuire rig to the man. While hovering over the tree, though, the UH-1 started taking heavy fire and had to break away. The Huey flew quickly to an open field, calling to the other slick to come get his passengers. The pilot wasn't sure the ship would fly back and didn't want to risk all their lives.

Rex saw the pilot move back to inspect the tail rotor, but then sprinted back to the cabin to report a sniper. Swartz moved in and killed the sniper, but each time the pilot went back to the tail, another sniper would fire. Finally, the pilot took off and flew the Huey back alone, at forty knots all the way due to severe vibrations, but the aircraft made it back.

They had to leave the soldier in the tree behind. Rex had carefully marked his position on the map and reported it when he returned. He never knew what happened after that. He always wondered.

LRRP insertions could sometimes be as hazardous as extractions. A battery learned that the hard way flying with the Vietnamese King Bees. The King Bee was an old Sikorsky H-34 helicopter, turned over to the Vietnamese after becoming obsolete for U.S. forces. The fat, old chopper had piston engines and looked like farting stink bugs as they belched smoke and rattled through the air. All the same, they did journeyman service for the ARVNs.

It was New Year's Day 1970 when they were inserting a six-man Special Forces team into Cambodia. The initial insertion went fine, and the choppers headed back to base. Part of the way back, however, they heard the team leader whispering in a low voice over the radio to come on back and get them out.

The team had been dropped in tall elephant grass, and there they remained. As the gunships returned, the LRRPs refused to pop smoke because the enemy was too close. Instead, they spread an orange marker panel so the Snakes could spot their position from the air. The first pass was for spotting fire; on the second run the Snakes opened up, and the enemy fired back with everything they had.

In the middle of it all came the King Bee, hovering straight down into the middle of the firefight from three thousand feet.

"Not yet, King Bee," came the call. As the battle picked up pace, the LRRPs on the ground fired at the enemy from their position while the Cobras continued their gun runs. Again, the old Sikorsky dropped into the middle of it.

"Not now, King Bee!" and up he went again.

The battle raged on as the enemy began converging on the LRRPs, gaining strength despite heavy losses to the Cobras' vicious attacks. This time, King Bee came all the way down and plopped on the ground beside the panel. Everyone jumped on board, and the ungainly old ship rose out like a bubble in a cauldron.

Rex had a load of nails left, so when the King Bee cleared

the LZ, he flipped on the switch and butchered the NVA closing in on the site.

Back at Quang Tri, the Special Forces team jumped off the King Bee and brought handfuls of rocket shrapnel over to the Cobras.

"Hey, you guys want some souvenirs?" they laughed. All the glass had been shot out of the Sikorsky, and it was riddled with holes. The Vietnamese pilots were looking it over nonchalantly. They'd flown plenty of Special Forces support missions, and that one hadn't been any worse than the others.

For several reasons cross-border missions were, as a rule, somewhat hairier than the ones flown in country. The first was that the enemy had a warm welcome planned, even if you dropped in unannounced. Flights into Laos and Cambodia went square into the middle of carefully prepared and emplaced air-defense systems. The guns would be bigger, and there were more of them. Potential target areas had overlapping fields of fire, with gun positions placed in triangles around the perimeters. This allowed NVA gunners to engage aircraft with most of their weapons no matter what angle the approach came from.

Second, there were no friendlies close by to bail you out. If you went down, the only way out was by air, and the next chopper in faced the same smiling group that put you there.

The briefings pilots were treated to before such missions were nearly as frightening as the flight itself. A Special Forces officer would welcome them into operations and have them take a look at his map stand, usually covered up before the briefing began.

"Here's what we're doing and where we're going today," he'd begin, flipping the cover off the map. "We're putting a team in here," he'd add and poke a gnarly finger into a point on the map completely encircled by red dots. Those dots were known antiaircraft positions. There were so many that they merged on the paper into big red blotches. All around the target area. That was the scary part.

After one such briefing, Rex found himself flying a fire team into Laos, just beyond Khe Sanh, to find and destroy an NVA basic training camp that a LRRP team had located the day before. There had also been an air force Jolly Green Giant helicopter shot down in the area a couple days before, so they were listening on the guard frequency as well as on their own commo net. They often monitored the guard frequency to keep track of B-52 Arc Light strikes and to be aware of bogeys in the area. North Vietnamese MiGs were tracked and reported in relation to "Bull's-eye," which was Hanoi. The jets were tracked by radar and reported by speed, altitude, distance, and azimuth from Bull's-eye.

As Rex flew out to locate the camp and fire it up, he heard the guard frequency talking about bandits about a hundred miles south of Bull's-eye. That wasn't too far from where his fire team was, but he didn't think a lot of it. He noted the heading was toward him, though.

A little later, he heard the report again, 150 miles out on the same heading. Still no need for concern. The Snakes finally reached the objective and were vectored in by the LRRP team concealed in the jungle near the camp. Arming their weapons, the Cobras lined up on target and began their attack, firing rockets and raking the area with grenade fire and electric Gatling guns.

Coming around for another pass, Swartz picked up altitude to begin a diving run, than lined up on the racetrack. Just then, a huge jet fighter blasted across his canopy, right off the nose of the Cobra! "What the . . . did you see the markings on that?" Rex shouted.

It was an F-4 Phantom. A couple fighter jocks had been coming back from a mission and decided to have some fun with the helicopters. It scared the hell out of Rex. The Phantom pilots probably knew they were monitoring the bogey reports. It was too good a setup to resist the gag, and the Snake drivers fell for it. Once they got over the initial shock, they all had a good laugh. Afterwards, it was back to business.

As Rex Swartz's tour of duty in Vietnam drew near the magic twelfth month, he continued to fly combat missions. He could have stopped flying about thirty days short of his DEROS (date estimate return from overseas) and worked in operations or somewhere else productive, but he preferred to keep flying. He did, however, exercise the option to stay out of Laos and Cambodia.

True to form, one of his final flights in-country involved one crazy thing after another. It began during one of the few times that Camp Eagle was attacked during his tour. Rex was on two-minute standby when B-40 rockets came flying in on the base, doing nominal damage, but stirring everyone into action. The hot section launched and went out to find the source of rockets and eliminate the threat. They scoured the area all day, but found very little. The rocket fire stopped right after it began, anyway. By evening Rex and his gunner were tired and looking forward to sacking out. About 11:00 P.M. they were scrambled again.

Down by Da Nang, remote sensors had detected troop movement. They were sent to investigate, fed and clean, but still dog-tired. Flying there at night was a dangerous proposition. With cloud cover overhead blocking out the moonlight, it was black everywhere. To make their flight safer, Rex called artillery for illumination to lead the way to the target area. One after another, the big guns fired parachute flares from distant bases, providing a continuous string of burning lights to lead the Snakes through the night. It was as if giant temporary streetlights had been placed along the way just for him.

They reached the target area safely and fired up their ammo. They flew back and repeated the mission three times before returning to Eagle.

Rearmed and refueled, they were on the ground no more than fifteen minutes before they were scrambled again. This time it was a fire base being overrun. When they reached the coordinates, the battle was in full force. Rex could see jet contrails left by mortar rounds dropping on the base from the surrounding hills. NVA sappers in the wire were being cooked alive by huge bursts of fougasse set off by the defenders.

Cocked and loaded, the Cobras were ready to strike, but the commander on the ground wouldn't let them. He still had patrols out and didn't want them killed too. So the Snakes had to orbit and watch the battle progress. Soon, the VC were inside the compound, doing damage and killing people before they were killed in turn. Swartz called down and told the commander that he could see the flash of the mortar tubes and would be glad to destroy them. Still a no-go. The man was concerned about his patrols. Rex never did get a chance to aid the base.

They orbited so long they had to go back to base to refuel.

Then they returned and flew in more circles. They ended up
flying all night before returning to Eagle. Then they were
scrambled again. Rex and his gunner were dead on their feet,
but they had to follow a Loach out on a visual recon mission. As they flew out, following the scout from a higher altitude, they took turns falling asleep. Not on purpose, either.
One of them would have the controls and begin to drift off.

"You got it!" he'd mumble, waking the other man in time
to take over. Then the other would fly a while until sleep
overtook his mind, and he'd nod off.

"You got it!"

Back and forth they went for over two hours, playing the
impossible game of sleeping in flight. Fortunately, it was an
uneventful mission, and they eventually made it home. And
went straight to bed.

Chapter 8

COBRA COMPANY COMMANDER

Capt. Lou Bouault (pronounced Boo-oh') was aggravated. He had fought for years to transfer from armored cavalry into aviation, finally getting to flight school, even through Cobra transition school. He'd come a long way since his first tour as an ACAV officer in Vietnam. Now, in September 1969, he was back, wearing silver wings on his chest and anxious to get some blade time in-country.

But Lou had too much rank to be a "peter pilot," flying front seat, and not enough rank to be an aviation commander. So he was stuck on the ground as S3 operations officer for the 1st Aviation Battalion of the 1st Infantry Division in Phu Loi. Things got worse when the S4 officer left and Bouault took over that section, too. He had no logistics experience, but rank seemed to matter more to the army than training.

He had a lucky break, though, in January 1970, when the commander of Bravo Company, the Longhorns, went home on emergency leave. Bravo was the Cobra company, and no one with AH-1 training was available to command it except, you guessed it, Captain Bouault. Bravo company commander.

Lou inherited six Cobras and six Charlie-model Hueys with the special 540 model rotor-head like the Cobras. The UH-1s lacked the beefed-up engines though, and couldn't perform near as well as the Snakes.

Unofficially, the 1st of the 1st was the only active "combat arm" of the Confederate Air Force, an organization dedicated to the preservation of vintage warplanes. The unit had indeed been issued a certificate which hung in the battalion's operations office, endorsing them as a CAF wing. Consequently, each Cobra had a rebel flag painted on the belly. A set of CAF wings—decals sent by the CAF—was on each side of the rotor cowling. Though the designation lacked official army blessings, it was a fun thing for the crews and added a nice touch to their morale and esprit de corps.

Because he already had one Vietnam tour, Lou was familiar with the conduct of combat operations and wasted no time getting into action. As commander, Captain Bouault flew missions in the front seat, needing to control the other aircraft in his flight without the distraction of piloting his own. Flight commanders generally flew in Hueys, but Lou found it difficult to keep up with a Cobra team unless he was part of it.

As he was fire team leader, the other fire teams also reported to him. While his pilot was concentrating on the firepower of the team he was in, Lou would be feeding the other flights into position and managing the overall battle.

Bravo Company's primary mission was aviation support. Unlike aeroscouts or Air Cav, they didn't usually seek out targets and then engage; they orbited on station and waited for a fire-support call, then attacked with guns and aerial rockets where they were needed.

In the Phu Loi area, at that time, the war was still in full swing. There were no politics to worry about when engaging targets, and missions were straightforward attack-and-destroy runs. Commanders enjoyed the freedom of using their own discretion and judgment. Despite the rigors of combat, Lou found himself in his proper element at long last.

Pilots cared about each other, too, whether they were air force, navy, or army aviation. As an example, a Mayday call was broadcast by an A-1 Skyraider pilot who was going down. Before Lou's Cobras could turn to the rescue or react, about seven other aircraft in the area said they were on the way. Cobra teams, Huey teams, air force and navy choppers all showed up for the rescue.

Most pilots operating in the south felt as though they never need worry about being stranded, because they were never alone. Cooperation was particularly good between O-1 Bird Dog spotter planes, F-4 Phantom fighter-bombers, A-1 Skyraider close-air-support aircraft, and the Cobras. The teams worked together to process a target for maximum effect. When the Longhorns assisted the air cavalry, Pink teams of OH-6 Cayuse scouts (Whites) and AH-1G Cobras (Reds) found a target and led the attack.

The scout located, identified, and lined up a target, such as an NVA battalion occupying a jungle area, then engaged with door guns and miniguns, harassing and drawing fire to test the enemy strength and locate strongpoints.

Then the Cobras moved in, firing rockets and raking the area with Gatling fire. Cobras were particularly accurate and effective on hardened point-targets like bunkers and trenches. When the jets or A-1s arrived, the choppers moved aside to allow an avenue of approach right up the middle of the target area. Bombs, napalm, and heavy guns from the fixed-wing aircraft saturated the area with firepower, obliterating many of the enemy and raining hell and jungle scraps all around them.

Then the Cobras moved back in, ferreting out and destroying survivors, hunting and killing those that fled, then finding more targets to start the cycle again. In a broader sense, tactical air strikes were for mass destruction of large areas, while Cobras were precise weapons of murderous firepower for detailed destruction.

Bird Dogs were another element of this cooperation. The O-1 Bird Dogs were often described as the deadliest airplane ever made. It's a curious title for a tiny high-wing monoplane with a 213-horse power engine. Completely unarmed, the little Cessna was slow, light, and very quiet. With only a map, a radio, and a pair of binoculars, the Bird Dog pilot was able to bring a world of shit down on any unlucky Communist who caught his eye. The O-1's primary mission was to direct artillery fires, but the tiny planes also brought tactical air strikes, helicopter assaults and even the horrendous Arc Light B-52 strikes.[8]

For his Cobra, Captain Bouault's favorite weapon was the XM-35 20mm cannon he had mounted under the left inboard weapons pylon. This gun was a giant version of the minigun in the chin turret, firing a much larger projectile with an explosive warhead. Deliciously accurate, the massive gun was so powerful that the Cobra airframe had to be strengthened to stand the recoil. Long, tapered ammunition canisters were strapped to the skids like saddlebags to feed the monster gun's 3,000 rounds per minute appetite. Lou always had one bird in each platoon equipped with a 20 to augment the total firepower of the team. There were limited numbers of the guns, so he wanted the best use he could get from them all.

In a fire team of three Cobras, the high bird would have the 20mm to back up the other two.

Other Cobras generally had nineteen-shot rocket pods on both inboard pylons and seven-round pods outboard. At Phu Loi, a full seventy-six-rocket load made it difficult to operate the aircraft because the climate was extremely hot, resulting in much thinner air.

Captain Bouault spent a short period at Lai Khe, engaged in a reaction-force mission. The procedure was for the pilots to do a complete preflight checkout, right up to, but not including, starting the turbines. They then stood by, fully-armed-and-fueled Cobras waiting, for a fire-support mission. They'd snooze in the operations shack, play cards, read, or whatever killed time, waiting for a call.

And it was stiflingly hot, so when the call finally came, the heavy-laden Cobras needed a special touch to launch in the thin air. The pilots had to slowly rotate the aircraft in circles just to get off the ground. When the Snakes came to a hover, the tail rotor ran out of countertorque needed to compensate for engine torque under the additional load. Full left-pedal just wasn't enough to keep the fuselage in line, so the Cobras had to carefully move out of the apron, rotating slowly as

8. Throughout the war, the VC and NVA feared no weapon more than the B-52 Stratofortress. Arriving unseen between 25,000 and 55,000 feet altitude, a flight of three B-52s could rain 150,000 pounds of huge bombs on enemy strongholds and troop concentrations, wiping them out in a single blow.

they approached the runway, and then change the direction of flight, still spinning in circles, as they began takeoff.

That wasn't the end of it, though, because the airfield was too short for the Snakes to get enough forward speed to launch. The Cobras needed translational lift; the point where ground effect, or the wind from the rotor bouncing back up, joins with the lift generated by forward speed and increased pitch on the rotor blades, and gives the helicopter an extra boost into the air.

Once translational lift is achieved, the chopper can speed up even more and climb up to a cruising speed and altitude. Under heavy load, extra space was needed, so troops at the base went to the perimeter and pulled the concertina barbed wire apart to give the Snakes more room to develop enough lift to jump over the edge. This made a gap big enough for spinning Cobras to dance through in circles. Once outside, the pilots dragged their skids along the ground, acting as a kind of rudder to keep the aircraft straight while speed built toward translational lift.

With the choppers finally in the air, the aerodynamics changed enough to allow safe forward flight at speed. The vertical tail fin that mounted the tail rotor was made in a cambered airfoil form that enhanced lift away from the engine torque. Once airborne, this effect, and the trimming quality intrinsic to the sleek design of the fuselage, sufficiently balanced out the tail rotor shortcomings. Production Cobras were later modified by placing the tail rotor on the other side of the tail fin, correcting the problem.

All the Cobras were finally in the air and proceeded directly east to respond to the mission call. The problem they were to fix was that of an infantry platoon pinned down by a Viet Cong bunker. The platoon had entered a trap set up to take advantage of a large bomb crater.

As the platoon had entered the area, they came under immediate heavy-weapons fire from the concealed bunker and quickly went to ground. Seeking cover, the soldiers moved to the crater, which seemed to provide the only shelter around. That was the VC plan. The crater had been plotted by the guerilla mortar teams and the falling rounds were already taking their toll of the Americans. For the coup de grace, Charlie was moving an assault team in under cover of the bunker and mortar fire to finish off the beleaguered Yanks. It was a perfect snare. Almost.

Captain Bouault called ahead on the infantry's radio frequency and told the men in the crater to stay where they were and keep their heads down. As the Cobras rolled in with weapons armed, they had no trouble finding the bunker, which immediately shifted the heavy machine-gun fire to the aircraft.

The gunships made several passes, firing two pair of rockets each time they lined up on the target. Lou led the three-ship fire team each time, suppressing ground fire with the minigun.

By the third run, he felt that they were making a pattern out of it, giving enemy gunners an advantage in laying their fire. After each run down the racetrack made by the rocket trails, they broke away to the left. This time, he broke to the right. Just as he did, the aircraft shuddered and wobbled, then continued its flight.

Now Lou was really ticked off. He had enough of that shit. And you just don't want to get a Cobra pilot pissed. On the next pass, he ran the Cobras in so close, holding his rocket fire to the last second, that he could feel the shock waves of the rockets exploding. The rockets from the aircraft behind him were coming in underneath his ship and hitting the same bunker. Each deadly Snake showed what it could do as it ripple-fired massive salvos of rockets at point-blank range into the bunker, which exploded as the lightened choppers peeled away at even greater climbing speed.

Relieved of their torment in a single thunderous blast, the infantry in the crater leaped to their feet and wildly cheered as the Cobras worked the wood line for Viet Cong survivors fleeing into the jungle.

When the team got back to Lai Khe, the pilots prepped for the next mission, rearming, refueling, and checking the choppers for battle damage. They all buzzed with excited talk about the mission. Bouault's pilot was first to notice what made their Snake shake and wobble during the third run on the target.

"Hey, Lou, look at this," he called, while Bouault was inspecting the rotor head.

"What is it?" Bouault responded and peered under the fuselage where the pilot was pointing. Right down the center of the belly was a long, shiny groove, as if a giant ice-cream scoop had run down the middle. It was between the skids, right under the fuel tank, and between the weapons pylons. Whatever had hit them left a long corkscrew scrape as it bounced off the sheet metal.

The two men looked at each other, realizing how close they had come to destruction. If they had broken left again instead of to the right, the hit would have gone straight in and blown them to bits, loaded with fuel and rockets.

It was a miracle, in fact, that the round hadn't detonated from the glancing blow. Unbelievable luck. Completing their flight check, the two men went to the base club and had a liquid lunch to calm their nerves.

They learned later that they had saved a lot of lives in the action. Lou and the pilot and the battalion commander, who was on the mission with them, all were awarded the Distinguished Flying Cross for the action.

Tactics used by the Cobras at that time were based on high-altitude diving attacks. Since the helicopters could carry so much ordnance, it was necessary to begin an attack higher up to have time to fire a greater volume of 2.75-inch rockets. The improved sights of the Cobra made this kind of attack more accurate than with the Huey. When a Cobra was locked on a target, it stayed there and delivered its fire accurately throughout the run.

The Hueys, on the other hand, lacked the Cobra's stability control and augmentation system and had a tendency to drift off. It was all the crews could do to keep the impacts centered in a general area. Huey gunners found it more accurate to mark a cross on the windshield in front of them and use that as a sight. The early flexible pantographic sights they used just weren't very good.

The Hueys were prone to all sorts of vibration, bouncing right, left, up and down, so Charlie-model pilots used what they called "interpolation," a mixture of interpretation and extrapolation. They just tried to find the middle of the wobble and fire into the center.

The Cobra was infinitely better, being designed as a weapons system with all the considerations of a stable firing platform, especially in light of the SCAS system that picked up where human error left off. It was truly a pinpoint weapon.

Used as aerial rocket artillery, the Snakes put a larger volume of explosives in a smaller area than howitzers were capable of doing. Once on station in a target area, they could do it faster in response to moving targets. Cobras didn't need the continuous fire adjustments of artillery, either. They were at the scene and could observe their own target effects.

A single Cobra armed with seventy-six rockets with seventeen-pound warheads was the equivalent of an entire howitzer battery. The minigun, with its high rate of fire and the 40mm grenade launcher gave more firepower than an infantry company. Mounted on the most advanced helicopter in the world, those formidable weapons could move around the battlefield wherever needed on short notice. It was the crowning achievement of the long development and implementation of the airmobile divisions. A rotary-wing fighter plane.

Time went by and Captain Bouault became more experienced with the Cobras. He noticed subtle changes occurring in himself. When he had first begun flying in country, Lou was amazed at the visual acuity of the old hands who had plenty of experience flying in the war.

"Hey, Lou," one might say, "look at the deer!"

From a few thousand feet up, Bouault thought he was being kidded. He couldn't spot diddly-squat that high up, and he'd say so. Just to make a point, the pilot would turn and descend to a spot where, sure enough, one or more deer would bolt and run. Now, only months later, Lou found himself locating minute objects at great distances. It was uncanny, but it seemed like his eyesight had actually improved.

Some of his habits needed changing, too. On a night mission he struck a match to light a cigarette and was rewarded with a violent swerving jerk of the chopper.

"Holy shit!" the pilot hollered into the intercom, "Don't *ever* do that again. Do you know what a tracer looks like coming at you in the dark?"

It seemed that the old adage "live and learn" was reversed here to say "learn and live."

Lou acquired another valuable lesson about Cobras at the hands of a crusty old instructor pilot.

It was said that there were two things that would kill you

in a Cobra: a full-load autorotation and loss of the tail rotor. The old IP taught Bouault how to handle the first emergency by doing an autorotation right into an enemy-held area.

"You got to trust this airplane to do what you want it to," he told his nervous student, "and you got to have guts!"

Well, guts were exactly what it took as they snapped along the ground, only twenty feet high, between a hedgerow and a tree line. The IP yanked on the cyclic, hopped over the trees, and landed softly on the other side.

"Now you do it."

Of course, Lou did very well, since if he didn't, they'd be stranded smack in the middle of nowhere.

Next lesson was tail-rotor failure. At the end of the airstrip at Phu Loi, a large bunker had been built to defend that end of the perimeter. The IP wanted to show Lou how throttle control could manage the aircraft when the tail rotor went out.

"Okay," he said, "Your tail rotor is gone and you're gonna die." With those words he took the chopper out over the other end of the runway across from the bunker, began a landing approach lined up on the strip, then backed off on the throttle for better control.

"Lou, I want you to grab the stick and hold it solid so it doesn't move. I won't be using it. And hold the foot pedals tight, too."

Then he flew down the runway and did a series of esses and turns, moving from one side to the other, swaying back and forth as the Cobra flew the length of the strip. All with the blade pitch and throttle on the collective lever.

As they continued, the engine rpm steadily fell off as each maneuver bled off more energy. By the time they approached the bunker, it seemed like the rotor was barely turning. They were lower than the bunker.

"You see how it works now?" the IP said. Lou choked out a muted, "Yup," just about where he thought they'd plow into the bunker, but the IP quickly rolled the throttle back up and gave the cyclic and collective a pull. That gave the Snake just enough of a hop to pop over the bunker and pick up speed as it swooped back down the other side and across the rice paddies. Nice touch.

In April 1970, the units of the 1st Infantry Division began to stand down as American forces started to withdraw from

Vietnam. Captain Bouault and the pilots of Bravo Company staged an air show for the troops and brass of the U.S. and Vietnamese forces as a going-away present. It meant the end of his command tenure, but they had a lot of fun, just the same. The highlight of the event was a V-formation fly-by with the Cobras and OH-6s. Loaded with colored smoke grenades wired to the skids, the pilots put on an aerobatic demonstration, performing maneuvers that simply aren't authorized.

At the high point of the display, five Cobras raced toward the reviewing stand at 180 knots, then Lou's center ship pulled straight up as two on each side climbed at increasing angles to the right and left, leaving a giant colored starburst design in the Asian sky. It was some hot shit.

By the end of the ceremonies, the sky was a giant quilt of colored smoke trails. The day's events were a fitting end to a successful command.

It was not, however, the end of Captain Bouault's tour in Vietnam. Lou was asked to take command of the 235th Attack Helicopter Company in Can Tho. There was no shortage of majors to take charge of the unit, but all the O4s who'd been asked had refused. The unit had severe morale problems when they found Lou, the spare captain from the 1st Division, who was just brash enough to chance it.

Upon arriving at his new base, Bouault was told to fire what seemed like the entire unit cadre. Cautious at first, he decided to get the lay of the land before making any drastic decisions, so Lou interviewed as many of the staff as would talk to him. He wanted a consensus on the *real* problems.

Lou finally decided there was no problem. What had been wrong was a senior officer, by then gone, a drunk who was abusive and inept, a flagrant alcoholic who frequently wandered the area in his undershorts. The soldiers knew they were good, but had been stifled by a lack of good leadership in the company. Lou simply gave them back their pride, and like a fairy-tale transformation, everything was great.

Having settled that, Lou got down to the business of running one of the largest Cobra companies in Vietnam. Based in Can Tho on the Ca Mau Peninsula, south of the Mekong Delta, the 235th AHC had over twenty AH-1G Cobras and was part of the 1st Aviation Brigade.

The 1st Aviation was formed, just for the Vietnam War, to support the straight-leg infantry in the conduct of airmobile operations. Scattered across the country, units of this brigade were among the last to leave when American forces finally pulled out in 1972.

Lou discovered quickly that things were done differently in this theater. One tactic was to send aircraft out in the daytime, usually Hueys and scouts, to drop duffel bags containing sensitive listening devices, or sensors called ADSIDS, in the Viet Cong's backyard.

When night fell, the Cobras launched and moved out on station. In Can Tho, intelligence analysts waited for signals from the listening devices monitoring enemy.

The Can Tho radar was a key element of the scheme, keeping track of the Cobras' precise locations and altitudes, then cross-referencing target data on their maps.

Cruising around two thousand feet, the Cobras were given a heading and range to the target. Targets were approached in a very long and slow dive, descending at only one hundred feet a minute.

The radar crew monitored the flight all the way, vectoring them right to the target and then saying when to open fire. The Cobras fired several rockets, then moved to the next target, closely monitored throughout the mission. This type of attack was known as H & I fire, or harassment and interdiction. As surprising as it seems, H & I was quite effective in limiting the size of enemy forces, making it difficult to gather in strength undetected.

Occasionally, intelligence would report that a previous night's mission scored some major targets, but usually it simply kept the enemy on their toes and nervous.

Night missions had become a common occurrence.

One evening in June, Lou's Snakes were called on to relieve enemy pressure on an ARVN base at Nam Can. The base, located on the Song Cua Lon near the extreme southern end of South Vietnam, was being assaulted in the dark by a large NVA force. There was simply no one else who could reach the isolated post available to assist.

Lou now flew out in the War Wagon, a UH-1H fitted out as the ultimate command-and-control, or C & C, ship. The War Wagon had radios to communicate on all necessary frequencies, so Lou could orchestrate the air battle, talk to the ground, and call fire from artillery and tac air.

It was also equipped on the right side with a huge six-bulb searchlight. Alongside the light was a detuned minigun from a Cobra, with a limited rate of fire to keep from shaking the Huey apart. On the left was a big fat .50-caliber machine gun, one of the most beloved weapons in any army. The M2 .50 caliber was easily the best heavy machine gun ever made. It had extremely long range, powerful penetration, and remarkable accuracy. Fifties had proven themselves in war after war, used everywhere from aircraft to infantry and at sea.

The ammunition on the War Wagon was stowed to balance the aircraft nicely for a level flight out to the war. Arriving at the battle, the War Wagon crew started kicking out flares to light the ground below.

The flares were hooked to a D-ring and then tossed out. The weight of their fall pulled out a pin and armed the flare, preset to burn at a given altitude.

Lou's flight crew set a series of flares for four thousand feet and sent them on their way. As the flares slowly floated down under small parachutes, the Snakes moved in below and began seeking targets. In the crowded airspace, each ship had to watch for the others darting in and out of the illumination, firing rockets at enemy troops and spraying bright red tracer streams from the miniguns.

Then artillery joined in, firing cannon flares that added a shimmer to the eerie scene. Aerial and cannon flares filled the sky with flickering points of orange light. Cobras slipped in and out like sharks in a feeding frenzy, punctuating the night with explosions and muzzle blasts. High above, the War Wagon shone its massive searchlight around the fire base perimeter as the big fifty devoured attacking NVA. Then things really got hot.

From nowhere and unannounced, the sky above started raining streams of flame down the center of a white-hot searchlight beam.

"Everyone, clear the area!" Lou called over the main frequency. In a moment they were gone. A brief silence fell across the night sky as the drone of huge engines hummed far above. Then the throats of massive guns coughed again. The new player was an air force AC-130 "Spectre" gunship, a

Hercules four-engine transport plane armed with two 20mm Vulcan Gatling guns, four miniguns, and a 105mm howitzer. Each of these weapons fired to the left side of the aircraft and slightly downward, aimed to converge at a given point where the million-candlepower xenon searchlight beam met the ground.

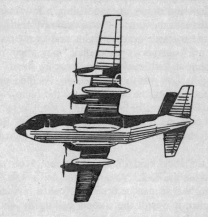

The wild Hercules circled a target at a specific altitude and poured huge volumes of heavy firepower into a target area. In the dark, it looked like bright red rain.

The Cobras and the AC-130 decimated the enemy formations, stopping them completely, and forcing the attackers to break away in a rout. It was a weird battle and a profound lesson in combat airspace management.

Other missions weren't so successful. Like a combat air patrol (CAP) mission that should have been a snap but became mired down in the politics of the zone they operated in. CAP was a strike team of Cobras that climbed to three or four thousand feet. There they remained, loafing about in an orbit of the day's sector, waiting for a fire-support call.

Lou was commanding a CAP team one evening when they spotted mortar rounds impacting on their own base. Then, to their surprise and delight, he spotted the muzzle pop and pinpointed the enemy mortars.

Coming around in a circle, the Cobras dived at the enemy

gunners to hit their positions. As required, Captain Bouault called operations with a quick report.

"Target in sight, firing at base," he radioed. "I've got the flashes, and we're attacking!"

Lou was thinking to himself as he talked.

"We finally got one!" he chuckled, since these mortar attacks were nearly impossible to stop. In the past, a few rounds dropped, blowing things up and killing a few men, then the enemy faded into the jungle. It was damn frustrating, and now they had the bastards dead to rights and in their sights.

"Break off," operations responded, "they might be friendly. Dive at them at low level and try to scare them."

Once again, Lou was to be pissed off. As the Cobras pulled away without a shot, he was back on the radio.

"This is Devil six. I'm landing, and I want to see the boss."

Back at base and standing before the colonel, Bouault was very nearly insubordinate as he demanded a logical explanation.

"What the fuck kind of a mission am I on here?" Lou shouted across the desk. "And who the hell is that?" Standing in the room was a man he'd seen before, a civilian. Lou began to realize it wasn't the colonel calling the shots.

"What is it you expect me to handle out there, sir?" he asked again.

"Just the shows we call you in for," the colonel lamely explained. "We wouldn't want to hit any innocent civilians, you know."

Captain Bouault knew by now that it wasn't worth the argument. The tall civilian was some kind of diplomatic advisor with more horsepower than a sack of generals. Rumor had it that he worked out of the American embassy in Saigon.

"Sir," Lou continued, "my show will be from four thousand feet from now on. And I'll call anything I see, first." With that, he stormed out of the operations shed, back to his Snake, and took off.

After launch, Lou regrouped with the other Cobras and took them all up to four thousand feet. They never went after a target again during CAP, except when specifically directed to. Anything else would be a farce.

Captain Bouault was beginning to realize why no majors were willing to command this unit. Twenty of the newest and hottest weapons systems in the entire U.S. Army should have officers waiting in droves to command them in combat. But, like the war itself, this dream command was being soured by arbitrary political whims and manipulations.

Lou didn't know it then, but the worst was yet to come. It was a day mission on the Ca Mau Peninsula they were called out for that began routinely.

At 5:25 P.M. on the evening of June 20, 1970, a light fire team of Cobras from the 235th left Can Tho Army Airfield.

Having just refueled and rearmed, they were heading for an area called Night Phantom South.

While reconning the river that crossed their northwest free-fire zone, the Cobras spotted twelve sampans off the coast.

The Cobras moved in to investigate, seeing three of the boats were steel-hulled, ocean-going types and that all the boats had fifty-five-gallon drums under tarpaulins on the decks.

The sampans were manned by all male crews in their twenties and thirties. No women, children, or animals. The lead Cobra, Shotgun 41, called for clearance to fire, although he doubted it would be granted. While they waited, the team flew back inland to scout some more.

Back at the Ca Mau tactical operations center, the American commander requested permission from the Vietnamese S-2 to open fire on the sampan flotilla. A quick check of their own units showed that the boats were not friendly and in a restricted area after curfew. Permission to fire was given, then relayed back to the Cobras.

The fire team asked twice for the clearance just to be sure and, both times were told, "Roger, you are cleared to fire." As the two Cobras and one Huey swung around and back for the sampans, the boats turned away and tried to make a futile run for safety. The three northernmost sampans were the fastest, so Shotgun 41 directed the team to them first. In the first target run with miniguns and rockets, the boats quickly returned fire with automatic weapons. To no avail.

Sinking the first boats, the Cobras worked south down the line of scattering sampans. All the men aboard were wearing brown shorts and firing with any weapons they could find. As each boat was hit, it erupted in fireballs of secondary explosions from munitions they were smuggling to the Viet Cong.

The Huey had a big chunk of the pie too, firing at a sampan

as three of its NVA crew ran into the cabin. The door gunner engaged with his M-60, the crew chief used an M-79 grenade launcher, and then a Car-15 submachine gun to kill a crewman who ran back out. The fire team sank nine sampans and left three burning. Thirty-five North Vietnamese soldiers died.

Mission completed, the aircraft returned to base.

For the next two and a half months, all the pilots and aircrews involved lived a nightmare of twisted legalities and misrepresented accusations.

Captain Bouault was visited by the theater Inspector General, the Vietnamese Inspector General, Department of the Army investigators and a myriad of other "concerned" parties questioning the sampan sinkings: "someone" claimed that the sampans were a simple fishing fleet that had been butchered by ruthless, trigger-happy chopper jocks.

It went beyond frustration. They had done everything right, followed the rules to the letter, but now, Shotgun 41, the pilot in charge of the fire team, was in serious jeopardy. Lou nearly lost the man as a pilot, since the poor chap was threatened with grounding and court-martial, and threatened to resign his commission himself. He said he'd never fly again if investigation is what you got for it.

The investigation went on and on, wearing down the nerves and patience of everyone. Lou was told the army was paying money to Vietnamese politicians who claimed the families of the dead sampan crews needed it. He was sure it lined their own pockets.

There's no telling where the whole thing would have gone had it not been for one man. A North Vietnamese lieutenant. He was captured by the South Vietnamese about ten weeks after the sampan incident. After extensive interrogation, the soldier got around to relating that he had come into the south on a sampan. He was shipping arms and munitions to the Viet Cong irregular forces in the Ca Mau area. Most of them were killed. By two Cobras and a Huey.

Ironically, it was the testimony of the enemy that put the investigation to rest and cleared the pilots. The final official report on the incident read as follows:

The Vietnamese are not concerned with this incident anymore. A different incident involving more sampans and bodies engaged by naval gunfire is causing the controversy. This occurred 30 miles south of our strike.

And that was the end of it. On that small piece of evidence, the entire matter was dropped as though it never occurred. None of the men whose careers were in jeopardy for so long would soon forget.

Another kind of lesson Lou's Snake drivers learned was that choppers could no longer fly high into a combat area and then dive in for the attack. The enemies' air-defense tactics were just getting too good.

So Lou and his pilots went to work developing and testing low-level tactics. Their approach was a bit different from that of other units, like air cavalry, since the 235th AHC had twenty-one Cobras and one Huey. No OH-6 or OH-58 scouts, just guns and a slick.

Flying low to the ground decreased the chance of being observed coming in, and the element of surprise was greater. The War Wagon Huey flew overhead at extreme altitude and talked the Snakes in to the target area. The single Huey flying alone attracted little notice, since thousands of ash-and-trash administrative flights flew every day throughout the country.

The Cobras came rolling in hot on the target to deliver their firepower with a minimum of exposure to enemy guns. Even with additional target runs, with the enemy expecting attack, the speed of snapping in over the treetops with guns ablazin' served to overcome the effects of enemy ground fire.

This was evident during a recon mission where Captain Bouault used the tactic to resounding success.

Flying at fifteen hundred feet, well into Cambodia, they spotted a white building alongside a canal. Intelligence reported it as a weapons and munitions cache, used as a transfer point for supplies moving from boats to trucks.

From his gunner's-seat command position, Lou started marking the checkpoints that would lead his fire team straight in to the target. Continuing "nonchalantly" on their way, Lou waited until the ships were out of sight of the building and swung the team around and down, onto the deck at treetop level. Then they poured on the power and built as much speed up as possible. It was a total surprise for the enemy.

The last thing the NVA regulars in the secret warehouse saw was the AH-1 fire team coming straight in at 150 knots. There was no time to fire at the helicopters or do anything but die.

Lou's ship was the first in, moving so fast that he got off a single burst with the minigun and fired two rockets, before breaking away. The next ship broke off quicker yet to avoid the immense explosion that followed. The two rockets from Lou's ship had gone straight in the front door and burst inside.

The result was a massive blast, totally out of proportion to a couple 2.75 rocket warheads. They struck such a large munitions stockpile that the two close-in Cobras were thrown upward from the shock of the fireball. It was over in seconds.

The Cobras made a pass of the area after the smoke cleared to see all that remained was flat ground covered with smoking debris. Plus several hundred automatic rifles firing at them from the surrounding jungle, so they climbed to altitude and moved away.

One thing Captain Bouault liked about the Cobra was its ability to absorb hits and keep flying. The Snakes he flew were hit many times, by small arms, shrapnel, and of course the time a large projectile creased his ship's belly. But he was never shot down.

Granted, most live-fire attacks he made produced holes in his aircraft, but the design of the Vietnam-era AH-1G was simple and robust. Today's aircraft are crammed full of high-tech electronics and fly-by-wire technology that is more vulnerable to chance hits; The AH-1G, on the other hand, had only a few places that, if hit, would disable the aircraft such as the tail rotor or the engine. Or the pilot.

Lou thought he had trouble once, bad trouble, that turned out to be an "entirely 'nuther sumpthin.' " With his strike team on a search mission, he was looking for targets or opportunity when they came under heavy small-arms fire. The team began low-level runs on the target area. Before long, Lou noted a real problem. They were still working a few bugs out of their tactics and found themselves crossing in front of one another, zipping close overhead and generally unsynchronized, so Bouault called them all out of the area to get organized.

On his command, the fire team lined up on his ship and moved back in to sweep the kill zone with rocket, 40mm, and minigun fire. The pass worked well this time, but Lou suddenly felt his Cobra shudder and heard something go *p-toom!* Next thing he knew, the panel was dead, the radio was gone, and so was their intercom. He leaned back and shouted to the pilot.

"You okay?"

"Yeah!"

"Let's get out of here!"

With that, they climbed to two thousand feet so they could autorotate if the engine failed and headed back to base, not knowing if they'd make it. Well, they did, and as soon as the ship was on the apron, the two men looked it over to see what damage they'd suffered. It was a single bullet hole. A rifle bullet had entered the side behind Lou and in front of the pilot, then crossed through the electrical harness, breaking a primary connector to the cockpit wiring. The aircraft was just fine, but the gauges couldn't show it, since they were without power. The bullet also shut down the communications equipment.

The rest of the fire team, busy with the attack, had no idea what happened, since Lou's ship simply dropped off frequency and disappeared. Everyone was pleased to find him and the other pilot safe and sound, once they'd returned.

It wasn't always so easy to make it back, though.

Lou sent two Cobras on a mission outside of Can Tho, and one took so many hits from ground fire that the pilot had to autorotate dead in the middle of the enemy force. The other aircraft, still armed and dangerous, did all it could to suppress enemy fire, which quickly concentrated on the downed chopper. They made as many passes at the swarming Viet Cong as they could, holding them at bay until more choppers could arrive and rescue the Cobra crew on the ground. But they ran out of ammunition much too soon.

It was then that the pilot in the air made a decision. He brought his Snake to a hover and dropped into the kill zone right beside the crew on the ground. Rushing to the Cobra, they opened the weapons bay doors on each side. These doors, used to load the minigun and 40mm, are hinged on the bottom and supported in the open position by wire cables, like the tailgate on a pickup truck. They were serving as seats now, with a pilot on either side clinging to the cable for dear life as the chopper lifted off.

And off they went, as the world's most powerful attack helicopter engaged the Viet Cong with the mighty firepower of two .38 pistols the rescued pilots were firing from their impromptu "gun platforms."

The men rode all the way home on their precarious perches at about forty knots. No one was injured except both Cobras. The rescue bird took hits all over, many close to the engine, but the sturdy craft could still fly as well as ever.

The ship on the ground took additional damage from two more Snakes that showed up just as the rescue was accomplished.

The Viet Cong swarmed over it once the other ship was gone and were caught in the open. It cost them. The wreckage was later lifted out by a CH-47 under the security of an ARVN rifle company. The wreckage wasn't retrieved because of its usefulness but to deny its explosives and weapons to the enemy. Another real concern was the communications equipment on the aircraft, particularly the KY-28 radio scrambler, a chunk of electronics that would be a real intelligence coup to the North Vietnamese and to the Soviets.

Then came the Cambodian incursion, lasting from April 29 until June 29. Viet Cong and North Vietnamese Army units had been building their strength all along the Vietnam/ Cambodia border, but in the Parrot's Beak area that extended like a boil into South Vietnam, the buildup was particularly extensive. Oblivious to Cambodian sovereignty, North Vietnam had constructed huge military complexes that served the forces they infiltrated into the south. From their cross-border sanctuaries, the Communists attacked and withdrew at will, harassing and damaging American and ARVN forces while minimizing danger to themselves.

At the invitation of newly installed Cambodian president, Lon Nol, the Saigon regime and its American allies planned a major offensive into Cambodia to cut out the bases like so many abscesses. Gen. Lon Nol, head of the Cambodian army, had recently seized power in a coup d'état, which overthrew long-time ruler Prince Norodom Sihanouk. Sihanouk had tried for years to keep his country out of the war, but his thirty-eight thousand-man army was no match for that of Hanoi, which also armed and supported a large insurgency within Cambodia.

Lon Nol's seizure of power was an act of desperation. He hoped that his support for the United States and South Vietnamese would bring them into Cambodia. It did.

On April 29, twelve thousand ARVN troops, supported by American artillery and aviation, crossed the border near An Loc and invaded. No sooner had they attacked than a larger-yet force of ARVN and American troops joined the fray. Over the following week, cross-border operations were initiated to the north and south at five more strongpoints.

The main target was the NVA Central Office South Vietnam near the town of Mimot. This was the major command for Viet Cong and North Vietnamese Army operations in III and IV Corps. The target area included an artillery command, security regiment, the 5th and 9th Viet Cong and 7th NVA divisions, and a shitpot full of support and training units.

If that wasn't enough, intelligence believed that massive storehouses of supplies were cached throughout the region. Eliminating these bases, decimating the enemy units, and destroying their carefully built up resources would have a profound impact for years to come.

It was during the Cambodian incursion that Captain Bouault and his Snake drivers locked in on the need for low-level flying tactics once and for all. The enemy had well-prepared air-defense networks set up around their camps. No approach was left uncovered, and the overlapping fires made it possible to engage helicopters from several angles at once.

All the same, Lou was surprised at the level of resistance they met. Rather than stand and hold their ground, the Communists elected to avoid contact. Even when caught in large numbers, they preferred to fight a delay, allowing their strength to melt into the jungles while small groups fired at the Cobras.

Lou was again flying front seat, leading his fire team in search of targets. They found plenty, though some fights were a bit trickier than others, often for curious reasons. One group of NVA chose to fortify themselves in a pagoda, set in a small courtyard, and were engaging ARVN troops when the Snakes dropped in. It would have been a small matter to drop artillery fire on their asses and turn them into so much meat. But the ARVN battalion was pinned down, and their commander was on the radio, asking the gunships to destroy the enemy without damaging the structure. It was the kind of job only a Cobra could do.

Lou called up two more fire teams for a total of six helicopters, then explained the attack plan to his pilots. "We're going to set up a big racetrack around this thing, and here's what we'll do. First we'll come in from one side and fire it up around the perimeter, then another side, another, and another."

It was the precision firepower of his Snakes that Bouault was counting on. The strongpoint was stalling the offensive in their sector, and he'd have to pull the cork out of the bottleneck.

"Follow my lead. I'll be the first heavy fire team, then two and three. We'll come down in a circle and make our runs. Enter after we start our dive. All breaks will be to the right, and move to the right as we shift to the next edge and the next and the next."

It was beautiful to watch as the graceful Snakes came around into their long dives over the tropical canopy. Starting comparatively low at one thousand feet, the rocket and minigun fire was placed exactly on enemy positions. Each round was precisely aimed on an identified soldier or gun on the perimeter.

As the next fire team began its run, the smoke trails traced white tracks from the air down to the now-frantic stronghold. As if in a deadly dance, the dipping Cobras choreographed an exact and delicately executed massacre of the defenders, each pass adding to the textured trails overhead and the brutal slaughter below.

The six Snakes were well into their steel maelstrom when a little O-1 Bird Dog shuffled lazily into the zone. He was just buzzing around looking for a mission, not realizing he had stumbled into a flaming pit of angry snakes.

Lou came up on guard emergency frequency, the common aircraft commo net, and said, "Bird Dog, look to your left and right!"

Even as he spoke, the little airplane pulled violently upward and rolled to one side, speeding out of the area. He'd been enjoying a pleasant spring day, and the sight of the burning hell below must have given him quite a jolt.

In the end, Lou's fire teams swept the area clear of enemy, and the advance on the ground continued.

Captain Bouault established a forward rearming and refueling point (FARP) inside Cambodia to expedite a return to the battle. The ordnance and petroleum products were trucked and airlifted in by tanker and Chinook and served as a forward airfield where every manner of helicopter set down for a quick reload and field-expedient repairs.

Chinooks might take as much as an hour to refuel, since the pumps weren't designed for aviation use. With their big, dual turbines still running, the CH-47s consumed fuel on the ground just a bit slower than the trucks could pump it in. When their own trucks finally arrived, operations went much faster. This forward airfield was maintained throughout the incursion.

As forces moved farther into Cambodia, they came upon huge hidden complexes that were apparently used as barracks, mess halls, office space, and giant supply depots deep in the jungles.

Contact with the enemy still seemed slight compared to the evidence of massive habitation. To the north of the Parrot's Beak, in the Tay Ninh area, the 1st Cavalry Division had launched its cross-border operation on the same day as the ARVN incursion. Both operations were preceded by Arc Light B-52 bomber strikes and long-range artillery bombardment. As in the southerly assault area, the enemy avoided engagement.

As armor and infantry advanced on their bases, the VC and NVA forces broke down into small groups and filtered into the jungles, deeper into Cambodia and away from the kill zones.

Most of the engagements happened as these fleeing groups were discovered and chased down by gunships.

On May 7, U.S. and ARVN troops entered Mimot and discovered what came to be known as The City. It was the NVA headquarters they hoped to find and much more. By the time all the captured gear was tallied up, thousands of tons of materials, vehicles, foodstuffs, weapons, and munitions had been located and removed or destroyed. On the downside, though, the majority of enemy troops had escaped into remote sanctuaries, safe to return when things calmed down.

The 235th worked an area from the Fish Hook near Snoul, down to Takeo. As far as they went into Cambodia, they stopped short of Phnom Penh, the capital city.

It was near Takeo that Captain Bouault lost the only Cobra crew of his time in command. His fire teams were leading a flight of slicks into an LZ, inserting ARVN troops for a mission forward. When the infantry was on the ground, the Cobras remained on station, providing fire support as needed. As they ran low on fuel or ammunition, a new team arrived to replace them and provide cover until the mission was completed.

The Cobra team's tactic was for one Snake to fly low and comb the area around the infantry for enemy. The other ship was high bird, generally armed with an under-wing 20mm gun to provide long-range heavy firepower. As a rule, the airspace above an active combat zone where helicopters were operating was off-limits to transient aircraft below twenty-five hundred feet. This allowed maneuver space for the combat flights.

Lou was in the high bird on this mission when he spotted a lone Huey coming into the area of operations. It was a four-star ARVN general, commander of the IV Corps down in the Delta. He was sight-seeing. Lou radioed the UH-1 and ordered them out of the area.

He thought nothing of it until later that day. Bouault's battalion commander had been saying he was tired of flying around in a Huey, so Lou offered him his front seat in the Cobra for the next mission. Three aircraft left for the mission. Only two came back.

What happened was the ARVN general had been rubbernecking around in the area again. Watching the Cobras from too low an altitude, his UH-1 had been hit by a Snake coming up from a rocket pass. The armed and fueled Cobra left a crater nine feet deep. One pilot had only three months in country, the other had served eleven months.

In the Huey, the four-star, a two-star, both pilots and key members of the ARVN corps staff perished.

Lou's battalion commander was devastated, feeling responsible since he was the ranking man on the mission. At services later, Lou assured him there was nothing he could have done. As expected, a major investigation followed. This time, however, the Cobras were exonerated right away. Small reward for the loss of two fine aviators.

A curious development of the Cambodian affair was the tendency of the pilots to enjoy the combat missions more. Many of the targets they attacked were simply abandoned structures, motor parks full of trucks but without troops, and large ammunition depots. The pilots truly enjoyed blasting the inert targets into smoldering scrap. There was often no danger of defending enemy guns so the pilots occasionally relaxed a bit on a mission. What really pleased them is that they didn't have to kill anyone.

Indeed, they were masters of their craft and had awesome destruction at their command, but the thought of slaughtering large groups of people gave them no pleasure. They had to do it frequently, they did it well, and with courage in the face of intense ground fire. But they didn't enjoy it.

So off they went, firing rockets into empty ammunition factories, ripping parked trucks to shreds with miniguns, and raking unoccupied barracks with grenade machine guns.

As the targets became ever more scarce, the Snake teams ranged farther and wider, locating retreating NVA. As was their duty, the pilots eliminated as many as they could before they escaped, then continued their hunt.

During just such a hot and furious search, Lou was leading his fire team along the treetops, looking for trails, equipment, and evidence of troop movements. The team made several contacts, and the guns were still hot, switches on the rockets armed. As trees and jungle snapped past them just under the skids, he caught a movement out of the corner of his eye.

Looking around, Bouault had a fleeting glimpse of figures dropping behind a cluster of fallen logs, seeking cover.

"Target," he said, "ten degrees to the left."

The Cobra team wheeled around and formed up behind Lou's ship, now beginning the gun run, bearing down on the target. Lou had the pantographic sight zeroed on the logs, waiting to hit the fire switch on the twin miniguns.

"Target, twelve o'clock," he said methodically as they bore

in closer. The cross hairs in his reticle were centered. Click. The pilot had armed the rocket pods. Only ten feet off the ground, the big choppers zoomed in at high speed until they were nearly on top of the target.

"Break Off! Break Off! No Target!"

Lou had suddenly shouted the command at the last possible moment as the figures came into his view. Three small children. They were mere seconds from butchering children.

After a day of high-speed combat, moving from battle to battle, target to target, and obliterating men and machines by the dozen, Lou had come a split second away from committing a horrendous deed. He had even seen the fear in their eyes as they shivered behind the logs. It was a sight he'd never forget, a moment in time that would live in his mind for the rest of his life.

But only a moment.

Sighting puffs of smoke in the distance, they were off again. Back to the war.

The Cambodian incursion lasted until June 29 when, under severe pressure from the antiwar movement, President Richard Nixon withdrew American forces into South Vietnam. Four students at Kent State University had been killed by Ohio National Guardsmen, during a demonstration, and nearly one hundred thousand protesters subsequently marched on the Capitol in Washington, D.C.

The operation had been a resounding success, resulting in more than ten thousand NVA being killed by combined air and ground forces. Enough weapons, equipment, and material had been captured or destroyed to equip an estimated seventy-five battalions of communist troops. As with the Tet Offensive of 1968, a crushing blow had been dealt the enemy that would take them years to recover from. Yet, the Hanoi regime had achieved a political victory in the streets of America, just as Tet 1968 had done. Nixon withdrew forces sooner than expected, and the already weak Stateside support for the war dropped even more. Continuing media coverage of American boys killed and maimed in combat gave a one-sided account of the carnage. That, in turn, twisted the reality of a significant victory into the perception of sinking deeper into quagmire.

Capt. Lou Bouault and every man in his company thought

they had won and won big. It would take years for them to fully grasp, if ever they did, that the win had worked against them.

At the time, though, the 235th simply went back to Can Tho and, after downtime for maintenance, went back to its usual duties of recon, fire support, and attack.

Following the Cambodian operations, Captain Bouault was curious about what it cost the United States to kill a Commie. The enormous expense of maintaining our modern military machines must be staggering in operational expenses alone, not to mention procurement costs.

Not that he didn't think it important to be there, since the Viet Cong and NVA were ruthless and brutal. But for his own edification, Lou did a study based on five months of combat operations of the 235th.

Lou cataloged the numbers of missions flown, ammunition expended, enemy KBAs (killed by aircraft) and whatever else gave him hard numbers to formulate a legitimate equation.

He then figured the total costs and divided by the monthly body counts. The cost per kill varied significantly from month to month, but by adding them together and dividing by five, it cost $8,026.20 to kill the average Cong.

Lou had been in country for what seemed like a lifetime, but was in reality close to a year. His next major operation would be his final one before returning to the World.

The 235th had been invited to the South Vietnamese island of Phu Quoc. Located in the Gulf of Thailand to the southwest, Phu Quoc was closer to Cambodia. It had been a plush resort and vacation spot in the past, but was then suffering from an infestation of Viet Cong. Lou and his crews had been asked to serve as exterminators.

Captain Bouault had been told by his battalion commander to take the company and determine the extent of the problem. Upon arrival, they were greeted by an American advisor and Vietnamese officer, a Colonel Nom. Nom had once been a Communist and fought against the French at Dien Bien Phu. On the staff of the famous General Giap, Nom elected to stay in the south after the 1954 accords that divided North and South Vietnam.

He was now the senior man in charge of the ARVN garrison on Phu Quoc. With his help, the Cobra pilots set up a temporary rearming and refueling point similar to the one used in Cambodia.

To the south was a naval base and airfield.

Despite those installations, the army garrison on Phu Quoc had been isolated from the war on the mainland and lacked the levels of supply and support enjoyed by units inland. That made it difficult for them to detect and destroy the enemy.

The Viet Cong, it seemed, owned nearly two-thirds of the island. Whenever Nom had patrols out, they were harassed and attacked by VC, and it was all they could do just to hold their own. That was before the ARVN had real firepower on their side. Once the Cobras started regular patrols and alert fire teams, the situation reversed drastically.

Another thing the ARVNs lacked on Phu Quoc was a medevac capability. Lou had flown into the island on the War Wagon command-and-control Huey so he put it to work ferrying wounded ARVN soldiers back for medical attention. The effect on their morale was impressive.

The Cobras provided an additional capability for combined-arms operations that dramatically increased the effect ARVN troops had on VC formations. As contacts with the enemy occurred on the ground, Cobras moved in to decimate the bulk of the VC strength. The ARVN then overran their battered positions, driving them into the jungles or capturing large numbers of surrendering Charlies.

Each battle widened the area under friendly control and decreased the number of Communists on the isolated isle. Over time the VC became evermore fearful of the deadly choppers, learning all too well the dangers of being spotted.

This was evidenced by a lack of sniper fire during a medevac lift out of a clearing. South Vietnamese troops had been returning from battle, marching toward the island's capitol, Duong Dong. Tired and battered, they had fought well and won the day, but several of them needed medical attention fast. Coming to a large clearing, the troops were still in contact with the enemy, receiving sporadic sniper fire while firefights raged outside the perimeter.

Captain Bouault radioed the commander on the ground, telling him to bring his people into the center of the field. He'd take care of anyone who might try to stop them.

Lou brought the War Wagon down into the clearing to

evacuate the wounded while his door gunners pasted the wood line with the big .50 caliber on one side and the minigun on the other.

As soon as the chopper showed up, the enemy simply stopped firing. They were so afraid of being spotted and attacked by the fearsome guns, the VC allowed the lift to come and go, completely unchallenged.

Combat wasn't so easy back at Ca Mau, but this was a different war from area to area.

Lou's final battle on Phu Quoc came when a U.S. Navy destroyer came by one sunny day looking for some targets. It seems the little dreadnought was headed back to Pearl Harbor for a rearm and refuel. The ship's captain heard that the Phu Quoc garrison could use good old-fashioned naval bombardment.

"Do you have a target?" called the ship.

"You betcha!"

Lou and Colonel Nom had a laundry list of VC bunkers, caches, and other strongholds needing destruction.

From his position high in the sky in the front seat of a Cobra, Lou had a panoramic view of the ship as it fired salvo after salvo. A Gearing-class destroyer, the ship carried two double-gun turrets with 5-inch, .38-caliber rifles, and an additional six 3-inch guns in single and double open batteries.

Lou watched the mass of high-explosive projectiles launch in a huge flash. The ship shuddered, and the water beneath flattened from the blast. The shells hit their targets in giant clouds of flame and shrapnel, and concussion rings from each explosion rippled outward hundreds of feet, flattening trees and scrambling the brains of Ho Chi's minions.

No point on the island was safe from the big guns, and they were exquisitely accurate. Fast, too. The complex directors and electronics used to lay the big guns were quick to adjust fire as the pilots called in fresh targeting data.

By the time it was over, the Viet Cong lost most of their ability to wage war on Phu Quoc. The island belonged completely to the South Vietnamese.

As a salute to the naval gunners, Lou's Cobras flew in formation from behind them, low down on the wave tops, with Lou in the center at mast level.

Approaching the ship at top speed, the outer aircraft peeled away to either side, then climbed with Lou in the center flying straight up. The sailors went crazy, swarming onto the decks and waving wildly at the choppers. It was an unabashed display of camaraderie, a joyous celebration of comrades-in-arms.

Over the radio came a voice from the ship.

"It's been a pleasure working with you, gentlemen!"

Chapter 9

ARA COMMANDER

Capt. Jake Benjamin had a fixed-wing rating as an army pilot. He had trained in the T-41 Mescalero (an off-the-shelf Cessna 172), and the T-42, a military version of the Beechcraft B55 Baron. Once he logged enough flight time in those two aircraft, Jake went on to the U-6 Beaver and the O-1 Bird Dog, taking an IP course prior to leaving for Vietnam. What Jake was working for, though, was to fly the OV-1 Mohawk, the army's high-tech electronic warfare and surveillance aircraft. But the quotas for Mohawk school remained full.

Looking for other opportunities, he managed to find a shortfall in a Cobra transition class. After serving as an artillery officer in Vietnam in 1967, then serving a Stateside tour at Fort Sill, Oklahoma, he enrolled in flight school. Looking for a branch change, Jake had already completed airborne and jumpmaster school, plus his previous artillery career courses.

Upon completing primary fixed-wing flight training, he managed to squeeze in a four-month rotary-wing transition school to boot. Showing up at the school in uniform, Jake finagled his way into the course en route to Vietnam. After he graduated, he was told don't stop, don't call anyone, just get your butt to Vietnam. Which he did, showing up at Long Binh's 90th Replacement in March 1970. Since Jake was dual-rated as an instructor, he was requested, by name, for a job flying VIPs out of Long Thanh, about halfway between Saigon and Xuan Loc.

Jake was elated, since he'd likely be flying U-21 Utes, the army's version of the Beech King Air. This executive turbo-twin was a sweetheart to fly, and the job would be a real plum. Jake thought he might even get a shot at a Mohawk transition in country! Elation turned to shock when Captain Benjamin began processing out of the reppo-depot to his new assignment.

"Uh oh," the personnel specialist said as he went through Jake's file, "you're Cobra qualified. You'll have to go to the 101st. They need Snake drivers real bad." He was stuck: they'd have no problems finding someone else for the VIP billet, but Cobra pilots were in high demand. So Capt. Jake Benjamin was sent to the 4th Battalion, 77th Aerial Rocket Artillery in Phu Bai. Reporting in, he was sent to Camp Eagle to the north where ARA headquarters was. His new battalion commander informed him that he was the senior captain there, then asked him what he'd like to do.

"I guess I'll settle for one of your companies," Jake responded. The commander smiled and made him the executive officer of B Battery. The CO there was a major. Jake was in the XO slot for about a month, getting into the swing of things, when his company CO went to Hawaii on R & R. While the man was gone, the battalion commander called on Benjamin and told him that he finally got what he wanted, his own command. Jake thought he meant A Battery, down at Phu Bai at the time.

"You are now the commander of Bravo Battery," the colonel went on. Jake was taken aback.

"Sir," he said, "you have a commander for Bravo."

"I don't want to spoil his R & R," the colonel explained. "You're the commander." It had been the colonel's plan for some time to move the major out of the command slot, and Jake fit into his plan just right.

So Jake took over. He had seventeen captains and twenty-five warrant officers, plus enlisted support personnel, to fly and maintain his twelve Snakes. And he had their respect. A black officer in 1970 expected to encounter some bigotry, but Jake found no evidence that being black affected anyone's attitude towards him. Since they had all known him for a month by then, the men knew he was capable, fair, and professional. So he simply went about the business of commanding.

The unit's primary mission was fire support for combat elements in direct contact with the enemy. They launched with heavy ordnance and light fuel, about a thousand pounds.

They used two-, five-, and fifteen-minute hot teams to react to fire missions. Two crews remained on the flight line at all times, combat cocked. When the phone rang, three men ran to the Cobras, and one got the phone and the fire mission. Front-seaters climbed aboard and strapped in, energizing the radios, while the "pilots in command" (PICs) started and ran up the engines. When the turbines reached about 40 percent power, gunners took over the run-up, and PICs strapped in. At sixty-one hundred rpm, the backseat took over again and pulled pitch on the rotor blades. They were airborne before they reached sixty-six hundred rpm.

Front-seat then keyed up the mike and established commo with operations, getting the mission underway. Ops gave them a heading and range, sometimes encoding the transmission, and the Snakes moved out for the target area. Then the five-minute and fifteen-minute sections moved into the next faster response position.

If really heavy firepower was needed in the field, pilots were pulled out of the barracks, and everyone launched to support the grunts.

The ARA pilots called themselves "extended artillery," since the 101st was an airmobile division and frequently operated out of range of its own howitzers. Cobras were portable howitzers.

On some missions, they flew escort for slicks carrying Blue teams (infantry) to LZ insertions. The Cobras prepped the landing zones with white phosphorous rockets, sometimes shifting LZs at the last moment for deception. Then they suppressed ground fire and provided fire support on request. The Cobras remained on station as long as needed or until replaced by the next fire team.

Then there were Pink teams. A single OH-6 Cayuse (Loach) with a pilot and a door gunner/observer, would cruise low along the ground, looking for contacts. Behind it and higher were two Cobras, loitering along in reserve until the Loach found and developed a target. When the Loach took fire from the ground, it returned the favor with minigun or the door gunner. This generally drew more ground fire, exposing additional enemy elements to observation, revealing their strength and concentrations. At that point, the Loach gunner popped smoke grenades around the enemy, then zoomed away.

The Cobras then zeroed on the smoke, saturating the area with rockets, minigun, and 40mm as the Loach orbited the kill zone, looking for yet more Communists fool enough to take a shot at him.

Jake's first mission in-country was in the front seat. In the 4/77, it was a policy that the first fifty hours a new pilot flew were as gunner to familiarize him to combat while a more experienced pilot flew the aircraft. Farther into his tour, Jake flew front seat frequently to direct his fire teams easier, but this first mission was mandated up front. In training, Jake had usually been in the backseat, with a few check rides up front and to learn the guns.

But Jake had a problem. Captain Benjamin was a very tall man, six feet three inches, so he encountered some difficulty climbing into the smaller front seat. He had dealt with it fairly well back in training, but now he was on the two-minute hot team.

Jake hadn't considered the cramped space he had to jump into when a fire mission came through. It had been some time since he shoehorned himself into the gunner's seat, taking plenty of time to pack in his lanky frame, and by now he'd forgotten about it. Then the phone rang.

Sprinting for his Snake, Jake stepped up to the cockpit and swung his right leg in, then his butt. He couldn't get his left leg in. The PIC was already winding up the turbine as Jake struggled with his left leg.

"This ain't gonna work!" he said, and hopped out. Then he put his left foot in first and swung around to fit his right in.

No go. Jake jumped out, turned around, and dropped his rump into the seat, with both legs sticking out the canopy. Now he couldn't get either in since the sight was in the way. Jake squirmed and pulled until his right leg was partially in, but now he was twisted in the seat.

The pilot launched the Cobra with Jake hanging out of the open canopy. The crew chiefs below watched the whole show and laughed like crazy as the Cobra picked up speed and zipped away with Capt. Jake Benjamin still trying to mount up. At nearly five hundred feet, with the added incentive of altitude, he finally worked down behind the pantographic sight, getting his legs in the right places. Completing the process of strapping in, he was ready by the time they reached the target area, though feeling somewhat sheepish.

After that, Jake made a point of practicing rapid front-seat entry. Following a period of experimentation, he worked out a method whereby he swung the sight to the left so it was hanging out of the cockpit. Then he stepped in with his right foot and dropped into the seat. The sight was then swung to the right and he lifted his left leg in after it. Then he closed the canopy and strapped in. The system worked, and he stuck to it for the rest of his tour.

There were some days he didn't even get out of the aircraft; with missions jammed so close together, the aircrews remained aboard while the Snakes were refueled and rearmed with the engine running.

The 4/77 ARA was supporting operations in the A Shau north of LZ Sally when Jake was involved in nonstop missions. He flew three strikes, and sat in the aircraft with his pilot while they rearmed. They had a hot lunch in the ship earlier, and this time he was handed his mail while the Cobra sat humming, with the rotor spinning overhead. They didn't shut down the turbine because another mission came up. Jake didn't have time to read the letter, so he stuck it in his pocket as they launched again, heading back to A Shau.

When the two Cobras arrived on station, Jake took out the letter and began reading it. It was from his wife. He'd just begun when a call came over their frequency requesting a fire mission. Jake keyed his headset and responded, stuffing the letter back into his pocket.

"Are there any Snakes in town?" came the call.

"Roger," Jake came back. "We're two Snakes up the A Shau."

"We need your help," came the station again and gave its location.

"We're about five clicks east and on the way to your location," Jake responded as they wheeled the big gunships around to link up with the fire mission. Coming into the target area, Jake took the controls and armed the weapon systems. A Loach was in the area, so they made contact to see if he could mark the target.

"Roger, I'll drop smoke."

The Snake drivers verified the smoke color, and the Loach gave directions.

"From the smoke, one thousand meters north is a .51-cal emplacement."

"Jesus Christ!"

No wonder he marked it from so far back. The .51 cal was a big heavy machine gun made just for knocking down aircraft. The procedure applied to that kind of target was to come in together at one hundred knots, building as much speed as possible, firing rockets farther out and through the run, engaging with the turret closer in. The second Snake would be just behind and lower, firing at the enemy as the first Cobra broke away. An exposed belly was a tempting target, so the second Snake covered the lead ship when it was most vulnerable. The chase ship then broke early to avoid the ground fire altogether.

Jake's Snake was the chase bird, so he lined up behind the lead, and they began the run. He watched as the other Cobra proceeded down the target line, firing rockets, and following the racetrack in. Then the chin started pumping bullets as the speed of the two aircraft increased. As they continued to bore in closer to the target, Jake began to worry that the lead pilot was under the spell of "target fixation." That meant a pilot became so obsessed with destroying his target, bearing down on it, keeping his sights zeroed in, that he might forget to pull out and actually run his aircraft straight in like a kamikaze.

Jake shouted into the mike, "Break! Break! Break!" The gun emplacement was destroyed, but now they were doing nearly 160 knots. A second gun began firing on them just as the lead ship finally broke away. Jake kicked the pedal and went after the second gun. He knew the lead ship couldn't come back around in time to cover him, so Jake figured he had to get that gun before it got him. He decided that hitting it with everything would either destroy it or make the enemy gunners duck long enough for him to dodge out of the way.

As he swung in and started firing, a third gun opened up. They had been lured into a triangulated kill zone, and the trap was sprung. Jake heard a loud *whap!* and felt the Cobra shudder like someone had grabbed and shaken it.

"Goddamn it, I'm dead," Jake said flatly. He had the mike keyed, and it went over the air. His next actions were purely reflex. He didn't think about what he was doing.

By the time he realized what happened, he had an armful of collective and a big handful of cyclic, and the Cobra was rocketing straight up.

"Where are you!" came the call over their frequency. The lead ship was cruising around down below. He'd heard Jake's exclamation and was looking for a big pile of broken airplane. Jake looked at his altimeter, which read nearly two thousand feet. He started laughing.

"Where are you? Where are you?" It was the other Snake again.

Benjamin keyed his mike.

"I'm at two thousand."

"What in hell are you doing at two thousand?"

"Climbing."

"Where do you think you're going?"

"Home."

They destroyed two of the NVA machine guns, so they called it a day and headed back to inspect the damage to Jake's ship. There was a big hole in the nose of the Cobra and nothing else. Whatever hit him had gone through, damaging only the skin of the aircraft. The rest of the fuselage was peppered with AK-47 holes, but it was still a sound airframe. His crew chief grumbled about all the work plugging the holes.

Jake and the other pilots had a hairy story to tell, and everyone took pictures and relived the moment of glory. They went to the club and someone bought a round of drinks for the heroes. Jake picked up his glass for a toast. It was then that his hand started shaking uncontrollably. He turned away before anyone saw, then excused himself to the latrine. He went, instead, back to his hootch and let the jitters pass without being seen.

It was then Jake remembered the letter from home and, taking it out of his flight suit a final time, enjoyed reading it like no letter he'd ever been sent before or since.

To be a Snake driver was a unique and curious way to fight a war, having the best of some things and the worst of others. When Jake was off duty, he could relax, shower, and stay clean. There was a club handy for parties and drinks, and he had a nice comfy bunk to relax in. Not like the grunts slogging around in the boonies, constantly miserable. But while on duty, every launch meant he was going into combat. The battalion provided fire support for a huge sector of the country, so they always had missions, and every mission was real war.

His weapons were massively powerful and highly lethal, mounted on an advanced aircraft. The enemy he fought had fairly crude automatic rifles and machine guns and some simple rockets. But hundreds of thousands of them. Every time he flew into an LZ or kill zone, he flew through a wall of lead and high explosives. Risky business at best. The pilots who survived were the ones who never forgot the magnitude of the threat they faced and didn't get too caught up in the spell of high-tech whizbangery.

Jake had a friend who had so little time left on his tour, he gave his sheets, pillows, and other comforts away. He was going back to the World and wouldn't need them anymore.

Because the man had just completed a full year as a Snake driver in combat, Captain Benjamin was surprised to see him in flight gear the day before he was to leave.

"Why are you wearing that shit?" he asked. "You're going home tomorrow!" The guy shrugged it off with a chuckle, confident that one more mission wouldn't matter. He'd be extra careful, too. And he was.

He'd flown up north with another Cobra and "popped some caps on Charlie," then headed back to Camp Eagle. On the way back, though, they punched into some fog and became disoriented. The lead ship managed to find its way home by instruments, but the other one never made it back. The short-timer's bird. Last contact with him was when he said they were doing a 180 to find the backdoor on the fog. The 180 became a long, descending left turn as the physics of the air-craft took over where their senses left off.

A search party couldn't reach the crash site till next day due to weather and darkness. When they found the ship, the wreckage was spread over half a mile from the impact at high speed. Two dead pilots were returned to the United States.

What happened to that crew was the result of what was called the "tac-ticket." Many helicopter pilots during the Vietnam War had no instrument flight training and were not qualified to fly in IFR (zero-visibility) conditions. In order to get the large number of pilots needed for war in a short time, many were trained for VFR flight only, conditions with enough visibility to fly by sight. This was a tac-ticket because they were ready to fly tactically in a war zone, but not in commercial airspace under varying weather conditions.

Jake was instrument rated, since he was dual-rated with fixed-wing aircraft. But the AH-1G had only nominal gauges for IFR flight, so it took a skilled pilot to fly instruments in the early Cobras.

Occasionally, a pilot thought he was a bit more skilled than he actually was. Since Captain Benjamin was the battery commander, he'd find himself flying front seat for a variety of different pilots as he directed his fire teams on missions. It didn't matter which pilot, usually, but Jake did avoid flying with one pilot who was something of a cowboy. He'd flown with the guy once before, and to his profound aggravation, this show-off kid popped the Cobra up in the middle of a routine flight and did an unannounced hammerhead stall. They'd been flying along at cruise speed near the ground when the fellow suddenly pulled up the nose into a steep climb until the airspeed fell off and the rotor stalled. Then he hit the foot pedals and spun the Snake around 180 degrees just as gravity began pulling the ship down. With the aircraft facing downward now, it was the same as a diving attack, and the bird picked up speed until the pilot pulled back the cyclic and added enough collective to return to level flight.

"Don't ever do that with me in the aircraft again!" Jake said. It was a fairly common maneuver, but this was hardly the place to be fucking around just for shits and grins.

Jake looked at him in the cockpit mirror, making eye contact. The pilot gave him a funny look.

"Don't ever do that with me again. This ain't a damn hot rod, and we ain't back on the block!"

The pilot was a might bent out of shape about the incident, but he knew the captain meant business, so it wouldn't happen again.

Next time Jake was flying with this guy was on another A Shau mission. Returning from patrol, they were en route to Camp Eagle when Jake saw a flight of four slicks coming across their path from another direction.

"I got the aircraft," Jake reported, meaning he saw the slicks nearby. He then went back to reading a letter he had with him. Within a moment, he felt the Snake start to rise and roll to the left.

Damn, thought Jake, he's doing it again!

"What in the hell do you think you're doing?" Benjamin shouted, getting ready to chew the guy out.

"What do you mean?" came the reply as Jake looked in the mirror. He clearly saw both of the pilot's hands held up for him. At the same time, both Snake drivers said the same thing.

"You're flyin' it, aren't you?" Nobody was. Just the SCAS, which wasn't quite enough. Jake snatched the controls and immediately stabilized the Cobra before it ran away with them both. From then on, Captain Benjamin always used clear instructions concerning who had control of the aircraft, including a show of hands and affirmations whenever he switched back and forth. It became a small ritual designed to keep him alive.

Although it wasn't required of him as battery commander, Jake tried to accompany as many combat missions as he could. A lot of COs felt it adequate to set policy and plans and let the troops handle the dirty work, but he didn't want to send someone to a place he wouldn't go himself. Jake felt compelled to see what an area was like before committing his men, and he had more direct control, faster and more effectively, by being there.

B Battery, the Toros, was the best unit he'd ever been in. Each Cobra carried an insignia of a huge bull snorting rockets out of its nose. Jake was Toro-42 on the air.

At Camp Eagle he was Mr. Entertainment. Jake understood the nature of the drug problem that sapped the army's strength during the later years of the war. He knew that many soldiers who were bored would end up "doing" recreational drugs. To avoid that, he put the troops to work making a small theater, then made sure that movies were available to show in it. He put the first sergeant in charge of scrounging up lumber and building supplies and soon had everyone involved in the project on their off-duty time.

Following that success, he had basketball hoops constructed, then started shooting hoops with the troops. For the folks who weren't hot on b-ball, Jake began a softball team that soon became the regional champs. He had plenty of support from battalion HQ because his recreational programs worked well for physical training as well as morale. But Jake wasn't so naive as to think his efforts were enough to hold back the tide of drug abuse. He kept a sharp eye out and expected the men in the battery to police their own ranks. In an aviation unit, more than anywhere else, being stoned on the job could get someone killed fast. Ground crews needed to keep complex aircraft in safe, operational condition. They had to be alert to battle damage, paying attention to details on intricate machinery.

Armorers and fuel crews handled high explosives and flammables in a hot environment, where a single spark could ignite Armageddon.

The pilots' lives depended on alert, clear thinking. No. Jake had no sympathy for drug users. He had to get rid of one man who started out as a good soldier, a young sergeant who seemed bright and eager. Until he got hooked on heroin. Jake shipped him away, hollow-eyed and thin as a rail. A soldier from another unit was apprehended in B Battery selling dope. Jake made sure his next assignment was Fort Leavenworth, Kansas. B Battery stayed clean on Capt. Jake Benjamin's watch.

By early 1971, the program of Vietnamization was in full swing. The United States was handing the war back to the South Vietnamese army a bit at a time as U.S. forces gradually withdrew from the country. By then, American strength in country was 335,000, down from 536,000 at the peak in 1969. As infantry, armor, artillery, and support troops folded their colors to retire to the United States, aviation units remained to support the ARVN soldiers. As the American numbers decreased, the NVA grew bolder, building in strength in the Cambodian and Laotian sanctuaries. It was in those sanctuaries, particularly in Laos, that MACV commander Gen. Creighton Abrams decided to hit the NVA as hard as he could.

The strike would need to be bold and powerful to succeed. It could only be done with ARVN troops, since Congress had forbidden use of American soldiers in Laos and Cambodia after the Cambodian incursion of 1970. The operation would be called Lam Son 719 and it would be the most frightening thing to happen in Capt. Jake Benjamin's entire life.

The 4/77 ARA was tasked to perform a variety of combat missions, from troop-lift escort to fire support against designated targets. Their first target was the operation's primary objective, the Laotion town of Tchepone, about twenty miles into Laos on Highway 9.

That was Jake's first introduction to flak. Until then, he had encountered massed small-arms fire, heavy machine guns, and some automatic cannons. But not flak.

As the Cobras approached the target, balls of smoke began to appear in the air around them. At first, no sound came through the heavy plastic canopies of the Snakes, but as they drew closer, sound grew. It seemed thick enough to land on. Each ball of smoke meant a vicious sprinkle of deadly shrapnel. Jake flew into the flying steel while escorting a flight of CH-47 Chinooks carrying ARVN into the fray.

The Snakes prepped the LZ with suppressive fires, opening up with rockets and guns in a futile attempt to stem the flow of lead rising from the ground. The Communists had prepared a warm and hearty reception wherever they went in Laos, with overlapping rings of large caliber antiaircraft guns. Any place where troops might be inserted by helicopter, the NVA had covered with air-defense systems.

It was just such a welcome they received at this LZ. Despite the best efforts of his fire team, the first Chinook in took a direct hit and began to shake and wobble. On final approach and about two hundred feet up, already in flames, the big transport chopper rolled over on its back and dropped straight into the ground. It exploded, killing all thirty soldiers on board as well as the crew. The second big Chinook started taking serious hits as it came in, then broke away and cleared out of the area.

All the Cobras could do was to rake the LZ with rockets and turret a few more times before following the Chinooks back out. Jake and the rest of the Snake drivers were devastated at what had happened. A silent flight of angry men flew back to refuel and rearm.

For the remainder of February and into March, Lam Son 719 continued. Jake's Snakes continued troop escort into Laos. They flew Pink-team missions to locate and destroy NVA and fired thousands of rockets on fire-support missions around LZs with names like Lolo, Gina, Liz, and Sophie.

Curiously, when the Cobras were by themselves, they seldom drew fire until they chose a target to attack. Even on their own ground, the NVA didn't want to mess with Cobras unless they had to. The only other aircraft that commanded as much respect from the enemy was the AC-130 Spectre, or B-52 bomber.

Jake's respect, however, was reserved for the medevac pilots. They had balls of steel. Landing or hovering under intense and unending enemy fire, they risked their lives to get out the wounded. Captain Benjamin did his damndest to cover them when they went in to load the injured.

The NVA were tough, holding their ground, counterattacking, and surrounding ARVN units. The Americans did what they could to help out with air support from gunships and air force fighters, but the Communists had been building up the area for years and were more than ready for the invasion when it began. The turning point finally came on March 6, when a fleet of 120 Hueys inserted two battalions of ARVN infantry into the Tchepone area.

This largest-ever airmobile assault was preceded by a massive B-52 Arc Light strike and intensive bombardment by Cobras before the slicks reached the various LZs. Resistance was light, and only one Huey was lost.

By March 10, the last ARVN and American forces were withdrawn, and Lam Son 719 was declared a big victory for the South Vietnamese. Of course, the North Vietnamese claimed it as their victory, and the antiwar sycophants in the States agreed. The NVA lost over twenty thousand troops and thousands of tons of weapons and supplies. Their plans for a major offensive would be held back by more than a year.

The ARVNS had fifteen hundred killed. One hundred seventy-six Americans died, 107 helicopters were shot down. The battle proved one great truth, however: the ARVNs could beat the NVA, but only with a massive commitment of American air power to back them up.

After Lam Son 719, Camp Eagle settled back into its status quo: Hot sections launched for fire missions, movies were shown each evening, and pilots were briefed each morning. During one such morning briefing in operations, a pilot mentioned that he'd been shot at coming back in to land. There was nothing unusual in the comment, since nearly everyone had taken a sniper round once or twice coming into Eagle. For some reason, though, Jake got pissed off this time.

"Goddamn it," he shouted, "Next time, shoot his ass! I'm sick of takin' fire at our own base!" Benjamin didn't really mean it; he was just blowing steam. Security for the base was handled by ARVN teams in the surrounding jungles. An occasional sniper was to be expected. A Cobra, on the other hand, could do some serious harm to friendly folk if it wasn't careful. But the other pilots took him at his word.

Soon enough, two Cobras were returning from a mission when the pop of a single shot was heard far below.

"I'm taking fire!" called the lead ship as the second Snake wheeled around.

"I got him!" came the voice over the radio, just as Jake scrambled for the microphone to stop him. A long burst of minigun fire followed. They were never sniped at Eagle again.

One fire team was called on a mission in support of a fire base being overrun by NVA. By the time the Snakes showed up, the situation was critical, so the American advisor on the ground was calling a strike within twenty-five meters of his position.

The Snake drivers told him that it would be "danger close" as the code went. The man on the ground verified. He decided they would be overrun and killed unless they risked the rocket fire. The Cobras saved the fire base, destroying the NVA attackers, but killed two ARVNs in the process with the close-in fire.

An investigation followed, creating quite a stir and a good deal of hard feelings with the ARVNs. The battalion commander at the time wanted to smoke the pilots' asses. He and Jake had more than a few harsh words as Benjamin stood up for his men against the unyielding bureaucrat. The issue grew into a full-blown inquiry, but the advisor who called the strike stuck up for the pilots. He took full responsibility for the incident and went on to explain to the investigators that the Cobras had actually saved many more lives than the two friendly casualties they'd caused.

And that was the end of it.

Occasionally, a mission was noteworthy for what didn't happen as much as what did. Jake was flying front seat again when his fire team spotted what appeared to be several companies of NVA frolicking naked in a river. Though itching to mow them down, the Snakes were instead obligated to continue their assigned mission and cover insertion of a LRRP team.

The Huey dropped the men into the LZ while hovering, because there was no flat spot to land on, and then lifted out after dropping the team. "I got a one-to-one on the main rotor," the pilot called as they cleared the area. "Tree limb strike." The Huey wobbled as it flew, but it seemed they'd get him home.

Jake wanted to head back by way of the river and check on the bathing beauties again. About then, they heard a tiny voice on the radio. Just a whisper.

"We're in deep shit here. Come back and get us out." It was the LRRPs. The choppers turned around, and by the time they reached the LZ again, a battle was raging between the LRRP team and the bad guys.

This time, when the Huey dropped down into the hover-hole, it wobbled like a drunk sailor in a roller coaster. The Snakes jockeyed for position to cover the extraction, but the jungle canopy was too heavy to place fires accurately. The slick pilot came over the horn.

"Use your forty-mike-mike." he said, and began directing where to place it. Jake's pilot brought his Snake around to where they could lay the grenades to best effect and he began to fire.

"Bring it in closer."

Jake eased the rounds nearer the slick as the team climbed aboard.

"Closer," the slick pilot said again as the last man climbed on, then rose out of the LZ as the grenades burst where the aircraft had just been, killing enemy soldiers who tried to get a clear shot as the Huey sped away.

"Let's beat up the area before we go," Jake's pilot said. They saturated the trees and jungle with rocket and minigun fire before turning away.

No one was left back at the river, so they just went home from there. They were disappointed at missing the ultimate fish-in-a-barrel shoot.

Snake drivers seldom knew how many enemy soldiers they killed in action. In Vietnam, the measure of a mission's success was the body count for the troops on the ground. For lack of clear battle lines, objectives, and otherwise measurable results, tallying corpses became the yardstick for unit machismo.

There were times, after mass rocket strikes, that infantry went into the area to count the enemy soldiers nailed to trees, the ground, bunkers, one another, and anything else they were near when the flechettes exploded.

Somewhere in an office far away, a skinny clerk with Coke-bottle glasses was likely adding up the totals, comparing our stiffs to theirs. Someday, the men thought, he would issue a winning casualty-to-kill ratio so everyone could go home.

One of the last incidents that occurred in B Battery as 1970 drew to a close involved two of Jake's top pilots, a fellow known as J.R. and a good-looking young fellow known as Baby-San. J.R. was father of a young son back in the World and would proudly show photos of his little boy to anyone who'd look. His young wife sent letters to remind him that, no matter what, she and the boy would be there for him.

Baby-San was single, a guitar-playing ladies' man. In the evenings and at unit parties, he'd strum and sing the hits of the day, but liked to change the words around to fit the mood.

But the two pilots constantly insulted each other, picked fights, and argued, so Jake kept them apart. They were eventually sent to another unit south of Camp Eagle, and Benjamin thought he'd heard the last of the two.

It was after B Battery finally redeployed to Fort Campbell, Kentucky, that Jake heard the strange ending of J.R. and Baby-San. A friend who had been there bumped into Jake and related the story to him. Though Benjamin and most of the unit returned Stateside, a few pilots, including the dueling duo, had been reassigned to other units in country.

On a fire-support mission with their new outfit, J.R. was flying lead for Baby-San. Baby-San's ship was hit and went in, crashing among the enemy. J.R. saw Baby-San exit the burning Cobra and head to the tree line to avoid the advancing NVA, so he dropped down directly in front of the enemy in a hover. Using pedal turns to aim the weapons, J.R. butchered the Communists while a Huey came in behind to get Baby-San. Just as Baby-San climbed aboard the slick, J.R.'s Cobra took a hit from a heavy machine gun, rolled in inverted and burst into flames. The crew died instantly, and Baby-San saw it all.

Jumping off the Huey, he ran to assist, but there was nothing he could do. The crew chief and door gunner had to drag him, kicking and screaming, back to the lift ship.

Chapter 10

THE PINK PANTHERS

Like many high-school boys, John B. Cole dreamed of being a pilot. It wasn't his only choice of a possible career, but was high on his list. Like many young men his age, he enrolled in college after graduation to earn a degree and to avoid the draft. John went to Spokane Junior College in Washington state. During the days he attended classes, then worked a four-to-eight-hour job at night. And he partied whenever he could. For a year and a half, John juggled school, work, and carousing until he was sure the military draft was catching up to him.

He graduated with an associate degree in December 1967, then began his junior year, but withdrew from school in January 1968. He had decided to join the army and make his own job decisions instead of being drafted and ending up in infantry or something equally unfortunate. So he entered basic training on February 29, 1968.

Despite his voluntary enlistment, John didn't qualify for his first request, officer candidate school and flight school; he needed a college degree. His tests scores were high, though, and he was allowed to sign up for Special Forces, the Green Berets.

After basic, Cole went to Fort Bliss, Texas, for forty-seven weeks of intensive training to learn Vietnamese. During language school, Cole found that he was still eligible to apply for flight school as a warrant-officer candidate. He wouldn't need the college degree that held him back earlier because, by then, the army was desperately short of pilots. John applied and was accepted, so following his graduation as an interpreter/interrogator, he and his new bride, Vicki Mosely from his hometown of Richland, Washington, proceeded to Fort Wolters, Texas.

WO-1 John Cole graduated in the top ten percent of his primary flight school class, giving him the privilege of choosing his aircraft transition course. He chose Cobra school.

John went to Fort Rucker and completed the Cobra course, then signed out for a well-deserved leave. Afterwards, he departed the United States from Travis Air Force Base in California, proceeding directly to Vietnam.

Mr. Cole arrived at Tan Son Nhut Air Base in Saigon with the other rookie pilots on his flight. They laid over for several days as assignments trickled in for the more than fifty aviators. Some went to the 101st Division at Camp Eagle, another large group was picked up by a CH-47 Chinook and headed for parts unknown. John went to Pleiku with a group of five. Two of the men went to the 7/17th Cav and the other three, including Cole, were assigned to the 361st Attack Helicopter Company (Escort).

Of those three, Cole was assigned to Cobras, and the other two became scout pilots in the OH-6. Within two days of their arrival, one of them died in a midair collision that killed everyone in both aircraft. The other pilot died several months later in combat when his aircraft exploded in midair from enemy fire.

When Cole first signed in at the 361st, he avoided telling anyone about his interpreter/interrogator training because he was worried it might interfere with his flying. He made the mistake, however, of telling a major he met while in-processing that he'd done some enlisted time at Fort Bliss. When the major asked what he'd done there, he told him about the Vietnamese language school. As it turned out, the major was the brand-new commander of the 361st, and immediately made Cole the domestic-hire officer. John was responsible for hiring and firing the hootch-maids, KPs, and other indigenous employees. Fortunately, it was only an extra duty tacked onto his responsibilities as a Snake driver.

The 361st AHC was called the Pink Panthers, after the well-known cartoon character. It was one of seven specialized aviation companies of the 52d Combat Aviation Battalion, which, in turn, was one of four battalions with the 17th Combat Aviation Group of the 1st Aviation Brigade.

The Pink Panthers were based in Pleiku, the provincial capitol of Pleiku Province. Pleiku sat near the center of a long valley, rich with fertile rice paddies and rivers, surrounded on all sides by rolling, jungle-clad mountains. It was located only thirty-six miles from the Cambodian border, but was linked to the coast by Highway 19 and to the north and south by Highway 14. The 361st shared a big, sprawling base called Camp Holloway with a variety of other units. Nearby were Pleiku Air Base and Camp Schmidt.

John's new platoon commander was Captain Watkins. He started Cole out, like all new pilots, flying in the front seat as copilot/gunner. The new men were then rotated among the various aircraft commanders to gain the benefit of their combined experience.

Early in Cole's tour with the 361st, bad weather limited the amount of flying the unit was able to do. All the same, the missions between the storms taught him what the Pink Panthers were all about. The first thing he learned was no one carried maps or personal effects on any mission, because all of their activities were classified. What they *did* carry was something the pilots referred to as a "blood chit." This was a ten-by-twenty-inch piece of heavy, white silk printed with the image of an American flag. Below that was a message, written and repeated in English, Burmese, Thai, Laotian, Cambodian, Vietnamese, Malayan, Indonesian, classical Chinese, modern Chinese, Tagalog, Visayan, French, and Dutch. It said, in all these tongues;

I am a citizen of the United States of America. I do not speak your language. Misfortune forces me to seek your assistance in obtaining food, shelter and protection. Please take me to someone who will provide for my safety and see that I am returned to my people. My government will reward you.

An average flight would begin at a small airstrip and base to the northwest called Dak To. Dak To sat in a mountain valley next to the Krong Poko River and was only sixteen miles east of the tri-border junction of South Vietnam, Laos, and

Cambodia. It was a key staging area for clandestine operations into the neighboring countries.

Typically, the Cobras flew into Kontum to await a go-ahead for a mission. When the call came, the pilots would be briefed before takeoff, then link up at the Dak To airstrip with a flight of slicks carrying LRRP teams of the 5th Special Forces. The seven-man teams were comprised of six mercenaries and one American Green Beret.

Once the entire force was assembled at Dak To, they all waited for a call from the "covey," an air force OV-10 Bronco or 0-2 Skymaster. These were forward air controllers, called FACs, flying inside Laos or Cambodia, watching a target. Covey watched the enemy until the target was ready, then radioed for the strike force at Dak To. As the helicopters raced to the attack, the FAC called for "fast movers," an air strike by jets or A-1 Skyraiders to soften the enemy just before the strike force arrived.

The force came in high, with four Cobras and two or three Hueys paired into two teams. As the fast movers broke away, two high-bird Cobras rolled in for rocket runs, generally firing flechettes in salvos to nail down everything in the LZ. The second pair of Snakes then set up a racetrack of rocket runs to keep the slicks covered as they worked their way down into the triple-canopy jungle to insert a LRRP team. With no open space available, the soldiers frequently had to rappel from ropes hanging under the hovering Huey. It often took several minutes to complete, so the Cobras were critical to the safety of the Huey and the LRRPs. Everyone on the mission, including the Snake drivers, wore MacGuire rigs in case they were shot down and needed lifting out.

Sometimes, an instant LZ could be made with a huge, special-purpose "daisy-cutter" bomb rolled out of the back of a transport plane. The giant ten-thousand pounder detonated ten feet above ground and cleared away enough foliage for several Hueys to land. But that option was not always available.

Once the first slick was in and out of an LZ, the second Huey would generally be the one to start catching enemy fire. If the resistance grew too intense, the insertion would then reverse and become an extraction to get the teams back out before they were all killed on the ground. If resistance was light, the teams would melt away into the jungle, avoiding contact with the enemy, to complete whatever their mission might be. All the aircraft then returned to Dak To to stand by until the LRRPs radioed an okay or requested an extraction. Their calls would be relayed by a permanent radio relay station hidden inside Laos atop a 3,301-foot peak seven miles from the Vietnamese border. It was strategically situated above the Se' Sou river, providing observers with a clear field of view stretching thirty miles into the Attopea Valley. It was often called the "Eagle's Nest" and helped maintain contact with LRRPs, aircraft, and clandestine operatives inside Laos.

If the LRRPs got into trouble, the choppers went right back in and pulled them out, shooting like crazy while taking fire from all quarters. They never needed to call for clearance to return fire, though, because they weren't really there, for all practical purposes. It was all classified. Nor was the enemy supposed to be there, in neutral Laos or Cambodia, so who could complain if a few hundred NVA got zapped while they attacked Green Berets and mercenaries being pulled out?

Nearly every day, two teams went into Laos and one into Cambodia. When Cole was assigned to the Cambodian insertion, the strike force worked out of Duc Co instead of Dak To. Duc Co was seventy miles south of Dak To, but sat only eight miles from the Cambodian border. On these missions, the air force usually provided A-1 Skyraiders, known as Spads by the army pilots. The original Spad was a World War I fighter plane, and although the A-1s were not that old, their design dated back to the end of World War II. The A-1s served well in Vietnam because the old straight-wing, piston-engine attack birds could carry huge amounts of guns, rockets, and bombs and place them very accurately on the enemy. Spads remained on station much longer than jets and could absorb a lot of damage and remain airworthy. The only folks who didn't like them were the North Vietnamese and the Viet Cong.

Pink Panther missions out of Duc Co were otherwise much the same as those from Dak To. Except for a few strange ones that remained unexplained. John flew one such flight with a light load of ammunition but as much fuel as his Cobra could carry. His instructions were to fly along a specific azimuth until he spotted a certain landmark, then open the canopy and drop a Coke can he had been given on a specific location. He assumed the can contained a message, but he never looked inside. The pilots talked to no one throughout the journey, and they saw no one at the drop site. He didn't know if it was received or not; John just did his part, and that was that.

Sometimes the Snakes would be vectored in-flight to an Air America plane en route to a drop site. Air America was the Central Intelligence Agency's own air fleet, then masquerading as a commercial carrier. The plane would reach its target, drop a small bundle or package into the jungle by parachute, and simply fly away. And the Snakes would go home. The CIA pilots talked by single-sideband radio directly to their Saigon headquarters, completely off the military FM communications channels. Cole never communicated with their aircrews, headquarters, or operatives on the ground.

The 5th Special Forces gave them a few curious missions, too. The LRRP teams frequently snatched prisoners out of the enemy's ranks and brought them back for interrogation. The Cobras flew escort. NVA soldiers led a brutal and spartan life, so the Americans gave the prisoner medical attention, excellent food, clean and comfortable accommodations, and attempted to *chieu hoi* him to our side. *Chieu hoi* meant open arms and was the name of a program instituted to allow Communists to switch sides for a big cash award and lots of other benefits.

The converted Commie then became a Kit Carson scout or was returned by helicopter to become a double agent. He was expected to find secrets or commit acts of sabotage, then return to a predetermined site for pickup. The pilots never knew what to expect when they arrived.

A converted prisoner may have helped set a trap for them, or he might still be friendly. When a slick was on the ground, the Cobras could only provide a certain amount of security to the exposed and vulnerable crew. The crew chiefs on the choppers seldom took any chances and would knock the guy out where he stood, check him for booby traps, then haul his limp ass back to the chopper. If the *chieu hoi* checked out okay when they got him back, the man got his reward and a new life. If not, and he was found to have booby traps, bogus information, or just plain nothing, he was handed over to the South Vietnamese for interrogation.

John escorted a prisoner snatch deep into mountainous country in Cambodia that yielded two male nurses from a huge concealed hospital. The area was watched by LRRP teams for several days and was so remote Cole couldn't believe anything was there. Except for the massive antiaircraft fire they encountered. Despite the resistance, the two prisoners were excited and happy to be captured. They literally jumped into the chopper, anxious to be on their way. Both prisoners had neat haircuts, clean and pressed uniforms, and were a wealth of intelligence information.

In mid-September 1970, Mr. Cole flew a series of combat missions that didn't go as smoothly as the nurse snatch. It was an operation called TAILWIND, which involved Marine Corps CH-53 Jolly Green Giants. The objective was to place a company-size force deep into Laos, using the big CH-53s, which could carry fifty-five troops apiece. The force being inserted was about 130 mercenaries and their American advisors.

The Pink Panthers began the operation with a move to the strip at Dak To. As they waited for the airmobile force to gather, John and the other pilots were surprised to see a flight of seven Marine Cobras roll in and land near them. As the aircraft shut down, the army pilots noted that full colonels and lieutenant colonels were dismounting the twin-engine AH-1J Sea Cobras. The jarheads seemed to put some real high-rollers in their Snakes! Following them came four massive CH-53s, bringing the chopper population at Dak To up significantly.

There now sat on the strip twelve UH-1s, four AH-1Gs, seven AH-1Js, and four CH-53s. Someone noted casually that the collection of aircraft would make a hell of a mortar target.

As the flight crews waited for the mission go-ahead, Cole found a semicomfy spot atop a pile of rocket crates and attempted to catch a short catnap. He had just drifted off into a light sleep when he heard the first explosion. *Whump!*

What's going on! he thought as he jumped to his feet. In his month and a half in Vietnam, Cole had never heard incoming mortar fire. *Whump! Whump!* He saw the explosions down the strip and then heard a searing *whoosh* that cut his nerves like a hot knife.

"God!" he said, just as a huge blast erupted nearby. Cole fairly leaped into a nearby bunker, only to find it completely full of other aircrewmen. He raced down to the next bunker and found it crammed full of people, too. The mortars and rockets continued to pound the strip as John continued his frantic search for a hole to jump into. Finally he ran back to the original bunker, where his commander looked out at him.

"Hey, can you guys make room for me?" Cole shouted. The major stroked his chin and said slowly, "Weeeellll, maybe. Hey, you guys. Do we have room for Mr. Cole?" John could have strangled him as the laughing group squeezed tighter to let him in.

Two of the pilots tried to reach their aircraft and take off. The attack was coming from "Rocket Ridge," appropriately, and someone needed to suppress the enemy's fire while more gunships could get in the air. The first crew to try didn't make it, cut down by a mortar round. Someone finally got in the air during a short lull in the attack. John's AC made it to their ship and was untying the main rotor when he heard another rocket launch. Leaping into a nearby ditch, he just missed being hit as the enemy rocket detonated between two helicopters. One Cobra blew to pieces, showering Cole's ship with shrapnel and burning fragments.

Cole's AC now found himself trapped in the ditch as fires on the rocket pods began cooking off and launching his own 2.75s right over his head. He was partially safe because the rockets wouldn't arm until they flew well past him, but he was in grave danger from the launch blast of the projectiles. And the Cobra might explode. By then, the airfield was nearly deserted as everyone had either evacuated their aircraft or was attacking Rocket Ridge. Sitting in the bunker by himself, John was suddenly greeted by his AC, leaping in like a frog on a griddle. Covered with dirt and mud from the ditch, he began to relate what happened. Just then, a giant, flaming explosion rocked the ground. Solid flame covered everything outside the bunker and Cole shouted, "Son of a bitch! We just took a direct hit, and I'm gonna die any second!"

It wasn't a hit on the bunker, though. It was the Cobra self-destructing as flames reached its filled fuel cell, igniting fuel and explosives alike into a monster fireball. The detonation was the loudest thing he'd ever heard. As soon as it was clear outside, the other pilot hopped out of the bunker and onto the last Jolly Green Giant as it departed.

Cole stepped out of the bunker and looked around. Everyone was gone. Everyone but him. He could see Cobras working the ridge for rockets and mortars, but the enemy troops were likely gone by now, back into their tunnels or fleeing into the jungle.

"Son of a bitch," he said again. Eventually, a CH-53 stopped by and picked him up, then returned him to Camp Holloway. The big operation would be postponed for a while. John thought about his experience at Dak To and how badly it had scared him. He had been involved in plenty of combat and always kept a cool head, but the mortar and rocket attack at the little airstrip scared him more than anything he'd ever done. He realized it was because he couldn't fight back. If he had weapons he could bring to bear on his assailants, Cole felt he could tough it through anything, no matter what the risk. Take that away, and he felt exposed and vulnerable.

The operation was reconstituted and began again on September 11. The insertion force was going in to seek out weapon and supply caches stockpiled for transport down the Ho Chi Minh trail. It was understood through "rumor control" that the whole operation was being managed directly out of General Abrams's office in Saigon. Although it was a joint army/Marine/air force/ARVN operation, the command element was army.

Outbound from Dak To again, the strike force reached the objective as fast movers completed their bomb runs. Cole was flying front seat in a light fire team of two Cobras as they began gun runs to prep the LZ for the CH-53s. On the first pass, his AC didn't fire because a bullet penetrated the canopy right beside him, distracting him from firing the 20mm cannon mounted under the wing. The pilot shouted at Cole to fire with his 40mm and minigun. On the next pass the AC still didn't fire, but told Cole to use the turret weapons, so Cole energized the chunker and started spraying grenades.

Suddenly the whole aircraft went crazy. A solid, thumping series of loud bangs, accompanied by smoke filling the cockpit, occurred just as the canopy flew open and his instruments went crazy.

Goddamn, thought Cole as he tried to close the canopy, we're dyin'. This is it! Just as the commotion began, his forty stopped firing, and he didn't know what happened. He didn't know who hit who or what. As the Snake pulled up and away, he said, "What in the hell was that?"

The AC said, almost nonchantantly, "Oh, I forgot to flick the switch up on the gun panel." John suddenly realized it was the 20mm's firing that caused the whole commotion. He hadn't been in a Cobra firing one before, so he didn't know he should hold the canopy closed. Later Cobras were reinforced because the big Gatling had a strong muzzle blast that knocked open the canopy, buckled the side plates, and filled the cockpit with smoke. The switch in question was a selector that cut out the other weapons when the twenty was firing. John later came to love the big twenty for its power and accuracy, but that day he had a few harsh words for it and his AC.

Due to heavy resistance, it took a good part of the morning to insert the company. As the Cobras completed gun and rocket runs, more jets waited up high to blast the surrounding jungles with bombs and napalm. The helicopters moved away for the air strikes, then back to attack again. As the army snakes went about their deadly business, Marine Cobras attacked enemy forces on the other side of the LZ. As darkness fell, the insertion was completed, and the aircraft turned away to their respective bases. Every man knew he'd be back at dawn, refueled and rearmed, to take up the battle where it had left off. The insertion had been difficult, and plenty of NVA remained in the area.

By the time they returned on the morning of the twelfth, four sets of fast movers had already been in and out, blasting North Vietnamese troops harassing the force on the ground. Mr. Cole was flying front seat with a secondary heavy fire team covering emergency-medevac Hueys going in for wounded soldiers. Because of a low weather-ceiling and rain squalls, the entire force flew in at low level, dodging mountainsides and gunfire alike for the entire forty-five-minute flight.

Cole's secondary team went as high as it could, holding overhead while the first Cobra fire team set up its racetrack. The leatherneck Snakes worked the surrounding hillsides to suppress fire, while the army Cobras rolled in hot. The leadship pilot in the primary fire team was the company commander, and on the first pass, all of his aircraft's hydraulic controls were shot out by enemy fire. Unable to move their flight controls, even with their feet on the instrument panel for leverage, they leveled the stricken ship just enough to crash into a nearby hillside.

Before they could get out, a Huey was right beside them, and Cole and his pilot set up a suppressive protection pattern over the crash site, pasting the jungle around them with rocket, grenade, and minigun fire. The rescue was over in just a few minutes, so Cole's Snake fired on the wreckage and destroyed what remained of the downed chopper. The wounded soldiers from the ground force were quickly pulled out, too. Which was fortunate, since the weather became worse, and the flight home was made entirely under instrument flight conditions. That was amazing in itself, since all the army pilots had tac-tickets and weren't rated to fly IFR. Because of their frequent seaborne operations, the Marines had instrument training, but the different elements of the fourteen-aircraft force went their separate ways once they were back in South Vietnam. The Marines went to Da Nang, the Pink Panthers split for Pleiku, and who knows where the air force went.

It was touch and go for many of the choppers, which spotted each other in the infrequent breaks in the clouds and barely maintained the same general heading. Sometimes, when a pilot actually saw another helicopter, he'd call and say, "Hey, I can see you at my two o'clock!" The response came back, "Nope. Not me. I'm still in the soup!" It was a miracle no one collided. As it was, several aircraft almost ran out of fuel—one Huey reached Da Nang with only four gallons left.

They tried several times to get back and extract the remainder of the friendly force, but the foul weather made it impossible to fly in. The force waited at Dak To throughout the thirteenth for a break, still breathing deep after the harrowing flight back the day before. Adding to the frustration, a young Marine accidently discharged his weapon and shot a Marine colonel in the leg. The colonel, one of their Cobra pilots, had been strolling along the Dak To airstrip when the incident occurred. He wasn't seriously injured, but it took him out of the war for a while.

By September 14, the weather had cleared, and the massive strike force rolled in. As usual, air force jets saturated the surrounding jungles with every manner of explosive available. Cole was again in a secondary fire team, providing security to the slicks and CH-53s while the primary team beat up the North Vietnamese harassing the LZ. Everyone was wearing a gas mask for this phase of the operation because the force on the ground had released a nonlethal knockout gas in the valley while awaiting the extraction. It was the only way they could reduce resistance enough to allow the choppers to reach them. It did the trick, but enough enemy remained functional to be a major threat.

Despite heavy fire from all quarters, the extraction was completed and the entire company was pulled out. As the last CH-53 pulled pitch and lifted out of danger, Cole was shocked to see a B-40 rocket streak out of the jungle and hit one of the engines on the giant chopper. Despite the severe damage, the aircraft made it out and began the flight home. The Cobras stayed close, even though they couldn't radio the pilot to determine his condition. Apparently, some of the CH-53's communications gear was out, but it seemed to have commo with higher headquarters. The big troop transport was carrying nearly forty troops and was laboring along on one engine. Within ten minutes, the battle damage overcame its ability to fly, and the Jolly Green Giant descended into the valley, making a crash landing and rolling over, still well inside Indian country. A second CH-53 came right in beside it and quickly loaded all the troops and aircrew aboard for a very crowded, but happy return flight. As with the earlier Cobra crash, John and the other Snake drivers made short work of the wreck on the ground, blasting it into flaming scrap.

They learned later that one soldier was still on board, but he had been pinned beneath the wreckage and was already dead.

The pilots and troops who participated in Operation TAILWIND were later told, supposedly by General Abrams himself, that it had been one of the most successful operations of the war. The ground force had uncovered huge caches of weapons, ammunition, and supplies, and major enemy camps, including a basic training center. As well, they seized large numbers of documents with important tactical information.

And, for his part, Warrant Officer Cole was recommended for the Distinguished Flying Cross. More than a year went by before the paperwork came back to him, though, and by then it had wandered the halls of mindless bureaucracy. Somewhere along the way, a faceless, nameless officer wearing the adjutant general "shield-of-shame" branch insignia, common to all pencil-pushing, bean-counting desk jockeys, had the award downgraded to an Air Medal with a V device for valor.

By October, Cole had learned enough about the 361st's mission, the area of operations, tactics, and combat, that he was certified an aircraft commander and began flying the aircraft from the backseat. Other than that, things didn't change much, as John soon found himself flying over Laos again. He was flying high bird, orbiting on station after expending a load of nails on a target, when air bursts that looked like popcorn began appearing around his Snake. He figured it must be a 23mm or 57mm automatic cannon firing at him around eight thousand feet.

"No problem," he radioed to the Snakes below. "Everything's looking good." Just as he spoke, the Cobra started vibrating, and a loud, grinding noise sounded just behind him. The rpm's started falling off slightly.

Cole started getting nervous, so he called the other aircraft and reported his dilemma. "I have a problem here. It sounds like I'm losing the transmission. Something's wrong." He told them he was heading for the Eagle's Nest, the remote base on top of an isolated peak inside Laos. It was the only place he could land where there were friendlies and a measure of safety.

"I'm flying over there to check it out," he told his front seater, a green kid who had just arrived. "If that thing seizes up, the rotor stops right now. We're in good shape as long as it keeps turning."

When he reached the peak, he brought the ship down to the tiny base from a high hover instead of using the usual slanting approach. Once he hit the helipad, he breathed a sigh of relief that the transmission hadn't frozen in flight, making the aircraft fall like a rock. Before he shut down, he called Camp Holloway. "You'll have to send maintenance out here to get this thing. I'm not flying it off this mountain."

Cole and his young protégé dismounted and inspected the entire aircraft. They found nothing. No damage, no shrapnel, no bullet holes. Nothing. Everything worked, too, and no warning lights had come on. By the time a Huey came to pick them both up, Cole had abandoned his search for the cause of problem, and he returned to Pleiku, leaving the lonesome Snake sitting on the rock.

Next day, a maintenance team flew out to repair the Cobra or, failing that, to sling-load it under a Chinook back into base. John was back in the officers club, later, when one of the men on the team caught up to him.

"Hey, man," he said, "that was pretty cool how you set that Cobra down there."

"Yeah," said John. "It scared the shit outta me!"

"Figured you lost the transmission?" the mechanic queried.

"Yeah."

"Lemme tell you what was wrong with it," he said, and gave Cole a short, but simple explanation.

"You lost a cockpit cooling fan." The cockpit cooling fan was a small blower powered by a short spline shaft from the transmission. Its purpose was to blow the cooled air from the climate control unit into the cockpit. It didn't affect the flight of the aircraft one bit, as evidenced by the fact they flew the Cobra home without doing any repairs at the mountaintop. Cole took a lot of crap for that one, finding himself the butt of numerous jokes from his jocular colleagues.

Another fluke was the time a 40mm round came up through the floor of the aircraft into the cockpit. They were firing on targets with the turret weapons, and a live grenade just popped in from nowhere. It lay on the floor, waiting to blow up, until the gunner found the nerve to gingerly pick it up and drop it out the canopy hatch. They never did figure a way it managed to enter the cockpit.

Sometimes a Snake took serious hits and continued to fly. Cole saw one of the Pink Panther ships catch a .50-caliber round through a rocket pod, through the wing stub, and through the main rotor blade, starting a fire in the rocket pod. The pilot salvoed the pod, blowing it clear of the aircraft with prepositioned jettison charges, and flew back to Dak To. When he shut the engine down and the rotor rpms fell off, so did the rotor blade, breaking in half as soon as the centrifugal load forces were gone. The big bullet had broken the main spar in such a way that the aircraft was able to fly back, but little else.

John had a few close calls himself. He was inspecting his aircraft after a combat mission and found a big bullet hole in the drive shaft to the tail rotor. It penetrated straight through the center of the aluminum tube, so he hadn't noticed the hit until the inspection. Should the shot have been an inch higher or lower and ripped the shaft off-center, it would have twisted in half and crashed the aircraft. Another battle-damage fluke was in his main rotor. The drag-brace bolt that held the rotor onto the hinge pin was half shot away, holding the rotor on by the threads alone; the nut head was sheared away. Cobras are beautifully designed birds—but without a rotor, they fly like bird shit, i.e., straight down.

Other Snake drivers had similar experiences. One platoon commander was carrying four hundred dollars in bills for an upcoming R & R when he took a hit through the bottom of his Snake. They found the entry hole and traced it through the ammo bay, up through the floor and then through the seat and cushion. They couldn't find the bullet until he pulled out his wallet and found a hole in it. Pulling out his cash, the projectile fell out of the wad of bills where it had come to a stop.

John's first lead mission was no less bizarre. His fire team escorted a flight of ARVN King Bee CH-34s into Cambodia. The Vietnamese aircraft were in the LZ extracting troops, taking heavy fire the whole time. Cole was laying patterns of cover-fire all around, using rockets with seventeen-pound warheads. Up to then, he had only used ten-pounders, which had a flatter trajectory. John fired a pair to the right and another set to the left of the LZ, then decided to put some over the top to the opposite side. They hit the trees right over the King Bee. The rockets curved down too fast, detonating in the branches, and showered the CH-34 with shrapnel and splinters.

John flew up close to the old Sikorsky as it rose up from the ground to see if they were okay. Inside the shattered canopy he could clearly see the pilot slumped over and covered with blood. Somehow, the ragged 34 made it back to Duc Co, but without the troops they came to get. John got on the radio and called for medical help for the ARVN aviator, then tried to find some fresh lift ships to go back for the troops across the border.

A couple of other King Bees came on line, so Cole took them back into Cambodia, while the injured pilot was flown to a hospital in Pleiku. By the time the ARVNs were finally extracted, the sun was falling fast as night came. The weary Cobra crew headed home against a squall line blowing in from the coast. They nearly headed the wrong way, toward Thailand, but the gunner noticed the radio magnetic compass was malfunctioning. Cole decided to just follow another of the aircraft and use a plain magnetic compass. As the weather became worse and total darkness set in, they found it impossible to keep the other choppers in sight, so he called Peacock radar, the big system in Pleiku, to vector his ship in. The radar was not working that night.

Cole was in radio contact with the two helicopters they tried to follow, but without visual confirmation, he couldn't use them for guidance and soon found his Cobra completely alone, deep inside Cambodia. His erstwhile companions eventually made it to Kontum, north of Pleiku, but Cole had to fly around lost, with a nebulous heading on a questionable compass in the pitch-black of night. He cursed the foul weather as he looked at his fuel gauge, now registering very close to empty. Then they suddenly broke into the clear. Right over Pleiku. John and his gunner laughed out loud as they saw the familiar lights and started down for the runway and their own cozy bunks.

John went to the hospital where the ARVN pilot he shot with the seventeen-pounders was recuperating. The man wasn't hurt as badly as he thought. A piece of shrapnel had cut through a small artery and sent blood spurting throughout the King Bee's cockpit, making things look worse than they really were. The ARVNs liked their fire support close and tight, but John felt like hell for hitting the very people he was protecting. The Vietnamese pilot didn't seem to care; he was pleased that Cole came to visit, but John was still depressed.

Cole decided to write a letter. It would be a letter of apology, and he'd send it through the ARVN commander to demonstrate his sincerity. He meant to explain exactly what happened, where, and when. Fortunate for John, his CO got wind of what he was up to before the letter was completed and delivered.

"What is the matter with you?" the major had asked him. "Can you imagine what might happen if the news media got hold of this?" He continued to rip his ass about the fact their missions were classified, shooting your allies, even by accident, can cause an international incident, and who the fuck did he think he was, anyway? By then John felt about two inches tall and twice as bad. But his CO was right. Accidents came with the turf; he just had to learn to live with them.

Some of the men found diversion in drunkenness and tomfoolery, and both were dangerous in a combat zone. Mr. Cole was checking the guards late one night when he found two of them passed out on the bunker. Sardine cans littered the area. He then heard raucous laughter overhead, so he walked up to the watchtower. Two soldiers sat there, drunk, laughing hysterically.

"So, what's so goddamn funny?" Mr. Cole asked. One of the men gestured towards the perimeter.

"Shit. He just put four rounds of M-79 out there, and he didn't miss that village once!" It was a friendly village. The problems that night didn't end there, either. At midnight, someone dumped a bunch of red smoke grenades in the compound, then fired into the air with a minigun from a Cobra. The night sky filled with tracers and red smoke, and the idiots doing it barely missed the guard tower, besides. It took a while to quiet things down after that, but if Charlie had wanted to hit the base that night it would have been an easy target.

The Pink Panthers had standby every night, a two-minute reaction team of two Cobras, armed, fueled and preflighted, ready for any kind of mission. Unlike other Cobra companies, there were no five- and fifteen-minute backups. Mr. Cole was on standby one night when a mission call came about 2:00 in the morning. It was an AC-130 who had expended its ammunition and scrambled the Cobras to cover a small outpost being attacked in the night. As the two Snakes arrived, the big air force gunship handed over the mission and gave them the radio frequency of the man on the ground.

And it was just one man. Cole saw a rather severe firefight going on below as green tracers converged in the dark on the base camp. Mortar rounds made regular orange flashes in the dark as they struck again and again. The single American told the pilots that his force had been all *chieu-hois* and mercenaries who ran off into the night when the fight got tough.

"Place your fire wherever you want," the doomed soldier calmly told them, "you can even drop it right on me, 'cause I'm down in the bunker. Just don't hit the village, 'cause I don't have permission from the chief."

Cole decided to rake the area with fire to keep the enemy out of the bunker, buying time while a rescue force was put together to get the man out. He was eventually extracted by a Huey and made it back to Pleiku unharmed.

By then, John was a certified aircraft commander, and part of his duties involved training junior pilots to a higher standard. Like any professionals, Snake drivers continued the learning process throughout their service, continually upgrading their skill levels. At any skill level, though, things sometimes happened that couldn't be anticipated. Cole was giving a young pilot his AC check ride when such an incident occurred.

The Cobra they flew was a later version of the AH-1G, improved with the new "tractor" tail rotor. This rotor was slightly larger and reversed to the right side of the vertical tail fin. Earlier Cobras had problems with tail rotor countertorque authority under load because the fin partially masked the rotor wash, reducing its efficiency. When the engineers moved it to the other side, they also increased its power with the larger blades. Cole was giving the check ride in his unit's first aircraft to be equipped with the new system. He thought it was great, giving a lot more left pedal and crisper control of yaw. The date was March 20, 1971, and the flight was done in conjunction with a relatively uneventful escort into Laos. Three

Hueys had inserted troops, with Cobras flying cover, taking some fire, but without losses, then returned to Dak To. As Cole's Cobra followed the slicks into the approach pattern, John decided to test his student. From his front seat instructor position, he added some right pedal and said, "Hey, you got a fixed right pedal setting. What are you going to do?"

The junior pilot responded quickly. "It really is stuck!"

John felt the controls again. They *were* locked up. He was about one hundred feet up and a quarter mile out of Dak To, over the river surrounded by jungled hills. John called ahead to the airstrip to clear the way for a Cobra with a "fixed pedal setting" so he could do a running landing. He intended to keep enough forward speed to counteract the torque, sliding on the skids like landing gear when he touched down. To align on the strip, though, he allowed it to make a long right turn, playing the throttle against the frozen tail rotor setting for the correct combination to bring them in line.

Before the maneuver was completed, the entire vertical fin, including the tail rotor, simply flew off the aircraft, and he went into an uncontrolled spin. The Snake made about eight complete circles before impact. John couldn't autorotate with no tail, and the ship still had nearly half its ordnance on board, so he waited until the last possible second and simultaneously rolled off the throttle to reduce the spin and pulled the collective for pitch to cushion the hit. The landing was solid and hard, over some tall bamboo, and nose-in on a hillside. The Cobra continued to fall down the hillside, rolling another one hundred feet, into the bamboo grove. Cole was knocked unconscious as his chicken plate struck him under the chin. The other pilot, shaken but unhurt, was pulled out of the aircraft by crewmen from a Huey, which quickly flew over to assist them. The Cobra had now started to burn.

Because the Snake lay on its left side, the rear-seat canopy had opened easily on the right. Cole's canopy was on the left side, pinned shut, and John lay motionless as the men tried to get him out. The fire continued to grow, threatening to detonate fuel and ordnance. In desperation, someone drew a .45 and shot the clear plastic to fracture it and facilitate cracking a bigger hole in the canopy. They finally retrieved him from the wreck, but not before he suffered third-degree burns on his left side and right elbow from the fire. He also had a compression fracture in his third lumbar vertebrae from the crash, as well as broken teeth, a split-open chin, and a cerebral concussion.

The other pilot had a slight burn on his ass, but was otherwise all right. John spent a week drifting in and out of consciousness in a hospital in Qui Nhon. He vaguely remembered seeing his last commander there, admitted earlier from wounds sustained in action. Other than that, Cole wasn't fully awake until he woke up in a hospital in the Philippines over a week later. He wouldn't be going back to Vietnam, being shipped through several hospitals en route home to the United States. One was in Yokota, Japan, where his bunk was next to a young infantryman who had been wounded in combat.

"You got your Purple Heart, yet?" the fellow asked him.

Cole was still feeling pretty bad and just mumbled. "Hell, not that I know of. I don't think so."

"Well, here, have one of mine," the soldier went on. "I got three of 'em!" and tossed a medal to John. Cole picked it up and looked at it.

"How in hell did you wind up with three?" he asked, mildly curious.

The man pointed to a couple places on his body and said, "I got shot here, and I got shot here."

"Well, what about the third one?" John said.

"I got my scrotum shot off."

All at once John felt great. He didn't hurt anywhere and felt like a million bucks to boot. The young soldier's wounds weren't a cure for his own injuries, but that was when he started recuperating.

John completed his hospitalization at the Madigan Army Medical Center in Tacoma, Washington, and was discharged on August 9, more than four months after the crash.

Cole eventually learned what had caused his Cobra to fail in flight. The crash investigation team completely ruled out pilot error, even complimenting the fast, professional manner in which they prevented a total loss of life and aircraft. The blame went instead to the sloppy work of one of the crew chiefs, a dope-smoking pothead who was more interested in getting a buzz than doing his job right. He serviced the tractor tail rotor before the flight and neglected to remove a roll of friction tape he absentmindedly parked on the rotor shaft.

When the rotor went back on, it didn't seat completely in place due to the tape's acting as a spacer. The tape was sitting inside a housing on a ninety-degree gearbox, so the pilots hadn't noticed it when they performed their preflight inspection.

During the mission that day, the vibrations and friction eventually caused the tape roll to disintegrate, leaving the rotor with overplay on the shaft. It finally failed completely and catastrophically by the time they arrived at Dak To, tearing the end of the chopper off at the tail fin. It was found several hundred feet from the crash site, providing mute testimony for the investigators.

Chapter 11

TASK FORCE
GARRY OWEN

First Lieutenant Roger M. Fox, Jr.'s first Cobra flight was a very unpleasant experience. It was such an uncomfortable and generally aggravating incident that Roger didn't care if he never sat in one again, nor did he intend to. It was June 1969, during his first tour in Vietnam. Fox was assigned to the lift platoon of the 114th Assault Helicopter Company in Vinh Long. When he started with the unit, it was still flying UH-1Cs as gunships and the UH-1H, which Roger flew, for troop lifts.

During Roger's time as a slick pilot, the 114th began transition to the AH-1G Cobra for their principal fire-support aircraft. Roger was at first intrigued with the new Cobras. He had spent the war being shot at without any means of fighting back. He had been shot down once, and just sitting in an LZ like a target was beginning to rankle him.

So Lieutenant Fox went to one of the gun-platoon leaders and managed to finagle a Cobra check ride. Roger planned to work his way into the gun platoon, getting out of slicks altogether, and become a Snake driver. Then he could fight back when Charlie got antsy. His check ride would be in the front seat, as gunner, with a WO-1 named Cutler, who he didn't know very well. Nonetheless, he looked forward to his chance at a "new career."

It began smoothly, with the first part of the day on escort missions prepping LZs for Blue-team insertions. As the day wore on, though, the ground fire became more intense. At one point, the Cobras took extensive fire from a heavy machine-gun position along a small river. The gun had to be removed to continue the mission, so the Cobras pulled back to formulate a plan. Fox had never attacked a huge machine gun like that one before. He was impressed. He could see it was a serious threat as the pilots discussed lining up for the run, who'd go in first, who would cover and which way they'd break off. He knew the gun was dangerous when they agreed on twelve hundred feet AGL as the break-off altitude.

Cutler seemed to think the machine gun was giving him his big chance to be a hero. When their Cobra began its run, firing rockets while Roger used the turret weapons, Cutler continued well past twelve hundred feet, all the way down to seven hundred. Roger got mad. They knocked out the gun, a big 12.7mm, but it put plenty of holes in the Cobra, too. Hanging right out in front, Fox felt more exposed and vulnerable than he ever had in a slick. He had a few hard words for Cutler.

To make matters worse, the climate control unit was shot out. The CCU was, basically, an air conditioner. It drew in fresh air at a vent in the base of the rotor cowling. The air was cooled and then forced through tubes to each pilot. A small round vent to the right and left of each man then blew the chilled air toward the aviators. As Roger soon found out, the system wasn't a luxury, it was for survival, since the pilot and gunner were enclosed in a clear Plexiglas canopy. The flaming Asian sun made the plastic like a magnifying glass, roasting the two men like buns in the oven.

In a Huey, Roger could just stick his hand out the window to deflect air into his face. Forward movement of the Huey kept a steady flow breezing comfortably around inside. Hell, if that wasn't enough, he could pull off the doors, too. But not the Snake—it wouldn't even fly right unless the canopy was closed tight, so Roger spent the rest of the mission sweating like a pig and cussing down Cutler, the CCU, the NVA, LBJ, Nixon, and Ho Chi Minh!

Not caring if he ever saw one again, Lieutenant Fox walked away from that Cobra. To his mind, the design was stupid, and if Cutler was the kind of people he had to contend with, he'd just stick to his slick. And so he stayed in Hueys, with the 114th AHC, until he was transferred to the 121st Assault Helicopter Company, the Soc Trang Tigers, as the S3 officer. The new assignment was good, in that he was promoted to captain while filling the position. It was bad, on the other hand, since he wasn't flying as much.

Fox managed to work in a few missions flying UH-1B gunships, but more often he was in the command-and-control bird flying a microphone on the C & C frequency. He fought to pilot a slick again, but remained in operations for three more months, till the end of his tour in February 1970.

From Vietnam, Captain Fox went to Fort Wolters, Texas, and became a primary rotary-wing flight instructor, teaching new pilots the basics. He spent more time in the hospital, too, from severe malarial attacks, but generally bounced back to flight status. After nearly fifteen months of training time, Fox decided to check on his status with the Department of the Army to see about a transfer. The army had just released a huge number of warrant officers from active duty as part of the winding-down of the war. Roger was concerned that such a large reduction in pilots could affect his career as a commissioned officer.

He soon learned he was scheduled to return to Vietnam when he crossed the eighteen-month threshold.

What's in it for me? was his first reaction. If he had to return to the war, he didn't want to be a slick pilot again since he still smarted from the sitting-duck syndrome. They offered him Chinook transition, which he declined, scout school at Fort Knox, to which he said, "Not just no, but hell no!" And Cobra transition. Fox thought about that one for a while. In the end, he decided that the ability to shoot back was more important than bad feelings he harbored for the Cobra.

"Okay," he said, "I'll take that," and was assigned a class date in July 1971.

He was surprised and pleased, once he was into the course, to find that a competent instructor and a well-maintained aircraft made flying the Cobra a dream. He soon fell in love with the machine and decided it would be a lot of fun after all. Roger enjoyed Hunter Army Airfield and the Cobra transition school more than he'd ever imagined. When he graduated, he went away feeling great, pleased with his choice of schools and what the future held for him.

Fox departed McChord Air Force Base in Washington state on 5 September 1971. Traveling with Roger were two of his friends, Tony D'auguillo and Lonny McCann. And two bottles of wine, which disappeared within an hour. The military-charter DC-8 made stops in Anchorage, Alaska, and Yokota, Japan, before finally landing in Cam Ranh Bay, Republic of Vietnam. The first thing Fox noticed when they arrived was the dilapidated state of the buildings, as though no maintenance was being done because of continuing troop withdrawals.

After spending the night at the 21st Replacement Company, Fox and his compatriots left the next day in a C-130 for their assignments. The flight jumped from Binh Thuy to Bien Hoa, where they stayed in the cheapest, sleaziest, most roach-and-rat-infested hotel in Southeast Asia. The final leg of the journey was completed the next day, on September 9, with a UH-1H flight to Bearcat, a major fire base that served as headquarters and home for the 229th Assault Helicopter Battalion.

Lonny McCann was assigned to the 23d Infantry Division, so it was just Roger and Tony D'auguillo who wound up in D Troop at Bearcat, an airstrip and fire base about halfway between Saigon and the coast. They'd *had* orders for H Troop, but a screwup at personnel sent them both to D. That was fine with them.

Since he'd been back in country, Roger was keenly aware of a big change from his previous tour. Everywhere he'd been was rundown and falling apart. No one seemed to care about fixing things or taking care of facilities. Discipline was lax, too, with sloppy uniforms and little military courtesy between the ranks. Only those things that kept soldiers safe and alive were given the attention needed to keep going—things like aircraft and weapons maintenance, latrines, showers, and mess halls.

The 229th was part of Task Force Garry Owen, a separate brigade organized from elements of the 1st Cavalry Division (Airmobile).

With Vietnamization of the war well underway, the numbers of American ground troops decreased, while the need for aviation grew, so Garry Owen was devised as a mini–airmobile division, much like the 1st Cavalry when it had been at full strength. But smaller and leaner. They called themselves the "Cav's Cav" since the name "Garry Owen" was taken from the famous cavalry song chosen by Gen. George Armstrong Custer. The song has long been the official U.S. Cavalry march.

TF Garry Owen was formed around 3d Brigade, which spent nearly six years in country as part of the 1st Cav. In April 1971, with a concentration of combat elements, plus assignment and operational control of combat support units, Garry Owen had become what Gen. Hamilton Howze had dreamed of almost a decade before, an air cavalry combat brigade. A key element of this brigade was the 229th AHB, including D Troop and Capt. Roger M. Fox, Jr., Snake driver.

He was also a Smiling Tiger, as attested to by the insignia on each side of each aircraft. Designed by Walt Disney Productions, the logo continued a tradition begun with Gen. Claire Chennault's Flying Tigers in the early years of World War II. Like those flyers in P-40s three decades earlier, the AH-1G pilots took pride in their name, too. Each Snake had a personal moniker similar to the nose art used on aircraft of previous wars. In the gun platoon, Roger's Cobra was "The Magical Mystery Tour," which was named after a then-new Beatles' album and Fox's year in the war.

D Troop was on alert every day, with Cobras, Loaches, and slicks full of packs ready to respond to any contingency. Missions ran the gamut of rescuing pilots to fire support and troop insertions. TF Garry Owen had some of the last American infantry to serve in the war, since that task had been handed mostly to the ARVNs. The Blue teams of the 229th carried little field gear into an LZ, since they were deployed strictly for assault operations. Each soldier carried ample water and as much ammunition as he could. Beyond that, the grunts wouldn't be needing sleeping bags, shelters, or shovels since they would drop in, kick ass, and leave in the Hueys. The ARVNs could hold the ground they took.

Fox was initially assigned as a slick pilot, since the company commander, Captain Lanning, needed more lift pilots than guns at the time of their arrival. Roger made certain Lanning gave him an out, though, because Fox was firmly set on being a Snake driver. The Cobra was the finest helicopter in the world, and if he was going to be a helicopter pilot, he would fly the AH-1G and nothing else. The deal he worked out with Captain Lanning was a real payoff for all the time he had spent as an instructor pilot. If Roger trained and certified six aircraft commanders, he could go to the gun platoon and fly Cobras. Tony D'auguillo was already there, so Fox went to work bringing lift pilots into his training cycle and getting them certified as ACs. Part of his deal with the CO was that he'd get certified for Cobras and be ready for business in the gun platoon.

It all came together by January 1972. Lanning had more than enough ACs for his Blue teams, and Roger was all checked out in Snakes. Even that didn't come easy, though. While getting some Cobra blade-time before the transfer, he was riding with a pilot named T. C. Ware. This fellow had multiple tours in Vietnam and had been to Cobra transition in Vung Tau when they first began the school. At the time Fox met him, Ware likely had more time in Cobras than most other Snake drivers in the army. A super guy and a super pilot, he was the man Roger took his in-country check ride with.

T. C.'s idea of a steep dive angle was different from most pilots. He felt that the usual approach exposed a pilot to ground fire for too long. Roger heard that Ware preferred to fly over the target, drop the nose straight down and let the rockets fall out of the tubes. Huh? Fox knew that must be an exaggeration. Sure, the guy probably liked a steep dive, but the story had obviously grown in the telling. Well, they were over a place called the Pea-Patch, near Bearcat, when he found out how close to fact the story had been.

Ware explained what he was going to do quite clearly before doing it. Even then, Fox was startled. He had never made such a steep, straight-down dive. Ware rolled the ship around, dropped the nose like a lead weight and went straight down with Roger in the front seat. Visibility up front is already phenomenal, but this made Fox feel like he was free-falling in open air.

The dive began at about three thousand feet, with Fox hollering to pull out all the way down. Ware pulled out in plenty of time, but it wasn't soon enough for Roger. Despite his quickened heartbeat and sweating brow, Roger realized he'd seen some remarkable flying skill from a superb pilot. He learned some valuable lessons that day. Roger kept his eyes and ears open around Ware, and picked up a lot of good advice and facts over time.

One lesson he taught himself was how to use the cyclic control in the front seat. In Hueys, the backseat of the Cobra, and every other helicopter he'd ever flown, the cyclic stick was positioned between the pilot's legs, just like the joystick in a fighter plane. It was because the Cobra gunner's cyclic had been moved to the short console on the right side that Fox had a problem. Roger had trouble relating to it, not only because of its odd placement, but also due to its short length and sensitive touch. He was especially uncomfortable when hovering.

Not one to ignore a problem, he figured out a way to deal with the front-seat cyclic psychosis he had created in his mind. He simply adjusted his thinking to imagine he had both legs to the left of a normal cyclic. Since his difficulty was borne of perception, this new perception seemed to alleviate the discomfort with the placement of the control. It seemed perfectly normal if his legs were to one side, so he never had a problem flying front seat again. Mind over matter.

Once officially a full-time Snake driver, Fox flew his first combat mission in the new job with WO Jack "Blackjack" Jordan. The task was to escort a convoy coming out of Xuan Loc on Highway 20 and heading north to Dalat in the mountains. Unlike the first Cobra Roger had flown in, back in 1969, the CCU in this ship worked exceptionally well, even forming ice crystals in the vent nozzles. In a mischievous moment, Jack had Roger look down at something so the vent would be close to his face. Then he flicked the blower motor to high, and Fox had a face full of ice. That got his attention, and they had a good laugh. The rest of the flight was less eventful.

In fact, most of early 1972 seemed pretty slow. Certainly, there was combat activity throughout the large area they supported, but the contacts were smaller and shorter than usual. Some of their missions were raids, or air-assault operations. Using the fully rounded red/white/blue concept of Cobras, Loaches, and slicks with infantry, D Troop was capable of awesome firepower and lightning strikes at high-value targets. If the planning phase was done as quickly.

They were alerted, on one occasion, to prepare for an important attack to rescue a couple of captured American Navy pilots. D Troop pilots never were briefed well enough by the time they moved to a forward staging area, getting in place for the strike. They waited at LZ Rock for seven days for the go-ahead. Rumor had it that a Special Forces colonel wanted his men to do the rescue, so some infighting went on while time slipped away. Too much time. The attack never happened. The bad guys kept their prisoners. D Troop returned to Bearcat.

Captain Fox had trouble with bad leaders on a few other occasions, like a fire-support mission to the old 11th Armored Cavalry operational area. Some ground Cav units entered the unsecured zone and met heavy resistance from the new tenants, NVA regulars in force. It was south of Xuan Loc, so Fox's fire team scrambled to relieve pressure on the troops in contact.

Coming up on the grunt push, Roger could hear a sergeant trying to direct placement of the Snake strike, but the infantry lieutenant had "lost it" and was frantically screaming incoherent instructions at the aircraft. Most of what Fox could understand was dead-ass wrong and would cause some friendly casualties if he complied. The wounded on the ground needed to get out fast, so Roger started to get testy with the lieutenant.

"Get off the radio," he told the officer. "I'm not talking to you."

That really set the guy off, but the needs of the moment were met by talking to the sergeant, getting clear instructions, and completing the entire mission successfully. Suppression fires were finally placed properly, breaking enemy strength, and the wounded were medevaced out.

When the Snakes returned to Xuan Loc to refuel and rearm, a colonel was waiting to speak with Roger. He was polite, but he was pissed, and informed Fox that it wasn't his place to chastise his people. He'd take care of that. Roger was apologetic, but firm in his assessment of the need to save lives, not follow protocol. The colonel was unconvinced, but sought no action against Fox. Roger, on the other hand, hoped the courageous sergeant back there on the battlefield wouldn't take a lot of crap for how he saved so many lives.

Over time, American units began pulling farther back as U.S. troops began to withdraw in earnest. President Nixon announced that American troop strength in Vietnam would be cut to sixty-nine thousand by May 1, so units were leapfrogging toward the coasts and major air bases. New fire bases were created to cover each withdrawal, then abandoned for newer fire bases closer to the "exits." As these bases popped up and then disappeared, the 229th screened the withdrawals, covered convoys, and delayed enemy forces. It went quite well, with limited contacts, and few large enemy elements being encountered.

But there were signs of large bodies of NVA moving in. D Troop was frequently working along the Cambodian border, mostly around the Tay Ninh area, and spotted pieces of tank trails, mostly obscured, throughout the area. They couldn't tell where the trails came from or where they were going, but it was definitely tanks. Something was up. The pilots continued reporting sightings, but the intel types back in Saigon weren't buying it. The men in the field had a much better handle on what was happening, because they were there. The decision makers in the rear told them everything was just peachy-keen and not to worry.

Fine, thought Roger, I'm taking an R & R in Hong Kong. He went to Hong Kong to forget the war, but woke up one morning to find the world had just gone down the toilet. North Vietnam had attacked the south in a full-scale invasion. At first Fox just figured the media was blowing the attack out of proportion so he elected to enjoy his five days in China. He had a big wad of money and was shopping for some of the men in the 229th as well as himself, so he didn't care to leave early.

But leave was soon over, and he found himself standing on the airstrip in Saigon. Fox was surprised that D Troop sent an aircraft right away to pick him up, since he'd planned to spend the night there. He was doubly surprised that they sent a Loach to get him. It was kind of strange. Captain Fox began to guess that things were rough on the flight from Saigon to Bien Hoa. It was a plain admin flight, but they took fire five or six times, flying at altitude. A week earlier, the same trip would have gone unnoticed.

He soon learned that they'd lost an aircraft, with three men killed in the crash. It was a Loach flying on the deck just north of An Loc. The bad guys nailed him. It was their first loss in what would soon become known to the world as the Easter Offensive.

Sensing victory in the wake of the huge American troop withdrawals, North Vietnam had infiltrated hundreds of thousands of soldiers into the south. Giant staging areas inside Cambodia and Laos were used to prepare a major thrust of infantry and armor deep into South Vietnam, capturing key cities and land. The invasion was the brainchild of NVA general Vo Nguyen Giap, commander of the Viet Minh when they defeated the French at Dien Bien Phu in 1954. Giap had not been so lucky in his battles against the Americans. He was now North Vietnam's minister of defense and commander in chief of the North Vietnamese Army. Giap's troops had their asses whipped at the Ia Drang Valley in 1965, in the Tet Offensive of 1968, and in the siege of Khe Sanh that same year. Whatever he had done to drive out the Americans had failed and cost hundreds of thousands of his soldiers. He wanted revenge. With the Americans almost gone and the Stateside antiwar movement ready to mobilize to prevent an American escalation of the war, he thought he could win big, and embarrass the imperialist American aggressors before the eyes of the world.

On March 30, 1972, the NVA launched the attack, assaulting in force against three major provincial areas. In the north, Quang Tri and Hue were targeted as units flowed in over the DMZ and in from Laos. Kontum and Pleiku faced attacks from the Cambodian side in the II Corps area, Tay Ninh and An Loc in the south.

Allied intelligence had anticipated some kind of major attack, but expected it on Tet in February. When that date passed uneventfully, readiness was relaxed and withdrawal continued. Gen. Creighton Abrams, the MACV commander, had even taken leave in Bangkok, Thailand, about the same time Captain Fox was in Hong Kong. No one thought the NVA would dare press for victory while the United States remained, even as our numbers shrunk drastically. By the time Roger Fox was back, it was open warfare throughout the area of operations. By the next morning, he was in the thick of it.

General Abrams, on the other hand, didn't grasp the scope of the offensive for several days after it began. Thirty-six hours after the initial attacks, he described the situation as "not critical at this time, but it appears to be developing." The 229th pilots were a lot closer to the facts than Abrams's downtown Saigon office. Roger was flying round-the-clock combat operations the moment he returned.

The only U.S. Army aviation available for fire support in the area were F Troop, 9th Cavalry; D Troop, 229 AHB; and F Battery, 79th Aerial Rocket Artillery—essentially, three aviation companies. On the ground, U.S. advisors were salted in amongst ARVN forces, but no American infantry units remained in the area to assist in the defense of An Loc.

Fox's first mission after returning from leave was a heavy Pink team (one Loach and two Snakes) visual recon through the Michelin rubber plantations near Tay Ninh. Roger argued against the VR. It was so far forward that no one could get them out if something went wrong. They were sent anyway. They planned to head up the west side of the plantation, then turn and make a run back in the direction of Bien Hoa to the east. If they were hit, they'd be headed toward home already. The team came in with the scout on the deck, the first Cobra between 750 and 1,000 feet above and behind, then the second Snake higher yet to cover the other ships. It was important to have the low bird near the scout in this area, since everywhere they turned might be a battalion-size greeting. The Snake had to be ready to bail out the "little bird."

The enemy's tactic against helicopter attack was to instruct every soldier to keep a thirty-round magazine in his weapon.

When a helicopter flew by, their leaders pointed in the air, straight up, in front of where the chopper was expected to fly past. On his command, everyone fired simultaneously, presenting a wall of lead for the Yankee dogs to fly through. With several hundred people firing thirty rounds each on full automatic, chances were good that several shots would find their mark. Aiming wasn't important.

Roger dropped farther to get close to the Loach, now just ahead and about fifty feet below. The scout made a turn to the right, then slowed, as though he spotted something, so Roger slid to the left and back around. In the middle of the turn he looked down to check his clearance. There sat a big, fat tank. For a fraction of a second, he was looking right down the tube of the elevated gun. In the next second he had gulped and continued his turn. Fox called the scout and reported the tank. They were now staring at rows and rows of thousands of AK-47 assault rifles standing at stack arms. Tents stretched back into the trees, and campfires burned everywhere they could see. It was eerie.

Eerie because of the sheer size of the encampment and the fact that not a single soul was in sight. Not a one. But he knew they were there.

"Zero-Niner-Zero, go," Roger said to the little bird.

"Pick up your heading and move out. If you slow down, I'm going to pass you!" They returned just as dusk fell, telling everyone it was something big out there and comin' this-a-way.

Next day, the first fire team out was a Loach and a Cobra flown by Capt. John Rahm and 1st Lt. George "Skip" Barsom. Their Snake had a defective fuel gauge, so Rahm accidentally splashed himself with JP-4 as the fuel cell topped up. Roger told him to trade flight suits, since he was on third-response section and had plenty time to change later.

"No thanks," Rahm replied, "I have a mission, and I gotta go." The mission was to the same area Fox had just been to only fifteen hours earlier. Roger went back to his hootch and made himself comfortable, lying down for a light nap. He hadn't been there five minutes when the alarm went off, and he heard people screaming they'd lost a ship. It was Rahm and Barsom.

All they knew was they were over the Michelin plantation

for about two minutes then called, "We're taking fire! Taking fire!" Then nothing. A fireball at around three thousand feet was reported, too high for small arms. They'd discover later what caught the Snake so high up.

Roger knew the major that sent them out was aware of what they'd find. Shit, he'd told the man himself about the equipment they'd seen the day before. The major was an intel type, though, and Fox figured the guy wanted to look like he'd deduced it all by himself. At the price of two good men.

For the rest of the day they tried hard to get in because someone had reported a signal from a survival radio. They couldn't get through the antiaircraft fire, the heaviest concentration of small-arms and automatic-weapons fire any of them had ever seen. Backed by five Cobras, three times they tried to get a medevac chopper on the ground, but ground fire was too intense, and they were repulsed every time. One Cobra finally got close enough to observe the wreckage from the air and determine that no one could have survived—the explosion, the impact, and the subsequent fire were all too great to live through. But the crew's survival was impossible. The pilots must have died when the ship first exploded.

D Troop had established a forward operating base and was staging operations out of Lai Khe, making operations to Tay Ninh and An Loc equally supportable. An Loc, and ultimately Saigon, were the primary objectives of the NVA invasion in that sector. Tay Ninh had been attacked in a feint to draw attention away from the real objective, An Loc. That became apparent when a follow-on thrust attacked Loc Ninh with a regiment of armor and overran it in a day.

The ARVN garrison fought hard, but was vastly outnumbered and, with the advent of Soviet-supplied tanks, outgunned. The Communists massacred the force of South Vietnamese defenders, killing nearly every man.

The ARVN commander, realizing he had to stop a drive toward Saigon, reinforced An Loc before it was surrounded and isolated by the NVA. At that point, everything north of Highway 13, except for An Loc and Quan Loi, was under enemy control. The ARVNs were finally able to hold the line, roughly along Highway 13, and begin pushing the bad guys back out to Cambodia. Without massive U.S. air support, however, the Communists might well have prevailed. The air

over every part of Vietnam was filled with American and
VNAF aircraft in huge numbers. Jets and attack planes came
from offshore carriers and bases in Japan, Thailand, and those
still in South Vietnam. Huge B-52 Arc Light strikes obliter-
ated massed formations of NVA divisions.

And American and ARVN helicopters fought side by side
against the tide of invasion. The enemy used weapons seldom
seen in the war before—Russian T-54 and T-55 main-battle
tanks, full-size, front-line armor with a huge main-gun cannon
and several machine guns. There were also large numbers of
PT-76 amphibious tanks and even a few World War II vintage
T-34s.

Fighting against tanks was a new experience for Roger and
the other pilots, but they soon developed tactics to counter the
steel monsters. At least one and usually two trucks with antiaircraft weapons followed the tanks. These trucks always carried at least twin-mounted .51 calibers, sometimes a quad
mount, and the tanks themselves mounted one or two
.51-caliber machine guns. Just for air defense. The bastards
had gotten bolder, but they still worried about Snakebite.

For the first time in the war, there was a real "front line"
as it would be called in wars past. An actual line on a map
that, if you went past it, you shot whatever moved. Coming
back, you were on the safer side again. Venturing over that
line was risky business, since ground fire was massive. But it
was a classic target-rich environment. Instead of guerrilla war

sifting secretly through jungles, the enemy could now be attacked in massed formations, exposed to American firepower.

Roger destroyed his first tank as it rolled down Highway 13 toward Chon Thanh south of An Loc. It emerged from a rubber plantation in a swirl of dust and started down the road, with two trucks close behind. Calling in a sitrep, the two Cobras of his heavy Pink team wheeled around to the attack, as the scout observed. While the Snakes came in from behind, the trucks immediately spun around to engage them with heavy machine guns. Roger believed in nailing everything down nice and tight before getting too close, so he launched a salvo of flechette rockets. It killed the crews in the trucks and made the tank button up. A pair of high explosive rockets destroyed the trucks on the first pass, and they lined up on the tank again. They began the run by sweeping the tank with another pail of nails, then hit it with a couple seventeen pounder HEs. Two more passes and several more rockets finished the chore.

Roger figured they destroyed it, and the trucks, since none of them moved for the rest of the day. He passed it a couple times on later missions, noting that someone eventually dropped a very large bomb there and probably claimed a kill for themselves.

For one mission, Fox got his hands on a batch of experimental missiles called Hardpoints. Designed to kill tanks, the damn things had been in a warehouse in the States for God knows how long while someone waited for a chance to try them out. Now was the opportunity, and between missions, Roger found them at the Lai Khe FARP. Loading up with a batch of nails, he snagged a load of Hardpoints, too.

About then, a major ran up, hot and bothered and asking why he was taking Hardpoints.

"I'm gonna use 'em." Roger grinned.

"But will you be shooting tanks?" came the anxious return.

"If I see any tanks, I'll shoot 'em."

"Well, Captain," the major began again, "you can't take these missiles unless you're using them on tanks."

"You don't understand," Roger replied. "If I find a tank, I'll shoot it with these rockets. If I find a bunker, I'll shoot the bunker. I'm not too proud." The major became so incensed that this upstart captain was taking his experimental rockets, he went for his sidearm to try and stop him. Not quickly enough. The door gunner of a nearby Loach was faster with his M-60 and held his weapon on the belligerent field-grade officer. He kept his weapon trained on the man until Fox was done loading the Snake. Not a word was said after that, as the muzzle of the machine gun projected the power of suggestion. Then they launched, leaving a frustrated officer on the ground below. The Hardpoints worked good on tanks, and bunkers, too. There just weren't many to go around, and they were quickly used up.

Sometimes a target was handed off to a bigger player. When Fox called a sitrep on a tank coming through a forest, he was told to keep it in sight, the air force would come and destroy it. That was fine with Roger, since he wouldn't have to get low and be exposed to ground fire. A dead tank was a dead tank, whoever killed it. They hung around the tank, popping a couple rockets at it to keep the crew busy, when Fox noticed big explosions bursting around the T-55. He thought it was his wingman, but a quick check proved it wasn't. Not even close. Then he noticed tracer flashes. Looking at the tank, he followed the line of shot up, then over his shoulder. It was an AC-130 Spectre gunship. The big plane was firing a 105mm *cannon*, plus its two 20mm and four 7.62mm Gatlings. Roger thought it hit mighty close to him, too. It damn sure nailed the tank.

As the weeks went by, D Troop was forced to modify its tactics as a result of intense small-arms fire. They now flew at three thousand feet, coming down only far enough to make rocket runs then climb back out and go home. That worked fine for a while. Until the day he saw seven aircraft explode and fall out of the sky in the space of a few minutes. As he watched in disbelief, each one flashed and fell to the ground into wreckage. No one knew what in hell was going on. At least none of the pilots.

It was D Troop's first encounter with the SA-7 Strela (Russian for "arrow"), a shoulder-fired, heat-seeking missile. Made by the Russians and given to the NVA, the small anti-aircraft missiles had been reported to the army brass by the air force. Somebody in Saigon didn't believe it, so the word wasn't passed to the pilots. And a lot of them died. It required an immediate change in tactics. The range of the SA-7 was eight thousand feet, so aircraft would fly either above that altitude or right on the deck. Nowhere in between. On a hot day, a Cobra would barely get that high. Some simply couldn't. As a result, everyone soon flew so low that they'd put the skids in the trees.

This maneuver addressed a number of threats they now faced, including the Strela. Flying low exposed the choppers to fire for only a few brief seconds, although they couldn't avoid it altogether. The Cobras flew as fast as they could, on full military power, then changed direction every twelve seconds or so. Twisting and turning as they raced through the treetops at high speed, the heavy Pink team spotted a target, made one pass, and sped away. When the enemy had a moment to prepare, ground fire was deadly, even for the few seconds of exposure. It was almost impossible, though, for the SA-7 to score hits when they flew this way. Too much time was needed for the missile's infrared tracker to acquire the heat signature of the exhaust plume, then more time to launch it. With trees in the way, too, it couldn't be done in the instant the choppers sped past.

Other tricks were tried that showed marginal success against the missiles. One was to grab a cloud and use it to mask the exhaust heat. If an aircraft had to climb, they'd go full power straight for a big cumulus and punch in as quick as possible. That worked if they made the cloud faster than the missile. If a cloud was available. Another dodge was to watch the missile coming, then autorotate straight down when it came near enough. The SA-7 couldn't turn fast enough to follow a ninety-degree change in direction. Success with that technique was debatable. Eventually, heat deflectors were designed that diverted the exhaust plume upwards and made the chopper harder to track. All the C & C birds out of Saigon had them installed and flew above the battlefield at ten thousand feet, once or twice. They even got medals for it.

In this part of Vietnam, the enemy didn't take helicopter pilots prisoner, so pilots counted on each other for backup. By now, D Troop was about 75 percent second-tour pilots who worked well together. Often, they didn't need radio calls, knowing automatically if something was wrong and what to do. They were a team and thought alike from working together so long. Most important, each man knew that if something went wrong, someone would be there for them. If worse came to worst, there wouldn't be two men on the ground, but rather six or more as the next crew came to make a rescue and also got shot down. The cycle would continue until enough firepower arrived to slaughter any opposing enemy. It was a circle-the-wagons-and-hold-the-fort-till-the-cavalry-gets-here mentality. And it really was the cavalry coming.

Some outfits weren't as tight as D Troop, though. Another unit had a flight of three aircraft go through the An Loc sector and only two came out—and they had no idea where the other ship was. Of course, it had been shot down. The crew got out, but both were found dead in a bomb crater. Executed. Because the unit didn't cover their own. That galled the men in D Troop. They knew they had no one but each other to look out for them, so they did exactly that to stay alive.

The pilots of all the services made sure to notify everyone in the area when they observed a threat to aircraft. The front-seater in the Cobra, when he wasn't firing the turret, was responsible for looking out for ground fire and Strela launches. If he saw a puff of white smoke on the ground, accompanied by a flash, he'd call out, "SAM launch," over the guard freq. It was interesting to watch the rest of the world when this happened. Because of the massive air support, navy and Marine jets, air force fighters, army and ARVN helicopters would be scrambling in every direction to dodge the missile. About the time they had the Strelas figured out, another threat came along.

Roger was escorting a mixed flight of American and ARVN Hueys that were reinforcing An Loc. At altitude, they swung out to the east of An Loc and were cruising along when it happened.

Crump.

A puff of black smoke appeared in the sky nearby.

Crump. Crump.

The enemy was reaching out to touch them at ten thousand feet. Roger recognized it right away. His dad had been a B-24 Liberator pilot in World War II, and Fox had grown up fascinated with airplanes and movies and books about airplanes. His father had described many times just what he was seeing now. Flak. Like a renegade film clip from *Twelve O'Clock High*, the flak burst around them in regular patterns that traced their route of flight. They cleared the area before the big gun below caught one the choppers with a burst. Although he couldn't tell just what kind of gun it was, Roger saw that it could fire a *looooong* way, so he didn't care to linger.

Next day, a fire team went back to destroy the gun. Fox caught a glimpse of its muzzle flash the day before and noted on the map where it was situated. Coming back, they figured it would be moved to a new site for its protection. For that reason alone, no one was looking for the gun where it had been the day before. Of course, that's where it was. As the gunships came into range, the big cannon started firing, catching the Snakes unaware until the fourth round hit one directly in the ammo bay. The flak round detonated inside the 40mm drum, and the resulting explosion literally blew the minigun box out of the aircraft, along with the bay doors and assorted shrapnel. The hydraulics and the SCAS went immediately to hell, requiring the strength of both pilots to move the cyclic enough for an autorotation. Fortunately, they were high enough to head south and execute a glide slope into friendly hands. The touchdown was rough, but they were all right and close to an ARVN unit.

That finished D Troop's last 20-ship. The 20mm cannon setup was such an ordeal to install and remove, it was easier to trade aircraft than to change the armament from a 20mm. Consequently, Snakes set up with 20s stayed that way most of their service careers. Most of D Troop's 20-ships were shot up in the An Loc battle, and now, all of them. The flak-bit Snake was hoisted out of the area within the hour.

The 20mm was especially handy for destroying trucks. The first time Roger fired one, he was with Tony D'auguillo. When the gun went off, the canopy flew open from the blast and startled them both. After that, the front-seater always held down the canopy when they were firing it. Since the trucks were armed with large machine guns, the 20mm made it possible to fire from a safer distance. In light of the heavy small-arms fire, this added advantage by keeping some altitude.

Airpower ultimately turned the tide of battle. Certainly, the beleaguered defenders holed up in An Loc and Quan Loi fought courageously against impossible odds. But those odds were honed down by B-52 Arc Light strikes; air force, navy, and Marine attack aircraft; massed artillery fires; and helicopter gunships. And the defenders in the cities under siege were resupplied regularly by air. The story was the same throughout Vietnam. Up north, they even had naval gunfire support from the American fleet. Wherever the NVA thrust into the south in their Easter invasion, their ranks were decimated by relentless bombing, strafing, rocket attack, and automatic cannon fire.

Battles and skirmishes continued throughout the remainder of the year as remaining enemy units struggled with the ARVN to keep a toehold in South Vietnam, but the Easter Offensive was effectively over by mid-May. The invasion had failed, costing many thousands of lives, mostly Communists, and huge quantities of tanks, vehicles, and weapons. Conservative estimates put the NVA's losses at more than one hundred thousand killed, fully one-sixth of their total losses since America entered the war. Half of their tanks and artillery were burned-out scrap on the battlefields. From a single offensive. Once again handed a stinging defeat, General Giap was replaced as commander of the army by General Van Tien Dung (Giap remained minister of defense until 1980).

American forces in South Vietnam were down to ninety-six thousand men in March and fell further to thirty-two thousand by October. In January of 1973, twenty-four thousand Americans remained, but the North Vietnamese still feared their power too much to invade again. Even as the last U.S. combat troops left in March 1973, with 150,000 NVA still in the south, the communist armies didn't have the strength to mount another offensive. From Quang Tri to Ca Mua, they were battered into retreat, going into hiding until the Americans were finally gone.

The Strela missiles had little effect on the outcome of the battles, despite their forcing changes in tactics and the loss of some aircraft. The M-72 LAW rocket, on the other hand, made a big dent in the NVA's armored thrust. Like the Russian-made SA-7, the American M-72 was a small, shoulder-fired missile. LAW stood for Light Antitank Weapon, a name the small rocket justly deserved. The LAWs were issued in large quantity to the ARVNs, who soon found that the little rockets would penetrate tank armor and detonate the tank's own internal ammo and fuel stores. Scooping up armloads of M-72s, the ARVN soldiers went out and littered the countryside with burned-out T-54s and T-55s.

Captain Fox, flying over the scarred battlefield after An Loc had been relieved, saw the broad expanse of shattered war machines stretched out below. It had been a different kind of war during April and May, more like the conventional battles of World War II, with giant armies locked in a death grip of firepower. Now they were back to chasing shadows, ferreting out company-size units and the occasional battalion. Ground fire was still vicious, but evermore isolated as the enemy limped back into Cambodia.

Roger noticed a strange white speckling over some large areas. Flying lower for a better look, he saw it was thousands of rocket motors, blown clear of the 2.75 warheads when they detonated. They fired so many that from higher up, the ground looked like it had been dusted with snow.

After the maelstrom of the Easter Offensive, later missions were less perilous. Some were even gratifying, being executed with ballet-perfect precision. Roger was in a heavy Pink team suppressing enemy elements along a riverbank. The Blues on the ground in support of ARVNs needed the entire opposite bank cleared "right now," so the two Cobras rolled in hot, tight, and close. Tony D'auguillo was flying wing, and he and Roger were in synch all the way through. Each Snake ripple-fired rockets on their target runs. Like giant strings of firecrackers, the pods lit up in rapid succession as the motors ignited in sequence and sent their deadly message into the trees.

It was one of the few times Fox dumped all his 2.75s in a single pass, and the backblast nearly slowed the Cobra to a crawl. The combined firepower of Roger's and Tony's Snakes churned up plenty of real estate and switched off the bad guys. They earned a "well done" from the troops on the ground and moved on.

Captain Fox and D Troop continued to screen the withdrawals from Vietnam until the end of his tour in September 1972.

In January 1973, after putting severe pressure on Hanoi with intensive bombing operations, President Nixon extracted a peace agreement from the North Vietnamese. By March, America had left South Vietnam alone to defend itself without our airpower or soldiers. As U.S. aid to South Vietnam was curtailed by Congress, the Soviet Union continued to help North Vietnam rebuild its military power.

The rest is history.

GLOSSARY

AA:	Antiaircraft.
AC:	Aircraft Commander.
ACR:	Air Cavalry Regiment.
Advancing blade:	The blade of the rotor turning into the direction of flight.
Airfoil:	The curved lifting form of a wing or rotor blade.
Angle of attack:	The angle at which an airfoil or aircraft strikes the air.
AO:	Area of operations.
ARA:	Aerial rocket artillery.
ARVN:	Army of the Republic of Vietnam.
Autorotation:	Emergency landing when a helicopter loses power.
B-40:	A Chinese antitank rocket.
Bde:	Brigade.
Bn:	Battalion.
Camber:	The arched side of an airfoil.
Cav:	Cavalry.
Centrifugal force:	The outward force exerted on a spinning object that imparts a linear stability to its path.
C & C:	Command and Control.
Chicken plate:	Aircrew body armor.
Chieu hoi:	A surrender program offered to VC/NVA.
Chopper:	Helicopter.
Cobra:	The AH-1 series of attack helicopters.

Collective:	The helicopter flight control which makes it rise and descend by adding or decreasing pitch to all rotor blades simultaneously.
Co:	Company.
Coning:	The tendency of a rotor disc to bend upwards under flight loading conditions.
Conex:	A large, square metal shipping container.
Cyclic:	The helicopter flight control which increases rotor blade pitch to one side while decreasing opposite pitch to cause the aircraft to move in a specific direction.
Deadlined:	Unusable until repaired.
DFC:	Distinguished Flying Cross.
Disc loading:	The ratio of rotor-disc-area to aircraft-weight.
DMZ:	Demilitarized zone.
Door gunner:	A soldier, usually enlisted, who mans an articulated machine gun on a helicopter.
Dustoff:	Medevac.
Extract:	To evacuate troops from combat by air.
FAC:	Forward air controller (OV-10, O-1, OH-6, etc.).
FFAR:	Folding-fin aerial rocket.
Flak jacket:	Nylon mesh body armor.
Flapping:	Up and down bending of the rotor blades while in flight.
FNG:	Fucking new guy.
Frag:	Hand grenade.
Ground effect:	Additional rotor lift from increased downflow pressure close to ground.
Grunt:	Infantry.
Gunship:	Certain types of armed aircraft used for ground attack.
Hq:	Headquarters.
Ho Chi Minh trail:	The route used by North Vietnam to supply and infiltrate troops into the south.
Huey:	The UH-1 Iroquois helicopter and all its variants.
Insert:	To place troops into an area by aircraft.

Jesus nut:	The threaded nut that retains the rotor to a helicopter.
JP-4:	Standard turbine aircraft fuel (kerosene base).
KIA:	Killed in action.
Lam Son 719:	A combat operation into Laos from February 8 to April 6, 1971.
Lateral cyclic:	A cyclic movement used to roll the helicopter.
LAW:	The M-72 light antitank weapon.
Loach:	Light observation helicopter (LOH).
Longitudinal Cyclic Pitch:	A cyclic movement used to move the nose up or down.
LRRP:	Long-range reconnaissance patrol.
LZ:	Landing zone.
MACV:	Military Assistance Command, Vietnam.
Mast bumping:	A teetering rotor striking its hub.
Minigun:	A 7.62mm electric-drive Gatling gun.
NETT:	New Equipment Training Team.
NVA:	North Vietnam Army.
OPCON:	Operational control.
Pegasus:	An operation conducted from April 1 to 15, 1968, around Khe Sanh.
Peter pilot:	Copilot.
Pink team:	A scout helicopter leading gunships to targets.
Pitch:	The angle of the rotor blade chord perpendicular to the rotor hub.
Purple Heart:	A medal given for combat wounds.
R & R:	Rest and Relaxation.
Red team: -	Attack helicopters operating without scouts.
REMF:	Rear echelon mother fucker (usually clerks and adjutant general branch officers).
Rotor:	The spinning wing assembly of a helicopter.
RPG-7:	A small, shoulder-fired antitank missile.
RVN:	Republic of Vietnam (South Vietnam).
SCAS:	Stability control augmentation system.
S-3:	Operations section or officer.

Sideslip:	A movement forward at an angle to one side.
Sitrep:	Situation report.
SKS:	A Soviet-style semiautomatic carbine firing 7.62×39 mm cartridges.
Slick:	A Huey configured to carry troops.
Snake:	The AH-1 Cobra.
Snake driver:	Cobra pilot.
SOP:	Standard operating procedure.
Spider hole:	A one-man foxhole with a camouflaged lid.
Stall:	A loss of airfoil lift due to an overly steep angle of attack, or flying below critical speed.
Teetering rotor:	A rotor with two blades mounted on a single horizontal hinge to facilitate controlled flapping.
Thrust:	The downward airflow of the rotor which causes and controls flight.
Torque:	The tendency of the rotor forces to push back against engine rotation.
Tracer:	A bullet that leaves a bright flash along its flight path.
Track:	Any tank or tracked vehicle.
VC:	Viet Cong.
White team:	Aeroscouts.
Willie Peter:	White phosphorous.
World, the:	Back in the United States.
Zap:	To kill.

BIBLIOGRAPHY

Drendel, Lou. *Gunslingers in Action*. Aircraft in Action Series. Carrollton, Tex.: Squadron/Signal Publications, 1984.

Drendel, Lou. *Huey*. Modern Military Aircraft Series. Carrollton, Tex.: Squadron/Signal Publications, 1983.

Fails, Lt. Col. William R. *Marines and Helicopters: 1962–1973*. Washington, D.C.: U.S. Marine Corps, 1978.

Heatley, Michael. *The Illustrated History of Helicopters*. New York: Exeter Books, 1985.

Mesko, Jim. *Airmobile: The Helicopter War in Vietnam*. Carrollton, Tex.: Squadron/Signal Publications, 1984.

Peoples, Kenneth. *Bell AH-1 Cobra Variants*. Aerofax Datagraph 4. Arlington, Tex.: Aerofax, Inc., 1988.

Richardson, Doug. *AH-1*. Vol. 13 of *Modern Fighting Aircraft*. London: Prentice-Hall, 1987.

Siuru, Bill. *The Huey and HueyCobra*. Blue Ridge Summit, Pa.: Tab Books, 1987.

Stanton, Shelby L. *Anatomy of a Division: The First Cav in Vietnam*. Novato, Calif.: Presidio Press, 1987.

Stanton, Shelby L. *Vietnam: Order of Battle*. New York: Galahad Books, 1986.

Summers, Harry G., Jr. *Vietnam War Almanac*. New York: Facts on File Publications, 1986.

Taylor, Michael J., ed. *The Illustrated Encyclopedia of Helicopters*. London: Exeter Books, 1984.

The Vietnam War. New York: Crown, 1979.

TM 55–1520–236–10: Army Model AH-1S (Modernized Cobra) Helicopters. Washington, D.C.: Department of the Army, 1980.

Tolson, Lt. Gen. John J. *Airmobility: 1961–1971*. Vietnam Studies. Washington D.C.: Department of the Army, 1973.

Trotti, John, and George Hall. *Marine Air—First to Fight*. Novato, Calif.: Presidio Press, 1985.

Turley, Col. G. H. *The Easter Offensive: Vietnam 1972*. Novato, Calif.:
    Presidio Press, 1985.
Vietnam Helicopter Pilots Association Newsletter. 4(5): (December 1987).
Zaffiri, Samuel. *Hamburger Hill*. Novato, Calif.: Presidio Press, 1988.